WITHDRAWN
UTSA LIBRARIES

P9-EEL-429

COMMUNITY
HEALTH
EDUCATION

Settings, Roles, and Skills for the 21st Century

Third Edition

Donald J. Breckon, MA, MPH, PhD
Park College
Parkville, Missouri

John R. Harvey, MPH, PhD
Western Illinois University
Macomb, Illinois

R. Brick Lancaster, MA, CHES
Centers for Disease Control and Prevention
Atlanta, Georgia

 An Aspen Publication
Aspen Publishers, Inc.
Gaithersburg, Maryland
1994

Library of Congress Cataloging-in-Publication Data

Breckon, David J.
Community health education: settings, roles, and skills for the 21st century/
Donald J. Breckon, John R. Harvey, R. Brick Lancaster.—3rd ed.
p. cm.
Includes bibliographical references and index.
ISBN 0-8342-0526-2
1. Health education—Study and teaching—United States. 2. Health education—
Teacher training—United States. 3. Community health services—United States—Management.
4. Public health personnel—Education—United States. I. Harvey, John R.
II. Lancaster, R. Brick. III. Title.
[DNLM: 1. Health Education—United States.
2. Health Promotion—methods—United States.
3. Community Health Services—United States. WA 590 B892c 1994]
RA440.5.B74 1994
610' .71 '073—dc20
DNLM/DLC
for Library of Congress
93-42924
CIP

The opinions expressed in this book are those of the authors and not of the Centers
for Disease Control and Prevention or of the United States Public Health Service.

Editorial Resources: Jane Colilla

Library of Congress Catalog Card Number: 93-42924
ISBN: 0-8342–0526-2

Printed in the United States of America

1 2 3 4 5

This book is dedicated to five special women in our lives. Our wives, **Sandra Breckon, Delores Harvey,** and **Mary Sue Lancaster**, have been longstanding sources of strength, encouragement, and renewal. Our major professors, **Dr. Mabel Rugen** and **Dr. Elizabeth Lockwood Wheeler**, helped to shape and guide the formative years of the entire health education profession. We publicly recognize the many ways that they have enabled us to reach the point where this book is possible.

Table of Contents

Health education and health promotion have come of age. There are thousands of professionally trained health behavior change specialists, and there are more than 300 institutions where new generations of such health education specialists are being taught.

Roles of health educators have been delineated and verified. Model curricula have been designed. Self-assessment and testing mechanisms have been developed. State professional organizations have been certifying those entering the profession, and national certification is being planned.

Master's degrees and doctoral degrees are available to those who wish to progress beyond entry level. Professionally trained health educators, with bachelor's, master's, or doctoral degree credentials, are readily employed. In addition, allied health specialists are increasingly being given training in changing health-related behavior.

The role of education in preventing or treating health problems is widely accepted. Future writers may well describe the late 1980s and the 1990s as the golden age of health education and health promotion.

Much progress has occurred in advancing the cause of health education and health promotion since we wrote the first edition of this book. We have been involved in leadership roles, and have experienced the widespread acceptance and use of our textbook. Textbooks are, in fact, an important part of collecting and disseminating the distilled wisdom of the profession. They reflect and help shape contemporary professional practice.

In the first edition of this book we presented descriptions of the various settings in which health educators practice, the roles they play, and the skills they need. Yet the settings, roles, and skills change rapidly, requiring textbooks to be revised. In the second edition we emphasized state-of-the-art professional practice, with attention to current problems and examples from current programs.

In this third edition we emphasize the 21st century, and the national "Healthy People 2000" project. The federal policy shifts that gave birth to this project, and the documents that grew out of this project, are rapidly changing the practice of health education. Quotes from the documents are used liberally in this revision, and the thinking of the Healthy People 2000 project staff is integrated into many chapters.

Certification of health educators was only planned when the second edition of this book was written. It is now a reality. Concepts essential for passing the certification exam are included in this revision. (Indeed, even the second edition is listed on the "Short Reading List" for the health education exam required for certification.)

The profession is taking a quantum leap forward, and textbooks and their readers must too, or risk being left behind.

Changes in the settings in which health education specialists practice are described. Health educators are working for and with organizations that did not exist a mere five years ago. This is especially true now with the President's emphasis on health (medical) care costs. Examples and other references are presented in this edition so that readers may become conversant with the contemporary scene.

New pressures, restraints, and opportunities are integrated with older but still commonplace settings. The growth of health education within group practice and clinics such as sports medicine is described, as is the extensive practice within health spas, weight loss programs, and so on. Educational roles in related areas have been added. Many health educators will find themselves working in or with such agencies. The recent explosion of health education in the public schools is explored. Primary prevention often starts in primary grades. Working effectively with schools is an essential component of many programs. Health promotion in the workplace has evolved from small beginnings in the early 1980s to major programs at present. Employee assistance programs are common at industrial and corporate sites. Support groups are the norm today, as are community organizations focusing on a variety of evolving health problems.

Health educators have new demands placed on them, as well as new opportunities. Educational technology is changing. Videotapes and videodiscs are widely used, as is computer-assisted instruction. Interactive videodiscs link computers and videodiscs, with a quantum leap in effectiveness being the result. Using technology effectively is an ever-increasing imperative.

Computers, too, have changed dramatically, providing more memory and user-friendly software at lower cost. Many opportunities exist to apply microcomputers to health education. Numerical computing is the least used but still valuable function of a computer by health educators. Many other innovative applications are available. Desktop publishing and databases can also have a major impact on the work of a health educator and are described. Computer networking and conferencing is a growing reality for the field.

Teleconferencing is yet another new emphasis. Satellite up-links and down-links are part of the jargon of the day. Yet, before people have learned to use the satellite technology, fiberoptic networking is beginning to replace satellite hook-ups. The way health educators interact with each other, the equipment they use, and the outcomes of such interactions are changing rapidly. The current state of technological affairs is discussed, as are projections into the immediate future. Much emphasis in this edition is placed on technological advances and the opportunities for application by health education.

Ethical issues are even more critical than when the first edition of this book was written. Acquired immunodeficiency syndrome (AIDS) is the major problem all public health and health care professionals are struggling to address. Ethical issues surrounding this disease are discussed, and illustrations from effective programs are used throughout the text.

Yet, despite the emergence of major health problems that require prevention or intervention and the emergence of new organizations and agencies, health educators will often have to sell themselves and their services. An emphasis of this edition is proactive strategies that both beginners and experienced health educators can use to get a job and to be successful in that job.

The theoretical models of health education have changed somewhat, some as a consequence of preference and fad and some as theory develops that better explains practice. The sophistication of professional preparation programs and of entry-level health educators has changed. Accordingly, more of the theoretical foundations undergirding practice have been included throughout. A feature of the third edition is an emphasis on underlying theory.

Finally, the view of the future has evolved. We can see more clearly the immediate future and can see farther than before. Health educators need to be future oriented. A best-possible-case scenario is presented because of a belief that positive thinking about the future leads to people helping to shape and mold that future. An optimistic view of the future also leads to pride in one's profession. That pride, when combined with knowledge and skill, leads to excellence in health education. Excellence in health education and health promotion results in better quality lives and in lives saved.

Acknowledgments

The material we have used in this manuscript has been prepared over a time span of approximately two decades. The original source of the ideas and materials has long since been lost. We acknowledge these unknown contributors, however, and regret not being able to attribute ideas to them individually.

We particularly acknowledge the work of Dr. Robert Bowman. Dr. Bowman developed or collected several of the items that we have included in this book. More important, he stimulated interest in methodology and skill development in his students in the School of Public Health at the University of Michigan before it became fashionable to do so. He has had a lasting, positive effect on our careers, and we gratefully acknowledge that contribution.

The preparation of teaching materials incorporated in this book has necessarily involved dozens of secretaries in several agencies. To them, collectively, we say again, "thank you." We especially acknowledge the work of Sandra Campbell, Marcia Matevich, Lorna Condit, and Virginia Bruch, who spent many long hours preparing the manuscript. Their skillful work, along with that of Marc Lancaster, made this an easier task and resulted in a better quality book.

The second edition was partially made possible by the timely and concise review of specific chapters from the first book by health educators from various settings and roles across the United States. Their insights and professional perspectives from the "real world" have been invaluable. These colleagues are Margaret Hall, Terry Hughes, Mary Sue Lancaster, Garry Lindsay, Mary Longe, James Lovegren, Robert Moon, Jon Rudy, Randy Schwartz, Randall Todd, Carol Vack, and Doug Vilnius.

The third edition also benefited from reviews by Karen Evans, Karen Glanz, Robert Goodman, Cheryl Cortines Lackey, and Randy Schwartz.

Part I

Community Health Education Past and Present

Health educators come from widely diverse backgrounds, drifting into the profession from nursing, teaching, social work, or other disciplines. They develop the skills to do the specific tasks that are required in a job description, but without formal training they may lack an overview of the profession they have joined.

Similarly, students preparing for careers as health education professionals need to become enculturated as to the foundations of the profession. In order to help shape its future, entry-level health educators need to know where the profession has been and where it is now.

The parable of the blind men describing an elephant based on their contact with the beast provides a much-needed lesson. Although each man's description represented an accurate account of his perception, the totality of the animal was much greater than the perception of any one person.

Part I provides an introduction to the profession. It contains a historical overview, a description of changes that have occurred, a definition of terms currently being used, and a discussion of some of the issues facing the profession, including those dealing with quality assurance, ethics, and related legal matters. The section also includes an introduction to the various professional organizations serving health educators. Thinking about these matters is an appropriate place to begin for all who seek an introduction to, or a review of, the practice of community health education.

Chapter 1

Current Perspectives of Practice and Professional Preparation

What is a health educator? Although this question can be answered simply, the answers given may be quite diverse. Indeed, it has been suggested that there are as many definitions as there are health educators.

Any response to the question usually reflects the biases of the respondent. It may also reflect the generation of the respondent, for the concept has evolved over time. Simplistic answers usually cause more problems than they solve and rarely provide the basis for long-term helpful relationships. Therefore, an appropriate place to begin a book on community health education is an exploration of what a health educator is thought to be and do and an examination of the underlying assumptions of these concepts.

HEALTH EDUCATION AND HEALTH EDUCATORS

Clair Turner, in his classic work *Community Health Educator's Compendium of Knowledge*, cited several early definitions that are still used today. He quoted a 1926 definition: "Health education is the sum of experiences which favorably influence habits, attitudes and knowledge relating to individual, community . . . health."[1] Turner went on to state that "community health education, then, is a learning process through which people in a community inform or orient themselves for more intelligent health action, and a community health educator is a person who helps to organize and develop community interests, study, and action toward the solution of health problems."[2]

These two definitions established that health education involves changing habits, and that to do so, attitudes must be changed as well. Information dispensing was a "necessary but not sufficient" part of this process. The definitions indicate that many factors influence health habits other than that which the health educator does or is able to control and that the final outcome depends on the sum or mix of these factors. Individual responsibility is also established firmly through reference to people informing themselves for health action and a health educator helping in the process.

The thinking of another generation of health educators is reflected in the report of the 1973 President's Committee on Health Education, which stated: "Health education is a process which bridges the gap between health information and health practice." It also suggested, by inference, that a health educator is one who is involved in "helping people . . . develop their lifestyles in health enhancing directions."[3]

These definitions build on earlier definitions but add new elements. Specifically, they seem to emphasize the idea of "process," that such changes do not usually come into being in a "one-shot encounter" but rather are developed over time. They reinforce the idea that health education is not concerned primarily with merely dispensing information, indicating that many people already know what they ought to do to be healthier. The definitions imply that health education is more concerned with motivation, attitudes, and beliefs, suggesting that although clients know what may be important, what they believe is more important, because this determines what they do about what they know. The idea of individual responsibility for one's own health decisions is reinforced, as is the idea that a health educator is a helper.

A few years after the committee issued its definitions, Mico and Ross advocated a stronger behavioral emphasis, stating that "health education is the application of behavioral science for improving the processes of health change and problem solving" and that a health educator is "any person who engages in a planned approach to the use of health education for individual, organizational, or social change."[4]

These definitions emphasized the fact that health education is planned change, that the focus should be on specific behaviors and on planning change in organizations and in society that promote health, as opposed to being limited to working with individual behaviors. A new dimension of health education was formalized in the definition, that of organizational development and political enterprises.

Another important work came out in 1980. In this work, Green and colleagues defined health education as any "designed combination of methods to facilitate voluntary adaptations of behavior conducive to health."[5] This definition reinforced that it was a planned experience, as indeed did the title of their book—*Health Education Planning: A Diagnostic Approach*. It also gave renewed emphasis to the concept of the individual making voluntary behavior change, de-emphasizing the more manipulative methods sometimes promoted by behaviorists.

The staff of the Role Delineation Project reviewed the aforementioned definitions and many others in 1980 and concluded that for purposes of their project:

> Health Education is the process of assisting individuals, acting separately and collectively, to make informed decisions on matters affecting individual, family, and community health. Based upon scientific foundations, health education is a field of interest, a discipline, a profession.[6]

In 1992, self-study materials for the Community Health Specialist Certification Exam singled out advocacy for emphasis:

> Community advocacy is a process used for social change. This process includes community organizing, coalition building, education of the community and the decision makers.[7]

> Health education advocates recognize and address barriers that impact successful health education interventions, promote self-help, community participation, capacity building, and health behavior change, and show sensitivity to needs of diverse populations.[8]

> Advocacy for health education also requires knowing the successes in the field, the effectiveness of interventions and conditions required to achieve successful behavior change.[9]

The 1990 Joint Committee on Health Education Terminology described a health educator as "a practitioner who is professionally prepared in the field of health education who demonstrates competence in both theory and practice and who accepts responsibility to advance the aims of the health education profession."[10] The report further reported that a Certified Health Education Specialist (CHES) is "an individual who is credentialed as a result of demonstrating competency based on criteria established by the National Commission for Health Education Credentialing, Inc. (NCHEC)."[11] This process is discussed later in this and subsequent chapters.

These selected definitions stress the fact that health education is a process, that individuals should retain control of the resulting decisions, and that the focus is on knowledge that clients need to make intelligent decisions. Although these definitions do not specifically criticize behaviorism, they also do not emphasize it, returning almost full circle to information dispensing and to leaving it up to the individual as to whether the information will be used.

HEALTH PROMOTION

Health promotion is a term of more recent origin, which has become widely used in recent years. Many people use the term interchangeably with *health education.*

Health promotion is most often defined as "the combination of educational and environmental supports for actions and conditions of living conducive to health."[12] The author of this definition stated that "environmental supports refer to the social, political, economic, organizational, policy and regulatory circumstances bearing on behavior or more directly on health."[13]

It is readily apparent that health promotion uses educational and regulatory approaches, so health promotion is, strictly speaking, bigger than health education. Confusion occurs because health educators have always used more than educational strategies.

Glanz perceptively stated, "While greater precision of terminology can be achieved by drawing a clear distinction between health education and health promotion, to do so is to ignore long-standing tenets of health education and its broad social mission."[14]

We will generally use the term *health education* because of the considerable overlap, although we acknowledge that there are differences. *Health promotion* is, however, used in Chapter 9, "Worksite Health Promotion and Employee Assistance Programs," because that term is more commonly used in worksite programs.

One responsibility emerges in all of the above cited definitions: to improve the quality of life. Health educators must help people have higher quality living in all of life's settings.

FACTORS THAT CHANGED THE PROFESSION

The certification of health educators came into being in response to (1) the growing marketplace interest in and demand for health education; (2) the tendency of some to call themselves or their staff health educators to satisfy this demand; (3) the evolving professional organizations that were becoming increasingly concerned about professional standards and quality assurance; and (4) the colleges and universities that were training health educators and were caught between the demands of the marketplace, the demands of professional organizations, and the restraints of their institutions.

The growing marketplace demands for health education occurred in response to a number of factors, most notably the consumerism movement and the inflationary spiral of the economy. Consumers were demanding a voice in decision making when it affected their health. Others were demanding the right to "self-care." Many people were showing increased interest and practice in such activities as exercise, nutrition, and stress reduction. Being healthy was becoming faddish and interest in having a high level of wellness was growing. All these facts required a knowledge base or, in short, health education for a growing segment of society.

The economy of the United States and of many other nations was in an inflationary spiral, and health care experienced more inflation than other sectors of the economy. Concurrently, there was evidence that health education had the potential to reduce health care costs and that it was cheaper to prevent disease than to treat it. With growing government involvement in financing health care, it became prudent to also have growing government involvement in preventing health problems. Accordingly, health education became a mandated service in some organizations and states and a recommended, rapidly growing service in others. Naturally, emphasis shifted perceptibly from cost containment to health promotion as the demand for limiting health care costs increased.

The law of supply and demand affects health education as well as other services and products. As the demand for health education increased, the numbers began to grow. Some agencies simply designated existing staff members as health educators and added this responsibility to existing job descriptions. This process was not necessarily done to circumvent the intent of legislative or accrediting bodies. Many of these staff members had been involved earlier in some form of health education, and the changing of titles was an attempt to stay current with the times. Furthermore, the definitions to this point in time did not spell out criteria or standards but instead, in functional definitions, suggested that people who engaged in these functions were in fact health educators.

The situation caused some uneasiness among many professionally trained health educators. People were calling themselves health educators and were functioning as health educators without benefit of formal training in the discipline.

More important, the emphasis on accountability was increasing, and the professionals knew that emphasis on health education at this time provided a unique opportunity to demonstrate that health education could change behavior, prevent disease and disorder, and do it in a cost-efficient manner. However, untrained people were being used in understaffed and underfinanced programs and in efforts that appeared programmed to fail. Many did not want this opportunity to advance the profession to go by without their best effort and realized that professional training was part of the answer. Although health educators recognized the need for any and all who were interested in health education, there was also a need for people who knew what they were doing and who had a good chance to be successful. Accordingly, colleges and universities began developing more undergraduate training programs for people who had already taken a few courses or who had a two-year degree to use in pursuing a baccalaureate degree. Also, colleges and universities that had baccalaureate degree programs began to develop health education graduate programs, to be available to those who had entered the profession without benefit of a baccalaureate degree in the field.

For several previous generations, health educators trained primarily at the graduate level in schools of public health. Regulating agencies developed and enforced standards regarding the establishing of a school of public health and the awarding of a master's of public health (MPH) degree. There was little interest or need to regulate health education training programs because they were included in the larger review of a school of public health.

In the mid-1960s, however, federally funded community programs mandated health education, with the outcome that existing health educators were "hired away" and the agencies had difficulty in filling the resultant vacancies. This sudden and large increase in demand gave rise to the increase in supply by colleges and universities. Universities with undergraduate programs in school health education reasoned that they could develop a four-year program that would produce a graduate who could do community health education. The number of such undergraduate programs has grown from a few in the mid-1960s to more than 300. Similarly, the number of master's degree programs in colleges and universities has proliferated rapidly.

The American Public Health Association developed standards for graduate programs offered in schools other than those of public health and began accrediting such programs in the late 1960s. The Society for Public Health Education, Inc., developed standards for undergraduate training programs and began accrediting them in the late 1970s. The Council on Education for Public Health, created in 1974, assumed the School of Public Health and other program approval activities of the American Public Health Association, including selected graduate programs in public health education. The Society for Public Health Education, Inc., and the American Alliance of Health Education have combined forces for an undergraduate approval process.

Colleges and universities faced severe problems of their own, in both finances and enrollment. The result of this crisis in higher education was that colleges and universities often were unable to implement the changes required for accreditation. Furthermore, accreditation agencies were proliferating, and many colleges and universities either could not or would not seek specialized or "programmatic accreditation," except in unusual situations. The university as an entity would seek accreditation but would operate on the assumption that individual programs would not seek accreditation.

The decisions had two kinds of effects. Many universities complied with the standards as best they could but did not seek accreditation because of the cost involved in doing a self-study, hosting the accreditation team for a site visit, and paying the annual dues to accrediting agencies. Such voluntary compliance did upgrade standards of practice and the profession. Other universities, however, continued to turn out graduates from programs with minimal curricular offerings that were staffed by faculty who were trained in other disciplines. Graduates of such programs called themselves health educators and had a degree in health education. Not surprisingly, many administrators hired such graduates, which in turn increased the emphasis among professional organizations on program accreditation.

The situation also resulted in a lot of dialogue among health educators, especially among those who were involved in training health educators, as to what health educators are, what their role is, and, by implication, what training they need. Could a program that had been training school health educators prepare such a schoolteacher to be effective in a community within the constraints of a baccalaureate degree? Could a person who was trained to function in a community setting also function in a hospital or industrial setting? Should health educators be licensed or certified? Should programs continue to be accredited or approved, or should the emphasis shift to certification or licensure of those who pass an examination system, regardless of where or how the basics were learned? These issues and others were part of the focus of the Role Delineation Project, which began operation in 1978. This project involved a large cross section of practicing professionals in verifying that the roles and skills were actually those used by practicing health educators.

Once the roles were verified, working committees formed to prepare curricular materials. Development of model curricula was begun to assist training institutions. A National Conference for Institutions Preparing Health Educators was held in the fall of 1982.

Guidelines and frameworks for the development of competency-based curricula for entry-level health educators were completed by 1985.[15] In 1987, the Metropolitan Life Foundation supported the development of a model for continuing professional education for health educators.

CERTIFICATION OF HEALTH EDUCATION SPECIALISTS

In 1988, the National Commission for Health Education Credentialing, Inc., was established. The commission is an independent nonprofit national agency with three main purposes: (1) to certify health education specialists, (2) to promote professional development, and (3) to strengthen professional preparation.

The commission began "charter certification" of individual health educators currently working in health education who meet certain academic and experience requirements. The commission began to administer the first credentialing examinations for health educators in 1990. The examinations are based on the defined competencies for health education specialists. The commission describes the benefits as follows:[16]

1. Attests to the individual knowledge and skills essential to the field of practice.
2. Assists employers to identify qualified practitioners.
3. Helps assure consumers of validity of services offered.
4. Enhances the profession.
5. Recognizes a commitment to professional standards.
6. Delineates the scope of practice.
7. Provides recognition to individual health education specialists.

Certification grants recognition to an individual who has met the qualifications for entry level health education professional. The standards have been specified by seven professional health education organizations and individual health educators.[17]

Those eligible for examination must have a degree from an accredited institution of higher education with a health education emphasis (minimum of 25 semester hour credits or 37 quarter hour credits).[18]

For additional information on the examination contact the National Commission for Health Education Credentialing, Inc., Professional Examination Service at 2175 Riverside Drive, Suite 740, New York, NY 10115.

The authors believe that development of a national process to certify health education specialists is one of the most important occurrences in community health education in the past two or three decades. Anyone who aspires to a career in the field should be certified as soon as possible. The certification is meaningful and should be proudly displayed on resumes and business cards. The certification process has had an impact on hiring practices, revision of professional preparation curricula, and availability of continuing education programs for health educators.

IN CONCLUSION

What is a health educator? A variety of job descriptions exist with differing skills required. The functions mentioned will not all be on the job description of any single health educator. Likewise, it is not expected that any single health educator will be expert in all areas, or that university training programs will develop specialists in all areas. Rather, a need is perceived, a job description is prepared, a health instructor is hired, and the final product is a blend of the perceived need and the interests and abilities of the health educator.

***

Suggested Learning Activities

1. List several important health problems and then brainstorm a list of skills needed to solve these problems.
2. Identify personal hobbies and other interests that could, if cultivated, be useful to a health educator.
3. Prepare a job description for an entry-level health educator that includes educational requirements, functions, and responsibilities.
4. Obtain a copy of *The Health Education Specialist: Self-Study for Professional Competence* and review it, especially the self-assessment exam.

NOTES

1. C. Turner, *Community Health Educator's Compendium of Knowledge* (St. Louis: C.V. Mosby Co., 1951), 11.

2. Ibid.

3. *Report of the President's Committee on Health Education* (New York: Public Affairs Institute, 1973), 19.

4. P. Mico and H. Ross, *Health Education and Behavioral Science* (Oakland, Calif.: Third Party Associates, 1975), xxi.

5. L. Green, et al., *Health Education Planning: A Diagnostic Approach* (Mountain View, Calif.: Mayfield Publishing Co., 1980), 11.

6. Health Education and Credentialing: The Role Delineation Project, *Focal Points* (July 1980):6.

7. S.G. Deeds, *The Health Education Specialist: Self-Study for Professional Competence* (Los Alamitos, Calif.: Loose Canon Publications, 1992), 8.

8. Ibid.

9. Ibid.

10. Report of the 1990 Joint Committee on Health Education Terminology, *Journal of Health Education* 22, no. 2 (1991):103.

11. Ibid, 104.

12. L. Green and M. Kreuter, *Health Promotion Planning: An Educational and Environmental Approach* (Mountain View, Calif.: Mayfield Publishing Co., 1993), 17.

13. Ibid.

14. K. Glanz, et al., *Health Behavior and Health Education: Theory, Research and Practice* (San Francisco:Jossey-Bass, Inc. Publishers, 1990), 9.

15. *A Framework for the Development of Competency-Based Curricula for Entry-Level Health Educators* (New York: National Taskforce on Preparation and Practice of Health Educators, Inc., 1985).

16. *Certification of Health Education Specialists Charter Certification Phase* (New York: National Commission for Health Education Credentialing, Inc., 1988).

17. S. Deeds, *The Health Education Specialist,* 115.

18. Ibid.

SUGGESTED READING

Bedworth, A., and Bedworth, D. 1992. *The profession and practice of health education.* Dubuque, Iowa: Wm. C. Brown Publishers.

Deeds, S.G. 1992. *The health education specialist: Self-study for professional competence.* Los Alamitos, Calif.: Loose Canon Publications.

Guinta, M., and Allegrante, J.P. 1992. The President's Committee on Health Education: A 20 year retrospectum on its politics and policy impact. *American Journal of Public Health* July, 128.

Healthy children 2000: National health promotion and disease prevention objectives related to mothers, infants, children, adolescents, and youth. 1992. Washington, D.C.: U.S. Government Printing Office.

Healthy people 2000: National health promotion and disease prevention objectives. 1991. Washington, D.C.: U.S. Government Printing Office.

Report of the 1990 Joint Committee on Health Education Terminology. 1991. *Journal of Health Education* March/April.

Chapter 2

Future Perspectives of Practice and Professional Preparation

The 21st century is almost here. At the beginning of the last millennium, cataclysmic events bordered on mass hysteria. Religious movements started, armies of the poor wreaked havoc in Europe, and the end of the world was anticipated. People were terrified of facing an uncertain future.

Few people expect such events to reoccur this millennium, but it is an unusually good opportunity to look ahead, to make predictions, and to shape the future. Various public health personnel have already looked ahead and have developed plans for the year 2001. Community health education is a significant ingredient in plans for the future.

INCREASED PREVENTION EMPHASIS

Many of the health problems the nation will deal with in the balance of this century and into the next are fully preventable.

> If tobacco use in this country stopped entirely today, an estimated 390,000 fewer Americans would die before their time each year. If all Americans reduced their consumption of foods high in fat to well below current levels and engaged in physical activity no more strenuous than sustained walking for thirty minutes a day, additional results of a similar magnitude could be expected. If alcohol was never carelessly used in our society, about 100,000 fewer people would die from unnecessary illness and injury.[1]

These are but a few examples of how mortality rates can be affected. Similar examples could be cited for morbidity rates. Even AIDS, the scourge of the 1990s, is almost entirely preventable, as are most other communicable diseases. Most chronic disease rates can also be impacted by prevention programs.

PAST SUCCESSES IN HEALTH EDUCATION PROGRAMS

Progress in professional preparation in conjunction with targeted comprehensive efforts of federal, state, and local agencies, has resulted in improved practice of health education, with significant results. Major decreases have occurred in heart disease and stroke mortality, due in large part to hypertension detection and control and a decline in cigarette smoking. Accidental injury and death rates have declined rapidly. Infant mortality rates, although still much too high, are at a new low. Major reductions in cervical cancer have occurred, and some decrease in lung cancer has been observed. *Healthy People 2000* states

> Virtually all these conditions are preventable. Mobilizing the considerable energies and creativities of the nation in the interest of disease prevention and health promotion is an economic imperative.[2]

> Health promotion and disease prevention comprise perhaps our best opportunity to reduce the ever-increasing portion of our resources which we spend to treat preventable illness and functional impairment. Smoking, for example, is the single most preventable cause of death and illness in the country. Smoking-related illnesses cost our health care system more than $65 billion annually.[3]

PUBLIC POLICY CHANGES

National reports are of major significance to the profession. While they may be viewed as "job security" to some health educators, they should also be viewed as a professional imperative, one which, if not met, could lead to the decline of the profession. Never in history have so much broad-based support and policy support and so many dollars been directed to prevention programs. At this writing in 1993, the two significant documents are *Healthy People 2000: National Health Promotion and Disease Prevention Objectives* and *Healthy Communities 2000: Model Standards: Guidelines for Community Attainment of the Year 2000 National Health Objectives.*

> *Healthy People 2000* is a statement of national opportunities. . . . It is the product of a national effort, involving twenty-two expert working groups, a consortium which has grown to include almost 300 national organizations, all state health departments, and the Institute of Medicine of the National Academy of Sciences, which helped the U.S. Public Health Service to manage the consortium, convene regional and national hearings, and receive testimony from more than

750 individuals and organizations. After extensive public review and comment, involving more than 10,000 people, the objectives were revised and refined to produce this report.[4]

The need for national health objectives was recognized and emphasized during the 1970s. Advocates planned for the objectives to be national in scope because a coordinated effort between the 50 states was required to accrue enough critical mass to show impact. Impact was likely to be demonstrable if the states focused on the same priorities. Certainly, federal and state prevention resources could also be focused on whatever priorities emerged from the process.

The objectives needed to be measurable to provide for accountability. Moreover, governmental agencies were largely responsible for collecting and reporting morbidity and mortality data; so an effort was made to use these measures for baseline data. The significant impact on such rates has been in large part responsible for increasing emphasis on health education.

The first report published in this series was *Healthy People: The Surgeon General's Report on Health Promotion and Disease Prevention.* Soon thereafter, it was followed by *Promoting Health, Preventing Disease: Objectives for the Nation,* which established targets to be accomplished by 1990. *Healthy People 2000: National Health Promotion and Disease Prevention Objectives,* published in 1991, focused on objectives to be accomplished by the year 2000.

As the health promotion titles of the publications indicate, more than educational strategies are emphasized. In fact, objectives are organized into three types: health status, risk reduction, and services and protection.

NEW IMPERATIVES FOR HEALTH EDUCATION

Although health educators should be conversant with all three types of objectives, they should thoroughly understand the risk reduction objectives, which are designed to "reduce the prevalence of risks to health" or "increase behaviors known to reduce such risks." The risk reduction objectives are included in Appendix B of this book for ease of reader access. It is strongly suggested that virtually all written or oral community health class work be related to one or more of these objectives. These are state and national objectives and students who work with them thus become part of a national project. Also of importance, these objectives are what future employers will be implementing. Using the objectives in class projects is a good way for faculty and students to further integrate practice and professional preparation. It is also an outstanding way to prepare for job interviews. Regardless of how health educators become conversant with them, no health education student should graduate without being familiar with the objectives and being able to discuss community programming that would help the community meet those objectives.

In addition to being categorized by type, the nation's health promotion and disease prevention objectives are grouped by age group and special populations. These subgroups and the related morbidity and mortality rates help practitioners to focus on narrowly defined target groups with group-specific intervention. These strategies are also likely to increase impact and to result in demonstrable rate decreases nationwide. Indeed, if these special populations are not reached with effective, culturally appropriate programs, many of the objectives for the year 2000 will not be achieved.

CDC's PATCH

The U.S. government's Centers for Disease Control and Prevention (CDC) has developed a Planned Approach to Community Health (PATCH), which is a facilitating, collaborative, community-based program. This program is an extension of the Healthy Communities 2000 philosophy and has a proven track record.

> The PATCH process has demonstrated that principles of the large, controlled community-based programs can be carried out at the local level. Communities are able to organize themselves for action, collect, analyze and interpret local data, set priorities and objectives, and implement and evaluate interventions.[5]

> Such programs have documented changes in behavior and risk factor levels, but their long term impact on disease and mortality is known.[6]

The CDC has funded numerous PATCH projects. The data continue to be collected and analyzed, and the effective projects are diffused throughout the health education system. In April 1992, *The Journal of Health Education* focused its issue on PATCH, with a theme statement: "Community Health Promotion: The Agenda for the '90s." It is an excellent reference to use to become better acquainted with PATCH and with successful local applications of it.

HEALTH CARE REFORM'S IMPACT ON PREVENTION

Health care reform has been a major issue in the decade of the 1990s as the cost of health care continued to increase faster than inflation. Both the Republican administration and the Democratic administration called for health care reform. The Republicans responded primarily to the needs of business and industry, which experienced financial duress due to health insurance cost increases in the double digits annually. The Democrats responded primarily to the growing proportion of the population not covered by any form of health insurance due to unemployment, self-employment, and other financial reasons. There was some political overlap, of course, and other factors were involved. For example, both political parties did agree that a major element was the cost of health care providers protecting themselves against lawsuits. Although some states have taken initiatives, little has yet occurred on the federal level to reform the nation's health care delivery system.

From a health education perspective, a significant issue is how much emphasis is placed on prevention. Without question, the United States has the best health care in the world for critically ill patients. Traditionally, more than 95 percent of the nation's health care dollar has been spent on acute care rather than preventive services. This policy issue continues to be raised. What would happen if more of the dollars now spent on the terminally ill were spent on preventive health services for children? Of course, family members of terminally ill patients want the best treatment possible for their loved ones, but then so do the parents of infants and children in need of preventive services.

There clearly is a need to engage in health care cost containment. The tendency sometimes is to cut preventive services, perhaps because it is hard to count and report illnesses or deaths that have been prevented. It is relatively easy to continue the practice of spending most health care dollars on critical care. Expenses for long-term care of the elderly with chronic diseases are also rapidly escalating in importance. More patients now survive medical crises and therefore need more long-term care at prohibitively expensive rates.

The problems are complex, and the policy discussions will continue well into the 21st century. There simply is not enough money to meet all needs, and so prioritizing the nature of health care expenditure will continue to weigh on politicians, particularly as expenditures impact employers, the very young, the very old, and the very poor. One constant remains, and it was eloquently stated by Louis Sullivan, former Secretary of the U.S. Department of Health and Human Services:

> We would be terribly remiss if we did not seize the opportunity presented by health promotion and disease prevention to dramatically cut health-care costs, to prevent the premature onset of disease and disability, and to help all Americans achieve healthier, more productive lives.[7]

IN CONCLUSION

The view of the 21st century is exciting from our present vantage point. Chapter 28 projects trends and offers considerable speculation on what the future will be like. The more substantive question, however, is what the 21st century's perspective of the decade of the 1990s will be. The answer to this question depends in large part on the nature of professional preparation programs in the next several years. Many leaders of the 21st century are currently enrolled in college and are among those who are reading this paragraph.

***

Suggested Learning Activities

1. Compare the major health problems of the 19th and 20th centuries. Identify the most likely health problems of the 21st century. What trends are evident?
2. Compare the health education approaches in the 19th and 20th centuries. How will they likely change in the 21st century?
3. Discuss the merits of altruism as the basis for public health policy. Compare the relative merits of altruism and economics as the basis of public health policy.
4. Review the risk reduction objectives in Appendix B. Become conversant with their format and the sections by which they are organized. Identify three categories of personal interest to you.

NOTES

1. *Healthy People 2000: National Health Promotion and Disease Prevention Objectives* (Washington, D.C.: U.S. Government Printing Office, 1991).

2. Ibid., 6.

3. Ibid., v.

4. Ibid., i.

5. Preface, *Journal of Health Education* (Special Issue, April 1992): 133.

6. Ibid.

7. *Healthy People 2000,* vi.

SUGGESTED READING

Community health promotion agenda for the '90s. *Journal of Health Education* (Special issue, April 1992).

Healthy communities 2000: Model standards: Guidelines for community attainment of the year 2000 national health objectives. 1991. Washington, D.C.: U.S. Government Printing Office.

Healthy people 2000: National health promotion and disease prevention objectives. 1991. Washington, D.C.: U.S. Government Printing Office.

Chapter 3

Professional Organizations

Health education as a profession is in a constant state of growth and change. As indicated in Chapter 1, there is a wide variety of issues related to professional preparation and practice of health education. Often, professional organizations are the most effective vehicles to use in responding to administrators and policy makers. One need only look at the efforts of various national professional organizations for health educators regarding the development of standards, training, continuing education, quality assurance, and ethics to realize the breadth of critical issues facing the profession.

The individual health educator, whether a new graduate or a veteran, needs to keep abreast of the ever-changing issues facing the profession in order to maintain a grasp on contemporary developments in the theory and practice of health education. Indeed, professionalism is an important function of health education, particularly in light of certification and credentialing requirements. One method of accomplishing this is to participate actively in one or more professional organizations.

There are more than 17,000 members combined in the eight health education units of seven national organizations that constitute the Coalition of National Health Education Organizations.[1] The functions of professional organizations, the role of the health educator in such organizations, the types of professional organizations for health educators to join, and the current issues facing those organizations are explored in this chapter.

FUNCTIONS OF PROFESSIONAL ORGANIZATIONS

Professional organizations enable their members to coalesce concerns, promote growth and progress through research, provide opportunities for individual professionals, enlarge the scope of the field, and provide opportunities for individual professionals to contribute to progress in the field. The vitality of any professional organization is based on both the service it provides to members related to the items just mentioned and the active participation of members within the organization.

Professional organizations vary according to field, orientation, membership criteria, scope, and service. However, the following common threads of function can be found in most organizations.

Research

Professional organizations provide a forum to promote and build a viable body of professional research on which to base preparation and practice. This is accomplished through the publishing of research in the professional journals of the organizations and by the presentation of papers at professional meetings. Some organizations also underwrite or sponsor opportunities to develop and review research findings. In all facets of research there is usually a strong level of cooperation among universities, practitioners, funding agencies, and the professional organizations.

Standards of Preparation and Practice

Many professional organizations develop and maintain standards of preparation and practice in their respective fields. Role delineation, criterion-referenced examinations, university program approval, peer review, accreditation, and professional registration and credentialing have all been topics of major discussions and meetings since the mid-1970s. Sometimes membership in an organization is predicated on a person's academic preparation, experience, or both. This, too, is a method of addressing professional standards.

Continuing Education and Professional Meetings

Members of professional organizations can participate in professional meetings and in continuing education programs. These activities give the practitioner an opportunity to become aware of current trends and research and to compare notes and share ideas on mutual problems with colleagues. Members may also be able to earn university credit at workshops sponsored by professional organizations. Credit is also given to participants needing continuing credentialing education units for Certified Health Education Specialist renewal.

Professional Policies, Politics, and Advocacy

Professional organizations are the leading voices for the field when national or state policies, legislation, or funding requires input from the profession. Members are represented by organization officers and staff in the discussion of key issues that may impact directly on the profession or on the delivery of health education services. Most organizations have standing committees on legislation and policy development at whatever level they function. Professional organizations are expected to represent their members in particular and the profession as a whole in a wide range of issues and forums.

The role of professional organizations and their respective members regarding policy advocacy has been gaining credibility. Examples of this function are providing testimony to public meetings or legislative hearings; taking stands on smoking, AIDS, or the public health aspects of nuclear war; and actively participating in setting national policies such as the year 2000 objectives for health promotion.

For health education, membership in a professional organization is voluntary, and therefore the viability of any organization relies heavily on the vitality and active support of its members. The increase in growth that most of the organizations have enjoyed has provided impetus to the development of paid staff support. The cost of providing a wide range of member services has caused an increase in dues, fund raising, and, most recently, exploration of consolidation and sharing of resources among organizations.

ROLE OF THE HEALTH EDUCATOR IN PROFESSIONAL ORGANIZATIONS

Health education professionals face careers of constant change with regard to trends, places of practice, professional expectations, employer expectations, and societal demands. Keeping up with these changes falls not only in the purview of professional societies and the services they provide, but also in the purview of the professionals themselves.

As a professional, the health educator is expected to maintain a level of professional competence in both content and method. By actively participating in professional meetings, keeping up with the literature, exchanging ideas with colleagues, and using peer review when available, the health educator can grow professionally.

Participation in professional organization varies, based on each person's needs and experience. For the entry-level professional this may be meeting other health educators, comparing classroom theories with practical applications and problems, and making job contacts. For the experienced health educator, this may be sharing research, serving on organizational committees, maintaining collegial networks, and providing leadership to the organization and the profession.

The changing needs of any professional after graduation from college may be expressed as follows:

When the young professional moves into the field, the prime responsibility for learning passes from the professional school to the graduate and to the associations to which the graduate belongs. The very first thing the young professional may discover is something suspected all along: Professors did not completely prepare the student for the real affairs in life. The voice of the aggrieved alumnus is always loud in the land and, no matter what the profession, the burden of complaint is the same. In the first five years after graduation, alumni say that they should have been taught more practical techniques. In the next five years, they say they should have been given more basic theory. In the tenth to fifteenth years, they inform the faculty that they should have been taught more about administration or about their relations with their co-workers and subordinates. In the subsequent five years, they condemn the failure of their professors to put the profession in its larger historical, social, and economic contexts. After the twentieth year, they insist that they should have been given a broader orientation to all knowledge, scientific and humane. Sometime after that, they stop giving advice; the university has deteriorated so badly since they left that it is beyond hope.[2]

TYPES OF PROFESSIONAL ORGANIZATIONS FOR HEALTH EDUCATORS

The history of health education and the changing settings in which it is practiced have led to the development of various professional organizations for health educators. To date, these organizations have evolved along the traditional practice lines of school health and community or public health education. However, new work settings for health educators and the broad concept of health promotion have seen a growth of new organizations specific to patient education, behavioral psychology, prospective medicine, and other fields in which health educators may now be found.

In 1972 the Coalition of National Health Education Organizations was created to address the mutual needs of the member organizations in a federation mechanism. The creation of the coalition was stimulated in 1971 by meetings called by the Executive Council of the then School Health Division, American Alliance for Health, Physical Education, Recreation, and Dance. Another major influence was the recommendation from the President's Committee on Health Education, appointed by President Nixon in 1971, which encouraged the coalition concept.[3]

The coalition comprises professional organizations that have identifiable memberships of health educators and a major commitment to health education. Membership includes eight health education units of seven national organizations. These organizations are American College Health Association (Health Education

Section); American Public Health Association (Public Health Education and Health Promotion Section and School Health Education and Services Section); American School Health Association; Association for the Advancement of Health Education; Society for Public Health Education, Inc.; Association of State and Territorial Directors of Public Health Education; and the Society of State Directors for Health, Physical Education, and Recreation. The abbreviations and major publications of these and selected other organizations are listed in Table 3-1.

The coalition has a primary goal to "mobilize the resources of the health education profession in order to expand and improve health education, whether community based or occupational, or whether it involves patient education or school health education."[4] Headquarters for the coalition is the National Center for Health Education in New York City. The coalition has listed five major purposes:[5]

Table 3–1 National Professional Health Education Organizations

Organization	Abbreviation	Publication(s)
American College Health Association, Health Education Section	ACHA	*Journal of the American College Health Association*
American Public Health Association, Public Health Education and Health Promotion Section and School Health Education and Services Section	APHA	*American Journal of Public Health,* PHE and SHE section newsletters; monthly newsletter, *Today's Health*
American School Health Association	ASHA	*Journal of School Health*
American Society for Health Care Education and Training	ASHET	*Journal of Health Care Education and Training;* quarterly newsletter, *Dateline*
Association for the Advancement of Health Education	AAHE	*Health Education*
Society for Public Health Education, Inc.	SOPHE	*Health Education Quarterly, SOPHE News and Views*
Association of State and Territorial Directors of Public Health Education	ASTDPHE	
Society of State Directors for Health, Physical Education, and Recreation	SSDHPER	
International Union for Health Promotion and Education	IUHPE	Quarterly journal, *Hygie*

Note: Other major journals for health educators include *American Journal of Health Promotion, American Journal of Preventive Medicine, Health Values,* and *Health Education Research, Theory and Practice.*

1. To facilitate national-level communications, collaboration, and coordination among the member organizations
2. To provide a forum for the identification and discussion of health education issues
3. To formulate recommendations and take appropriate action on issues affecting the member interests
4. To serve as a communication and advisory resource for agencies, organizations, and people in the public and private sectors on health education issues
5. To serve as a focus for the exploration and resolution of issues pertinent to professional health educators

A health education professional may choose to join one or more of the various professional organizations. The major focus, membership, and other facts about the member organizations of the coalition are discussed briefly in the following paragraphs.

American College Health Association

The American College Health Association (ACHA) is made up of professionals and institutions of higher education dealing with health problems and issues in academic communities. It promotes continuing education, research, and program development related to educational institutions. With the increased amount of health education programming in college and university health services, ACHA has become an important forum for health educators functioning in those settings. For additional information, contact ACHA at 1300 Picard Drive, Suite 200, Rockville, MD 20850.

American Public Health Association

The American Public Health Association (APHA) is the largest and oldest professional health organization in the United States. It represents the major disciplines and specialists related to public health from community health planning and dental health to statistics and veterinary public health. APHA has two primary sections of interest to health educators: the Public Health Education and Health Promotion Section and the School Health Education and Services Section.

The Public Health Education and Health Promotion Section has more than 2,000 members and is one of the largest sections of APHA. It is concerned with providing input on public health education concerns to the overall APHA organization and its various sections and state affiliates. It is a major sponsor of scientific papers related to health education during the APHA annual meetings.

The School Health Education and Services Section, like the Public Health Education and Health Promotion Section, provides input to the APHA organizations on matters related to comprehensive school health. Such input includes the traditional areas of school health education, school health services, and healthful school environment. This section also sponsors major scientific papers on school health during annual meetings of APHA. For further information, contact APHA at 1015 15th Street, N.W., Washington, DC 20015.

American School Health Association

The American School Health Association (ASHA) is the primary professional organization concerned with issues related to school-age children. School health services, healthful school environment, and comprehensive school health education are key areas of concern. ASHA provides the major forum for discussing school health issues through annual, regional, and local affiliate meetings as well as through publications and journals. ASHA provides leadership in professional preparation and practice standards for school health educators, school nurses, physicians, and dental personnel. For further information, contact ASHA at P.O. Box 708, 1521 S. Water Street, Kent, OH 44240.

American Society for Health Care Education and Training

The American Society for Health Care Education and Training (ASHET) is a membership organization representing a diversity of health care and educational organizations for the purpose of promoting awareness of the educational needs common to all health care personnel, facilitating continuation of professional development in management, and encouraging participation in national health care issues. Health educators in medical care settings find this organization particularly helpful. Local chapters in large cities present programs for professional development. The organization also is linked to the American Hospital Association. ASHET can be reached at 340 N. Lakeshore Drive, Chicago, IL 60611, or (312) 280-6113.

Association for the Advancement of Health Education

The Association for the Advancement of Health Education (AAHE) is part of the larger American Alliance for Health, Physical Education, Recreation, and Dance, which comprises more than 43,000 professionals in sports, dance, safety education, physical education, recreation, and health education. The association has a membership of more than 6,500 professionals from schools, universities, community health agencies, and voluntary agencies. It promotes comprehensive health education programming in schools, colleges, and community settings. AAHE's full-time staff maintain close contact with federal legislative issues. For further information, contact AAHE at 1900 Association Drive, Reston, VA 22091.

Society for Public Health Education, Inc.

Founded in 1950, the Society for Public Health Education, Inc. (SOPHE), has represented a major leadership role in public health education, both nationally and internationally, and is the only independent, free-standing health education organization. The society was formed to promote, encourage, and contribute to the advancement of health for all people by encouraging research, standards of professional preparation and practice, and continuing education. SOPHE has local chapters throughout the United States. It has an approval process for baccalaureate-level programs in community health education and a code of ethics that is widely used in health education (see Appendix C). For further information, contact SOPHE at 2001 Addison Street, Suite 220, Berkeley, CA 94704.

Association of State and Territorial Directors of Public Health Education

The Association of State and Territorial Directors of Public Health Education (ASTDPHE) membership is made up of directors of health education in official state and territorial departments of public health. The association is primarily concerned with developing standards of health education programming at the state level and encouraging other state health education staff. It has been quite active in developing communication mechanisms on health education between state health departments and the federal government. The association is an affiliate of the Association of State and Territorial Health Officials. For further information on ASTDPHE, contact any state department of public health.

Society of State Directors of Health, Physical Education, and Recreation

The Society of State Directors of Health, Physical Education, and Recreation (SSDHPER) membership comprises directors of school health, physical education, and recreation in state agencies. Its goal is to promote comprehensive statewide programs of school health, physical education, recreation, and safety. The society works closely with the American Alliance for Health, Physical Education, Recreation, and Dance and the other members of the coalition. For further information, contact any state department of education.

International Union for Health Promotion and Education

Although not a member of the coalition, the International Union for Health Promotion and Education (IUHPE), formerly the International Union for Health Education, is an international professional organization committed to development of health education around the world and bears special mention. The union cooperates closely with the World Health Organization and the United Nations Educational, Scientific, and Cultural Organization (UNESCO) in a variety of international forums. IUHPE has four major objectives aimed at improving health through education:[6]

1. Establishing an effective link between organizations and people working in the field of health education in various countries of the world and enabling them to pool their experience and knowledge
2. Facilitating worldwide exchanges of information and experiences on all matters relating to health education, including programs, professional preparation, research, methods and techniques, communication media, and so on
3. Promoting scientific research and improving professional preparation in health education
4. Promoting the development of an informed public opinion on matters related to healthful living

The union has constituent, institution, and individual memberships and meets every three years for international conferences. Its journal, the *Hygie International Journal of Health Education*, is printed as a three-language edition (English, French, and German), as are other technical publications. For further information on the union, write the North American Regional Office, c/o P.O. Box 2305, Station "D," Ottawa, Ontario, Canada KIP5K0.

National Council for the Education of Health Professionals in Health Promotion

Another organization that warrants attention, but does not strictly constitute a professional organization for health educators in the context of those described above, is the National Council for the Education of Health Professionals in Health Promotion. Staffed by the American College of Preventive Medicine, its mission is to "assure that all health professionals are adequately prepared to make health promotion and disease prevention part of their routine practice."[7] As such, the council is working with academic institutions that prepare allied health, public health, and primary care professionals to enhance health promotion and disease prevention components in their curricula, accreditation, certification, licensure, and continuing education. For further information, write the American College of Preventive Medicine, 1015 15th Street, N.W., Suite 403, Washington, DC 20005.

National Association for Public Worksite Health Promotion

The National Association for Public Worksite Health Promotion (NAPWHP), formerly the National Association for Public Employee Wellness, is the only professional association whose mission is to serve the needs of coordinators of public sector health promotion programs. NAPWHP membership is available to health promotion professionals in state, local, county, and city government, as well as federal government, state-supported universities and colleges, and school districts. It has a newsletter and annual meetings. For further information, contact the Council of State Governments, Iron Works Pike, P.O. Box 11910, Lexington, KY 40578-1910, or (606) 231-1868.

Association for Worksite Health Promotion

The Association for Worksite Health Promotion (AWHP), formerly the Association of Fitness in Business, exists to advance the profession of worksite health promotion and the career development of its practitioners and to improve the performance of the programs they administer. AWHP has over 3,000 members and provides a newsletter, job bureau, publications, and guidelines. The AWHP journal is the *American Journal of Health Promotion*. For further information, contact the Association for Worksite Health Promotion at 60 Revere Drive, Suite 500, Northbrook, IL 60062, or (708) 480-9574.

Washington Business Group on Health, National Resource Center on Worksite Health Promotion

A joint project of the Washington Business Group on Health (WBGH) and the U.S. Public Health Service Office of Disease Prevention and Health Promotion (ODPHP), the Resource Center's mission is to advance the state of the art in worksite health promotion and encourage adoption of health promotion and disease prevention policies and programs in worksites of all sizes and types around the country. The Resource Center maintains a computerized database on worksite programs, resources, and evaluation studies. For further information, contact the National Resource Center on Worksite Health Promotion at 777 North Capitol Street, N.E., Suite 800, Washington, DC 20002, or (202) 408-9320.

Wellness Councils of America

Wellness Councils of America (WELCOA) is a national nonprofit organization dedicated to promoting healthier lifestyles for all Americans, especially through health promotion activities at the worksite. It has a nationwide network of locally affiliated wellness councils serving corporate members and their employees. WEL-COA also acts as a national clearinghouse and information center on corporate health promotion. For further information, contact the Wellness Councils of America, at 7101 Newport Ave., Suite 311, Omaha, NE 68152-2175, or (402) 572-3590.

National Coordinating Committee on Worksite Health Promotion

Composed of national organizations representing employers and employee groups, the National Coordinating Committee on Worksite Health Promotion (NCCWHP) serves as a forum for networking and problem solving for the business and labor community. The NCCWHP includes federal liaisons from multiple departments and agencies. It examines emerging trends in worksite health promotion and identifies barriers and strategies to encourage implementation of worksite activities to achieve the goals and objectives of *Healthy People 2000*. For further information, contact the Office of Disease Prevention and Health Promotion, U.S. Public Health Service, Room 2132, 330 C Street, S.W., Washington, DC 20201, or (202) 205-8611.

The Health Project

The Health Project is a private-public organization formed to seek out, evaluate, promote, and distribute programs with demonstrated effectiveness in influencing personal health habits and the cost-effective use of health care services. The project has a Worksite Programs Task Force and Community Programs Task Force. In 1992, the project recognized what it considered the top worksite health promotion programs in the United States with the first annual C. Everett Koop Award. For further information, contact the Health Project, 1166 Avenue of the Americas, New York, NY 10036, or (212) 345-7336.

IN CONCLUSION

Professional organizations change from time to time. Professional organizations and their collective memberships provide a vital function in promoting professional preparation, standards of practice, research, leadership, and overall growth of health education as a viable health and education profession. Individual health educators can contribute to their own professional development as well as to the effectiveness of the professional organizations by active, consistent participation at the local, state, national, and even international levels.

The key to discussing professional organizations is service—service to their respective members and service to the public by improved health status through professionally planned and conducted health education programs.

***

Suggested Learning Activities

1. Write to one of the professional organizations discussed in this chapter and inquire about student membership.
2. List the health education professional associations that are active in your state and attend a meeting.
3. Arrange to have representatives of the coalition organizations attend class and discuss their organizations.
4. Compare and contrast the major journals for health education.

NOTES

1. *Directory of the Coalition of National Health Education Organizations*, 1990–91. (New York: National Center for Health Education, 1991), 1–8.

2. C.O. Houle, The Lengthened Line. *Perspectives in Biology and Medicine* II, no. I (Autumn 1967):42.

3. *Facts about the Coalition of National Health Education Organizations*, Information Pamphlet (Muncie, Ind.: Coalition of National Health Education Organizations, 1980), 1.

4. *Working Agreement, The Coalition of National Health Education Organizations*, October 5, 1979.

5. Ibid.

6. *International Union for Health Education Membership Pamphlet* (Ottawa, Ontario: International Union for Health Promotion and Education, 1983).

7. *Recommendations and Strategies for Educating Health Professionals*, Information Pamphlet (Washington, D.C.: National Council for the Education of Health Professionals in Health Promotion, no date).

SUGGESTED READING

Current Issues of *American Journal of Public Health, Journal of School Health, Health Education, Health Education Quarterly, Journal of Health Care Education and Training, The American Journal of Health Promotion,* among others.

Chapter 4

Ethical and Legal Concerns

Health education has been occurring for a long time. The Bible contains many stories and parables concerning health and cleanliness. Other religious and historical writings refer to behavior, clean environment, and methods to prevent illness as proper. Consequently, one of the major factors for the advance of civilization from the dawn of history to the present is that many people have effectively learned positive health behavior. A next step is to begin to demand services that result in improved health status. Yet another step is to demand that others practice good health behaviors.

Questions begin to arise about whether certain practices of health education are morally, ethically, and legally appropriate for today's society, in which an individual's rights are emphasized. For example, should a person be forced to participate in a treatment in order to protect groups of people? Should AIDS patients be provided expensive treatment at government expense, when the needs of children without the disease are neglected by the government because of the cost? Should the parents of all children attending public schools be required to have their children immunized against childhood diseases and those affecting expectant mothers? Or, should they be educated to want to do this? Should children be immunized against mild childhood diseases in which the disease itself may be less traumatic than the shot? What about a society that goes to the limit to protect and preserve all human life, whether genetically inferior or aged, and then educates its young to zero population growth and reinforces this by providing birth control and abortions? What about the ethic overtones of a public health program that involves testing for sickle cell anemia but that does not provide affordable educational programs or genetic counseling for those affected? Or, for that matter, is it proper for those not formally trained in the profession to take on the duties of and claim to be health educators? Is it ethical for individuals who believe that homosexuality is a form of deviant behavior to work with AIDS patients?

THE NATURE OF A PROFESSION

Attempts have been made for some time to establish the practice of health education as a true profession. Such recognition would certainly provide economic and professional advantages for those involved.

Wilensky stated that certain characteristics are necessary for an occupation to be considered a profession. He described a profession as "one which requires an abstract body of knowledge, a base of systematic theory, work which is challenging, for which long training is necessary, and which has a code of ethics and an orientation toward service."[1] Health education appears to meet these criteria. This book and others describe the abstract body of knowledge required for practice, as does the certification process. Numerous books and journals describe the base of systematic theory, including the journal *Health Education Research: Theory and Practice*. Certainly those in the field find the work both challenging and rewarding. The certification process generally requires a baccalaureate or master's degree, and doctorates are available. Clearly, long training is necessary. The Society of Public Health Education has adopted a code of ethics, and by mid-1994, the Association for the Advancement of Health Education is expected to have a similar code of ethics. The codes are discussed in the succeeding sections of this chapter, and the SOPHE Code is presented in its entirety in Appendix C. Finally, the entire emphasis is on service to others.

Health education *is* a profession. Now is the time to declare its legitimacy and put the issue to rest. With stature as a profession, however, come obligations to behave as professionals. According to Fromer, health professionals should meet the following criteria:[2]

1. The health profession is worked at full time and is the principal source of income.
2. Health professionals see their work as a commitment to a calling.
3. Health professionals are set apart from others by signs and symbols that are readily identifiable.
4. Health professionals are organized with their peers for reasons other than money and other tangible benefits.
5. Health professionals possess useful knowledge and skills based on an education of exceptional duration and difficulty.
6. Health professionals exhibit a service orientation that goes beyond financial motivation.
7. Health professionals proceed in their work by their own judgment. They are autonomous.

THE NATURE OF ETHICS

Ethical issues involve opinions on what is good or bad. Laws and morals assume there is a single correct behavior, whereas ethics deals with beliefs, values, and preferences of individuals or groups.

Ethics, by definition, is concerned with debatable and controversial issues. In a sense, ethical decisions are intensely personal. Even if one concurs with someone else's beliefs, the decision to concur is individual.

Decisions that affect groups of people are most ethical when they produce the following:[3]

- the greatest good for the most people (good motives and good results)
- justice (fair and impartially administered)
- utilitarianism (practical enough that it can work in foreseeable circumstances)

Individual behavior can be considered ethical or good if it

- increases trust among people
- promotes integrity and decreases deceit in relationships
- dissolves barriers between people
- increases cooperative attitudes
- enhances self-respect
- does not exploit others
- eliminates confusion and allows individuals to move toward respect

AREAS OF RESPONSIBILITY

The Public

Ethical and legal concerns dealing with the public vary from overall commitments to do public good to concerns with fairness and equality for each individual.

Green and Anderson referred to a worldwide recognition that the health of all people is intrinsic to international peace through the establishment of the World Health Organization (WHO) as part of the United Nations. According to Green and Anderson, a founding principle of WHO was as follows: "The enjoyment of health is one of the fundamental rights of every human being without distinction of race, religion, political belief, or economic or social conditions."[4] In many places, however, this right has not yet been translated into reality.

An interesting ethical dilemma is whether dollars currently spent to keep terminally ill patients alive as long as possible should be shifted to prevention programs.

The Profession

The National Commission for Health Education Credentialing has determined that Certified Health Education Specialists have seven areas of responsibility.[5] Working with individuals, groups, and organizations, they are responsible for the following:

1. Assessing individual and community needs for health education
2. Planning effective health education programs
3. Implementing health education programs
4. Evaluating effectiveness of health education programs
5. Coordinating provision of health education services
6. Acting as resources in health education
7. Communicating health and health education needs, concerns, and resources

Competencies listed under each of the preceding responsibilities require numerous judgments. Verbs such as *select, apply, distinguish, infer, seek, determine, match, compare, appraise, facilitate, translate, explore, recommend, analyze, stimulate, suggest, demonstrate, explain,* and *communicate* can all raise ethical considerations, as do verbs used in Health Education Credentialing, Inc., documents, such as *advocate, decide, monitor,* and *modify.*

With adequate preparation, the individual will be theoretically ready to face a complex world and always do the "right thing." But what is the right thing?

Determining proper ethical responses is not easy. Codes of ethics recommend that health educators maintain their competence through continuing education; through active membership in professional organizations; through review of research, programs, materials, and products; and through leadership in economic, legislative, and cooperative endeavors.[6]

Some of the ethical issues involved in the day-to-day functioning of health educators include those that violate moral and legal standards, those that help individuals but are unfair to others, those that do not involve the people who are affected, those that do not communicate possible positive or negative outcomes of a course of action (informed consent), and those that use coercion rather than choice.

Colleagues

The relationships between people working in the same profession may be crucial to the success or failure of its activities. Complaints in several health-related professions relate to the lack of honesty; the failure to develop mutual respect; and the tendency of some individuals to take advantage of clients, situations, and peers for personal gain. Is peer review needed as a mechanism to control behavior of individuals within the profession of health education? Green and Brooks stated that for effective quality control, "the professional association with a mandate from, or sufficient representation of, the members of that profession or discipline allow that association to provide acceptable peer review panels."[7] In his article entitled "The Seven Deadly Sins of Health Educators," Carlyon implied that there is a need for some mechanism for the health education profession to control its members' conduct.[8]

No acceptable plan has yet been developed for the enforcement of standards with health education organizations. Most writers on this subject recommend a conscious role-modeling effort by everyone within the profession.

Students

The quality of preparation of those who enter the field of health education is imperative to its success. Ethical concerns of this preparation involve mutual respect between teacher and student and teacher responsiveness to student interests, opinions, and desires. Every effort needs to be made to develop potential within individual students for high-quality contributions to the public's health and to create a culturally diversified profession.

Employers

Employers have a moral and legal right to expect their employees to be truthful. Health educators, after all, are attempting to help people change and develop a higher quality of life. Consequently, it is important that health educators be straightforward with their employees about their qualifications, expertise, experience, and abilities. They should act within the boundaries of their competence, accepting responsibility and accountability for their acts, which they should commit by exercising their best judgment. Failure to do so may not only result in their being fired from their jobs but also do damage to clients and the profession.

Research and Evaluation

Research implies discovery of ideas, causation factors, and consequences. Evaluation is used to change, promote, and develop better programs and activities.

A summary of the important aspects of ethical relationships and concerns for health educators is shown in Table 4-1.

Ethical issues discussed thus far of necessity involve the feelings and concerns of those presently practicing in the profession. As a result of a survey of its members, the Association for the Advancement of Health Education ranked the unethi-

Table 4–1 Ethics: Some Problem Areas and Concerns of Health Educators

Concerns	Primary Area of Application					
	Public	Professional Growth	Colleagues	Students	Employers	Research/ Evaluation
Protect individual rights	X			X		X
Be candid, truthful	X		X	X	X	X
Don't misrepresent/exaggerate	X		X	X	X	X
Limit of expertise	X	X	X	X	X	X
Ensure privacy/dignity	X		X	X		X
Involve clients	X					X
Treat people equally	X		X	X		
Keep abreast		X		X		
Be fair	X		X	X		X
Be responsible	X	X	X	X	X	X
Be a role model	X		X	X	X	
Give equal respect	X		X	X		X
Allow no adverse discrimination	X		X	X		X
Recognize potential	X		X	X		
Stress ethical practice	X		X	X		
Be accessible	X		X	X	X	X
Be realistic	X	X	X	X	X	
Provide meaningful experience	X			X		
Be honest	X	X	X	X	X	X
Be accountable	X		X	X	X	X
Use informed consent	X			X		X
Maintain confidentiality	X			X		X

Source: Based on "An Exploratory Survey of Ethical Problems in Health Education" by Janet H. Shirreffs and Elaine Vitello. (Unpublished manuscript developed for the Association for the Advancement of Health Education.)

cal practices that the respondents considered most serious. The results are presented in Table 4-2.

LIABILITY ISSUES

Educators have generally been considered a low-risk group for lawsuits, and that is certainly true of health educators as well. Society is becoming more litigious, however, and health educators are well advised to ascertain their liability insurance coverage. Some employers have such coverage for all their employees, and some professional organizations offer optional group liability insurance coverage. Home owner insurance policies often have options for liability insurance also.

Threats of lawsuits have caused many health care professionals to practice defensive medicine, ordering many tests to rule out even remote possibilities. Attempts are being made in the current round of health care reform to limit such practice. Yet, just as there is a need for physicians to practice defensive medicine, there is also a need for all health professionals to consider potential liability and conduct themselves at all times so as to minimize the risk of a problem.

In worst-possible-case scenarios, lawsuits typically name the organizations with the most money (the "deep pockets") as defendants. But anyone even

Table 4–2 Unethical Practices Considered Most Serious by AAHE Members*

Practice	Very Serious	Somewhat Serious	Not Too Serious	Not Serious
Manipulating or manufacturing research data	88%	1.1%	7%	—
Discriminating against clients/students on the basis of race, color, sex, or age	83%	6%	6%	1%
Knowingly misinforming students or clients	83%	5%	4%	3%
Failing to respect an individual's freedom to decline to participate in research or to discontinue participation	83%	6%	2%	6%
Failing to protect confidentiality of research participants, students, clients	80%	7%	2%	6%
Misrepresenting one's competence, education, or experience	76%	16%	6%	—
Conducting research on subjects who have not given their informed consent	73%	20%	9%	1%

*Information gathered from a survey of health educators who were members of AAHE.

Source: "An exploratory Survey of Ethical Problems in Health Education" by Janet Shirreffs and Elaine Vitello. (Unpublished manuscript developed for the Association for the Advancement of Health Education.)

remotely involved in an incident may be sued. Because health education is, by def-inition, prevention oriented, risk of liability is less than for those in health care. However, that does not negate the need for insurance and for professional conduct.

The most basic responsibility of any professional is to "do no harm." Certainly, that concept applies to health educators as well as to others. One implication of this concept is the need to ensure that clients are making the decisions voluntarily and are well informed about those decisions. Educators must not be induced to make decisions for clients or to pressure clients for the preferred behavior. It goes without saying that in most non-educational interventions, signed consent forms should be used. When in doubt, legal advice should be obtained, especially when developing new programs.

A more abstract issue relates to whether or not a health services professional should have done more than he or she did. Legal issues often arise over acts of omission, in addition to acts of commission. Again, the standards of practice will be the basis of comparison. If a matter goes to court, other health educators may be called to testify as to the professional conduct expected of a health educator in a given situation.

If, however, a client experiences a problem he or she perceives as related to something the health educator failed to do, the burden of proof is generally on the claimant to establish that the health educator did not follow normal standards of practice. Stated differently, the claimant must demonstrate that the health educator did not conduct himself or herself as "a reasonably prudent health educator" would have in the same situation.

Most of the ethical and legal issues stemming from health education practices, especially some newer challenges involving health promotion, are yet to be tested in the courts. If someone were to die, for example, of a heart attack after vigorous exercise or from jogging because he or she had been encouraged to do so by a health educator, is the health educator liable? Also, what is the liability of the organization for which the health educator is working?

According to Hanlon and Picket,

> Personal liability depends on proof of bad faith, which may be shown by evidence that official action was so arbitrary and unreasonable that it could not have been taken in good faith. Although obviously diffi-cult to ascertain, bad faith has been demonstrated to the satisfaction of the courts. If it can be proven that an agent willfully disobeyed the organization's instructions or policies which results in injury or unde-sirable results, then the agent is liable for damages.[9]

Health educators need to do their work without fear of litigation because to do otherwise is counterproductive. It must again be emphasized that seldom are health educators named in liability suits, and even less frequently are judgments rendered against them. However, all health service professionals must be conscious of the possibility of a lawsuit, and must always conduct themselves according to the standards of their profession. However, even health educators who follow the standards should carry liability insurance, because in a lawsuit, the court determines whether or not the standards were followed.

If health education programs expand as expected because of improved federal and state financing over the next several years, then legal suits from displeased clients will surely follow. This will be especially true if large amounts of money are involved.

CONTEMPORARY ISSUES

As is so often the case, a review of this chapter on ethics provides few concrete answers. What is ethical is, after all, a matter of personal belief.

Health promotion specialists are encouraged to examine their beliefs and practices. Professionals should discuss ethics frequently to clarify what they do believe. Conferences to discuss ethical issues in the practice of community health promotion provide opportunities for brainstorming, generating lists of emerging ethical issues.

A number of ethical issues have been raised in this chapter. Additional issues are emerging, many of which center around AIDS and minority group rights: Should the research and service dollars appropriated be commensurate with the severity of AIDS? Do some clients with AIDS deserve the disease because it was acquired through deviant behavior? Should staff be forced to provide services to AIDS patients despite their personal views toward the disease? Should ability to pay be the primary criterion on which to base the decision as to who gets treatment? Are rapidly growing minority groups receiving an increasing percentage of community health services? Are the needs of the elderly being adequately met? Are individuals who are concurrently members of two or three minority groups discriminated against? Are the rights of smokers being adequately addressed in smoke-free society programs?

Regardless of the answers to these questions and regardless of whether alleged discrimination is intentional, the question to ponder is, "If so, is it ethical? If not, what do my ethics require me to do about it?"

IN CONCLUSION

Satisfactory performance in health education endeavors continues to be paramount. The phrase *satisfactory performance* is certainly nebulous and will never be fully defined by the public or by health educators themselves. However, it is important that the profession continue to define and refine its rules and practices. *Profession, ethics,* and *rights* are words that convey the complexities and individual responsibilities involved.

***

Suggested Learning Activities

1. Compare medical quackery with health education quackery.
2. Apply the SOPHE Code of Ethics to current public health issues, such as AIDS, rapid-weight-loss clinics, and adequate health care for the poor.
3. Review the Proposed Code of Ethics for Patient Educators in *Health Values* and compare it with the SOPHE Code.
4. Interview a practicing health educator on his or her past or present conflicts between job demands and professional ethics.

NOTES

1. H.L. Wilensky, The Professionalization of Everyone? *American Journal of Sociology* 70 (1964):137.

2. M.J. Fromer, *Ethical Issues in Health Care* (St. Louis: C.V. Mosby Co., 1981), 6–7.

3. D.J. Breckon, *Matters of Life and Death* (Independence, Mo.: Herald House, 1987).

4. L.W. Green and C.L. Anderson, *Community Health* (St. Louis: C.V. Mosby Co., 1982), 562.

5. S.G. Deeds, *The Health Education Specialist: Self-Study for Professional Competence* (Los Alamitos, Calif.: Loose Canon Publications, 1992), 108–114.

6. Recommended Code of Ethics. Presented to the membership at the 1983 annual meeting of the Society for Public Health Education.

7. L. Green and B.P. Brooks, Peer Review and Quality Control in Health Education, *Health Values* 2 (1978): 191.

8. W. Carlyon, The Seven Deadly Sins of Health Educators, *Health Values* 2 (1978): 186-190.

9. J.J. Hanlon and G.E. Picket, *Public Health* (St. Louis: Times Mirror/Mosby, 1984), 136.

SUGGESTED READING

Arras, J., and Rhoden, N. 1989. *Ethical issues in modern medicine.* Mountain View, Calif.: Mayfield Publishing Co.

Balog, J.E., et al. 1985. Ethics and the field of health education. *Eta Sigma Gamma Monograph Series,* November .

Breckon, D.J. 1987. *Ethical aspects of life and death.* Independence, Mo.: Herald House.

Breckon, D.J., and Ledebuhr, K. 1981. Ethics for patient educators. *Health Values* 5, no. 4:158–160.

Clark, K.R. 1982. The implications of developing a profession-wide code of ethics. *Health Education Quarterly* 10, no. 2:120-125.

Fleishman, J.L., and Payne, B.L. 1980. *Ethical dilemmas and the education of policy makers.* Hastings on Hudson, N.Y.: The Hastings Center.

Friedman, E. 1986. *Making choices: Ethical issues for health care professionals.* Chicago: American Hospital Association.

Wing, K. 1990. *The law and the public's health.* Ann Arbor, Mich.: Health Administration Press.

Part II

Settings and Roles for Community Health Education

The community is a variable entity. It can be defined or described in many ways. It can refer to either large aggregates of people or smaller subgroups. Similarly, community health education can take place in all such settings and can work with a variety of groups.

Practicing health educators should be familiar with the various settings in which health education occurs. It may be that cooperative endeavors are possible and can evolve from a base of familiarity. It may be that job mobility will cause a person to change settings. Health educators should know what their options are and should be able to describe similarities and differences. Finally, professionals can learn from one another. Many of the skills being used in one setting can also be used effectively in another.

In this section, an overview is provided of the role of health educators in some of the more common settings. A practical description of typical functions is presented, compared, and contrasted.

Chapter 5

Healthy Communities

The term, *community health education*, is in widespread use and is generally preferred over *public health education* because the concept of community is more useful to health educators. (The nature of community is also discussed in Chapter 16 on community organization.)

THE NATURE OF COMMUNITY

Minkler pointed out that communities are usually thought of in geographic terms but supported Felin in stating the following:

> Communities may also be non locality identified and based on shared interests or characteristics, such as ethnicity, sexual orientation or occupation.[1]

Minkler also agreed with Hunter in saying that communities have been defined as social units that are (1) functional spatial units meeting basic needs for sustenance, (2) units of patterned social interaction, or (3) symbolic units of collective identity.[2]

Bracht referred to a community as "a group of people sharing values and institutions."[3]

> Community components include locality, an interdependent social group, interpersonal relationships, and a culture that includes values, norms, and attachments to the community as a whole as well as its parts.[4]

The definition suggests that a community is more than a randomly selected group of people and emphasizes that the key ingredient is in the values that are shared, as well as the places of employment, hospitals, schools, churches, governmental units, and other institutions that are shared.

Thus, examples of communities suggested by these definitions include cities or other governmental units, the Mexican-American community, the gay community, alcoholics, smokers, the blue-collar community, the educational community, the senior citizen community, the arts community, the religious community, and others.

From a health education perspective, the shared values and institutions are the key to developing health education strategies for risk reduction. An analysis of such shared values and institutions is a critical place to begin planning health education. (This topic will be the subject of Chapter 13.)

COMMUNITY STRUCTURES

Bracht also emphasized "systems" as a structure for understanding communities and suggested that they are generally based on cooperation and some degree of consensus. Bracht identified political systems, economic systems, health systems, education systems, and religious systems as examples.

> The view of the community as a system provides some insight into community organization for change. . . . change in one sector usually implies that adjustments or responses will eventually occur in other parts of the system.[5]

A significant aspect of this definition of community is that health education can occur in any of the systems (economic, political, etc.) and that it will eventually permeate the whole, if critical mass (a large enough base program to have an impact) is present. Moreover, an understanding of the total community and its subsystems is required if a health educator is to be successful.

> The advocates of the system view argue that interventions aimed at changing the behavior of individuals are inadequate because the system is a more powerful and pervasive determinant of behavior and of health than decisions made by individuals operating in a supposed full choice situation.[6]

Bracht also suggested that a focus on individual behavior makes it too easy for conservative government to evade responsibility for social change:

> It also tends to lead to . . . charges of victim blaming, whenever ill health resulting from faulty life-styles (such as smoking) is seen as the responsibility of the individual rather than the result of the social pressures under which the individuals live.[7]

SETTINGS

With this perspective on community, it thus becomes apparent that a variety of community agencies are appropriate settings for focused health education programs, including governmental units, voluntary health agencies, health care providers, and employers. However, the fundamental point of this chapter is that regardless of the agency or institution that employs the health educator, and regardless of the specific target group of health education programs, the larger community and its political, economic, educational, religious, and health care systems all have to be analyzed, considered, and used.

The interdependence of people and the common elements that provide a sense of community are also the elements that usually have to be impacted in order to improve the health of people in that community.

LOCUS OF RESPONSIBILITY

A time-honored principle is that government is responsible to do for the people what the people cannot do for themselves. Thus, governmental units provide police protection, educational systems, clean air and water, safe food supply, health care, and so forth:

> Government is the "residual guarantor" of health services, whether they are provided directly or through community agencies. Every locale and population should be served by a unit of government that takes a leadership role in assuring the public's health. This concept has become known as "a governmental presence at the local level."[8]

It is therefore appropriate and natural for these units to be charged with the responsibility to establish standards for community health and to ensure that they are met. However, that is not to say that all programming comes from government, but rather it must come from a variety of community agencies:

> The government at the local level has the responsibility for ensuring that a health problem is monitored and that services to correct that problem are available. The state government must monitor the effectiveness of local efforts to control health problems and act as a residual guarantor of services when community resources are inadequate, recognizing of course that state resources are also limited.[9]

Healthy communities will always have multiple interventions and overlapping programs. The problems and opportunities are too great to be left to government alone:

Many of the activities . . . go beyond the activities customarily carried out by state and local governmental agencies. Even in those areas where health agencies are extensively involved, prevention is a shared responsibility of the public and private sector.[10]

It becomes readily apparent that the public and private sectors must coordinate their efforts to solve common problems so that the most efficient use of resources has the greatest impact on improving the health of the community.

ENABLING COMMUNITIES

As noted in health education credentialing documents, enabling strategies are critical to sound health planning and must be involved in participatory planning throughout policy or program development. Another way of describing this role is the "empowerment of communities," wherein the communities help determine priorities and implementation strategies. This approach avoids "experts planning for people," instead emphasizing consultants or advocates planning with people, in the true spirit of community, of coming together because of common interests.

Bracht concluded a discussion on this topic with the following:

The primary consideration in health promotion is not policy or education, but the ordinary people whose health is at stake. They should not just be "consulted" or "educated." They should be brought actively into the health enterprise in a significant way through the processes encompassed by the term "enabling."[11]

Bracht subsequently defined enabling as being "a matter of power, resources, control, and who sets the priorities."[12] Generally speaking, it means making it possible for individuals or groups of people to make good things happen in their lives.

MODEL STANDARDS

The concepts of advocacy are also addressed in *Healthy Communities 2000: Model Standards*. Although the community for the task force was the United States, a broad spectrum of people were involved in establishing the national health objectives. Moreover, the title of the document itself emphasizes that they are model, not absolute, objectives. The subtitle of the document is *Guidelines for Community Attainment of the Year 2000 National Health Objectives*, with *Guidelines* being the operative word. It indicates a direction that leadership may take. Although it is desirable that such leadership come from within, an advocate for health planning is often needed. This, too, is an important role for community health educators.

The opening pages of *Healthy Communities 2000* emphasize an action step: determining local priorities. Moreover, although most of the model standards are restated without change from *Healthy People 2000*, there are numerous blank spaces that communities are encouraged to fill in with appropriate target dates or with quantitative descriptions of target goals:

> Communities are encouraged to establish targets based on their own situations and when possible establish targets that are more ambitious than the national reference.[13]

Of even more significance, the task force added a section of "Community Implementation" objectives and measurement indicators. One such objective focuses on community participation:

> By _____, each community will utilize open participatory processes in developing community health policies and plans.[14]

Similarly, a subsequent objective states the following:

> By _____, a mechanism will exist in the community to ensure that official health agency staff will be trained in facilitating open processes to obtain public advice and guidance.[15]

Accountability is also stressed throughout, with appropriate evaluation indicators suggested. In reference to the above two items, the indicators are "evidences of public participation, documentation of action taken as a result of such input, existence of training programs, and documentation of training provided."[16]

IN CONCLUSION

Healthy Communities 2000: Model Standards provides a concise listing of Activities for Implementation as follows:

1. Assess and determine the role of the health agency.
2. Assess the lead health agency's organizational capacity.
3. Develop an agency plan to build the necessary organizational capacity.
4. Assess the community's organizational and power structures.
5. Organize the community to build a stronger constituency for public health and establish a partnership for public health.

6. Assess the health needs and available community resources.
7. Determine local priorities.
8. Select outcome and process objectives that are compatible with local priorities and the *Healthy People 2000* objectives.
9. Develop communitywide intervention strategies.
10. Develop and implement a plan of action.
11. Monitor and evaluate the effort on a continuing basis.

The book provides several pages of elaboration on these 11 steps. It is readily apparent that effective health educators have to understand the concepts of community as well as be intimately acquainted with the community they serve. Moreover, advocacy and community empowerment are essential skills to be developed, primarily through planning with people rather than for people.

Students preparing to enter the profession in the United States must be very familiar with *Healthy Communities 2000: Model Standards.* Using the concepts of community and the model standards as advocated is sound health education practice. It is also sound learning theory to use these model standards and impact indicators in various class projects.

***

Suggested Learning Activities

1. List the various communities of which you consider yourself to be a member.
2. Are there any health education programs that are part of the above-mentioned communities?
3. What individual or groups have enabled you to have the level of good health that you enjoy?
4. List three communities in which you currently feel comfortable working.

NOTES

1. M. Minkler, Improving Health through Community Organization, in *Health Behavior and Health Education: Theory, Research and Practice,* eds. K. Glanz, et al. (San Francisco: Jossey-Bass, Inc., Publishers, 1990), 261.

2. Ibid., 262.

3. N. Bracht, ed., *Health Promotion at the Community Level* (Newbury Park, Calif.: Sage Publications, 1990), 47.

4. C. Bell and H. Newby, *An Introduction to the Sociology of the Local Community* (New York: Praeger, 1971), 32.

5. N. Bracht, *Health Promotion,* 48.

6. Ibid., 31.

7. Ibid.

8. *Healthy Communities 2000: Model Standards* (Washington, D.C.: American Public Health Association, 1991), xviii.

9. Ibid., 443.

10. Ibid.

11. N. Bracht, *Health Promotion*, 43.

12. Ibid., 12.

13. *Healthy Communities 2000,* 19.

14. Ibid., 6.

15. Ibid.

16. Ibid.

SUGGESTED READING

Bracht, N., ed. 1990. *Health promotion at the community level.* Newbury Park, Calif.: Sage Publications.

Patton, R., and Cissell, W. 1990. *Community organization: Traditional principle, and modern applications.* Johnson City, Tenn.: Latchpins Press.

Chapter 6

Health Departments and Other Tax-Supported Agencies

Tax dollars are used to support a wide variety of health programs at the local, state, national, and international levels. Without question, this is an appropriate expenditure of tax dollars. To paraphrase Abraham Lincoln, it is the responsibility of the government to do for the people what they are unable to do for themselves.

One of the oldest and most prestigious of such tax-supported agencies is the health department. Typically, it hires more health educators than do other tax-supported agencies, especially at the local level, and will continue to do so because of the community emphasis in *Healthy People 2000* and *Healthy Communities 2000*.

Local health departments in the United States came into existence during the 1700s. They preceded state and federal agencies because several large cities in the colonies had severe health problems. Responsibility for health is the responsibility of the states, according to states rights theorists, but states typically organize themselves into a series of city, county, district, or regional health departments.

Local health departments are mandated in the United States by various state laws. They may exist in a city, a county, or a group of counties. Their charge is to reduce the risk of or alleviate conditions that cause community health problems and generally to work to improve the health of the residents in the community.

From the early days to the present, public health workers have recognized that the two most important components of such a public health program are enforcement and education. Even though police power exists and can be used as necessary, public health workers recognize their inability to be in all places at all times to enforce good health practices in the public and private sectors. It is necessary, therefore, to emphasize health education to enhance voluntary compliance with recommended health practices.

HEALTH EDUCATION IN LOCAL HEALTH DEPARTMENTS

Health educators have been—and sometimes still are—communications specialists. Increasingly, however, they are moving into the arena of planning interventions that combine community organization, organizational development, group process, communication, and other skills. Most health education programs usually include a variety of interventions and methods that are carefully integrated and timed. For clarity's sake, these activities are presented separately here. In actual case studies they merge in varying degrees, as judged appropriate. Professional judgment as to what is needed and what will work best remains the most important ingredient of any health education program.

Local health departments are changing organizationally to meet new challenges. Traditionally, they have had at least two major divisions. These divisions have various titles, but their responsibilities center on those required by law: to provide personal health and sanitation services. Personal health services are provided by public health nurses, nutritionists, vision technicians, and other specialists. Sanitation services are provided by sanitarians, environmentalists, or environmental engineers.

In recent years, many, usually larger, local health departments reorganized to provide emphasis to chronic disease prevention activities. Sometimes called health promotion/disease prevention sections, health educators, epidemiologists, public health nurses, and nutritionists combined forces to address such areas as smoking cessation, weight reduction, cholesterol control, exercise, and worksite health promotion. Other departments have formed statistical, planning, and epidemiology sections or special AIDS sections to meet local needs.

Health educators working in a local health department are in somewhat of a dilemma. They need other health department personnel to recognize and emphasize the educational component. Yet because education is everyone's responsibility, some administrators believe that an educational specialist is unnecessary. This is definitely not the case. Health education specialists are needed to plan, conduct, and evaluate educational activities that cut across the divisions. They are needed to conduct the public relations and marketing functions. Additionally, they are needed to work with members of the community to help them identify their health needs and develop programs to meet these needs.

Health educators in local health departments are usually a service component to the other divisions. On organizational charts they are often listed as either being in the administrator's office or as reporting directly to the administrator, indicating the importance of working with all department units. They may also have responsibility for providing direct program services of their own, such as school education consultation, injury prevention, or other health promotion programs. In fact, a common problem faced by health educators in such a situation is that of finding time to respond to the requests of department heads and the administrator or health officer and still implement programs that the health educator wishes to initiate. It is possible—and indeed somewhat common—to spend so much time responding to perceived crises that there is no time to prevent them.

Another problem related to being partially a service component is balancing time and energy between the divisions. Where time and energy is spent is often determined by politics, personalities, and personal preferences rather than by the priorities as perceived by the educational specialist. For example, if members of funding agencies or the board of health want to emphasize a specific problem, or if the public demands that attention be given to a program that happens to be in the news, such as problem pregnancies, it is difficult not to give such requests preference over personal priorities. Or, if a department head is somewhat dominating, intimidating, or powerful because of position or influence, undue pressure may be brought to bear on the health educator to engage in projects that are of interest to that individual or the division he or she represents. Health educators need to be aware of both political and departmental agendas and look for opportunities to incorporate that information into planning. It is also very important to educate the other "players" about the role of health education.

Nonetheless, health educators are obligated to plan their time and programs so as to present a balanced view of the health department and to deal with most if not all the problems of the community in somewhat of a defensible sequence. Obviously, planning a yearly calendar with emphasis given to various departments at appropriate times of the year is important for many reasons, as described in Chapter 21, "Public Relations and Marketing." Yet the calendar must remain flexible to permit attention to problems and opportunities as they arise.

Working with Environmentalists

When health educators collaborate with environmentalists, their work is usually with some form of potential pollution or disease-causing process. It may involve the development of educational materials for specific clientele. On one occasion, literature, a slide tape presentation, some transparencies, or a display regarding such topics as water wells, sewage disposal systems, and purchase of resort property may be required for a builder's show. On other occasions, materials dealing with proper sanitation and food handling procedures may be needed for restaurant owners or employees of food service establishments. Similarly, materials may be needed for swimming pool operators or for people wanting to sponsor a church supper as a fund-raiser. Health educators also plan, and perhaps conduct, classes for food handlers, contractors, septic tank–cleaning establishments, and so on, in coordination with environmentalists and others in planning and implementing the program.

Material may be prepared on such problems as pollution, contamination, toxic wastes, and disease transmission. Obviously, training or work experience in biology and chemistry enables a health educator to work effectively with this division. Equally important is the ability to let the sanitarians be "content experts" and the educator be a "process" specialist. Certainly, educators need to have their materials reviewed several times by experts in the field for accuracy and appropriateness of emphasis. Some health educators enjoy working with such problems and spend a significant amount of their time on them by preference.

Since the Love Canal toxic waste case and other community-centered problems, more attention has focused on links between environmental hazards and human health problems such as cancer and birth defects. This has resulted in more emphasis on community health education. Many of these situations are highly emotional and require skilled communication with local communities to interpret technical information quickly and accurately.

The escalating reaction (and occasionally overreaction) to environmental hazards has occasioned the development of "risk communication." When an environmental disaster occurs, communication must be extraordinarily cautious but accurate. Litigation will often emerge, and media statements may be made by attorneys on both sides of the case. More important, the people served by governmental agencies have a right to know the risks they are experiencing. Overstating the risks, however, may cause panic or other adverse reactions. Those involved with the case must be careful not to overstate what is known, to use statements about the risk made only by credible experts, to use qualifying phrases (e.g., "it is presently believed"), and in other ways to balance accuracy with the need to know and the concerns associated with litigation. Health educators who work with environmentalists are encouraged to read the literature on risk communications, and to discuss it with appropriate agency personnel.

Working with Public Health Nurses

Nurses and others engaged in personal health services meet with numerous opportunities for health education and may call for such services often. Problems they face vary widely: the nutritional status of high-risk infants, the needs of homebound stroke patients, substance abuse in the schools, sexually transmitted diseases and AIDS, glaucoma in the elderly, the need for immunization, an epidemic of head lice, hearing or visual difficulties, nutritional problems, and so forth. They also often see and investigate cases of child abuse and other forms of domestic violence.

In addition, public health nurses are taking a more active role in health promotion and cost management in the community. Nurses often are the strongest proponents for better prenatal, infant, and maternal care programs, as well as for programs that serve the aged. Home visits, school visits, and clinics place nurses in direct personal contact with a cross section of the public who need personal health services. Often they serve in key positions on community or agency boards and committees. In these roles, an educational need usually exists, as well as a need for direct service.

Again, some health educators prefer working with nurses and the problems they face and spend a great deal of time meeting the needs identified by nurses, either by personal preference or by job description. As with environmentalists, the services needed vary. Requests may be made for specific materials not commercially available, for consultation on a problem, for someone to conduct educational sessions for pregnant teens, or for prepared materials for the mass media. One attractive part of working in a local health department is the diversity of people and problems that the professional staff encounter.

Working with Planners and Epidemiologists

Many health departments have staff planners and epidemiologists to provide planning, surveillance, and evaluation support for all department programs. These may be solo professionals or entire units, depending on the size of the department. The increased need for measurable objectives and targeted evaluations in health education make it important that health educators work closely with these colleagues in developing programs. Much can be learned and shared regarding the planning and evaluation process.

OTHER JOB-RELATED CONSIDERATIONS

Because they are expected to assist a variety of personnel with a variety of problems, health educators are often placed in areas of inexperience. Time restraints prevent them from becoming "experts" on topics that are unfamiliar to them. Therefore, it is imperative that health educators develop elaborate filing systems The files ought to be in a format that is useful to the individual and agency. Most important, they should be kept up-to-date with newspaper clippings, pamphlets, journal articles, and other pertinent material. For example, if a windstorm causes a power outage that may last for several days, there is an immediate need for information to be disseminated through the media giving precautions and recommendations. Such detailed information must be readily available in the files. There are also many national hotlines and company databases available for specific health problems or issues.

Health educators need to be able to work effectively with different kinds of people in different situations. For example, they may be working with physicians in private practice, with hospital personnel, with public school personnel, and with media personnel. Additionally, clients may range from the poor and disabled who need assistance to survive, to emotionally distressed middle-class families with temporary health problems caused by a combination of circumstances, to the wealthy who are about to purchase vacation property, to well-established business owners. All health educators need to be able to work effectively with a variety of people, but nowhere is this more important than in the local health department setting. The art of politics and advocacy becomes of importance when educating members of commissions and boards and elected officials about health promotion programs.

HEALTH EDUCATION IN STATE AND FEDERAL AGENCIES

Health educators are employed by state and federal health departments, albeit in fewer numbers. Although some of the responsibilities are similar, major differences do exist.

Whereas local health departments primarily serve their constituents directly, state and federal agencies primarily serve other agencies. Federal agencies tend to work with state agencies, state agencies tend to work with local agencies, and local agencies tend to work with the citizenry.

All state health departments and United States territorial health departments, such as those in Guam, Puerto Rico, and the Virgin Islands, have health education units. These units may be only one health educator in a bureau or division, or a large multiple staff unit unto itself. How these units are staffed and organized varies from state to state; however, most have relatively high visibility and placement in their respective organizations. Functions range from in-house program development and public information to managing large grants and programs in AIDS, smoking, cardiovascular disease prevention, and so forth. As discussed in Chapter 3, the primary professional organization for state-level health educators is the Association for State and Territorial Directors for Public Health Education.

Health educators employed by state and federal agencies find that successful and effective work experience in a local agency is useful background. In fact, civil service requirements for this type of employment often give preference to those people with such work experience and advanced degrees. Although this generally is true, there are entry-level positions in many state and federal agencies, and recent graduates will be well advised to take the appropriate civil service examinations to become eligible.

Communication skills are important for health educators at all levels but are especially so for those working at state and federal levels. Such people need to become adept at consultation, since much of their time is spent conferring with others on site, by telephone, or by mail. Statewide planning and resource development is imperative, as is networking with other state agencies. State and federal employees also usually need to develop their skills in grant writing, since their responsibilities may involve grant application review or consultation with those preparing grant applications. Because much of their work involves conferences, seminars, and other training functions, educational specialists at state and federal levels also need to be experts at planning conferences, conducting staff development sessions, and speaking in public.

Finally, health educators working at these levels of government need to develop skills in educating decision makers, or at least in monitoring the legislative process. Knowing how bills become law and which bills in process will affect health education provides excellent opportunities to enhance health education funding and support.

The skills mentioned above as ones needed by state and federal health educators are not exclusive to those levels. These skills are also required from time to time by local health educators. However, state and federal employees spend a larger percentage of time in these areas than do educators at the local level. Separate chapters are devoted to these topics in a later section.

HEALTH EDUCATION IN THE MILITARY

With the federal government advocating national objectives, it is not surprising that the nation's military also would be identified as a target group for health promotion. In one sense, active duty military personnel and the large number of civilians who work within the defense complex represent a unique opportunity to impact a significant subset of our nation's population with health risk reduction programs.

Military leaders have always been concerned about their personnel being nutritionally and physically fit, so that they can function at peak efficiency. Health promotion programs are now viewed as part of readiness strategies.

However, the more important consideration is the opportunity to contain (if not reduce) the cost of providing health care to military personnel. Health care costs have increased faster than inflation, as has the cost of military preparedness. (Presumably, the high cost of emerging technological advancement common to both health care and the defense industries is the primary cause.)

Since the "Cold War" ended, the nation's focus has been on "downsizing" the military and on shifting costs to "peace time initiatives." Defense Department budgets are being reduced in successive years, and so every area in which to reduce or contain costs will be examined, including health promotion.

The military is implementing programs so that health promotion

> 1) supports . . . total organizational efficiency by optimizing the performance of its human resources, 2) promotes and supports policy development and management efforts to contain escalating costs of the Department of Defense's corporate health benefits program.[1]

The role of health educators in military settings will not differ significantly from that in other settings. Military personnel, regardless of whether they are active duty or civilians, may be treated as a community. Indeed, military personnel, dependents of military personnel, and retired military personnel and their dependents often dominate the cities adjacent to military installations. Of course, military personnel are employees, so worksite programs are appropriate (see Chapter 9). Similarly, because the military has its own health care programs, opportunities also exist for various patient education programs (see Chapter 8).

It is not yet clear whether those working in health education in the military will primarily be enlisted personnel or civil service personnel assigned to military installations. It is clear, however, that health education and health promotion in military settings are increasing rapidly, that professionally trained health educators are needed to achieve maximum effectiveness, and that a new setting or career option is evolving for health educators.

OTHER TAX-SUPPORTED AGENCIES

Health educators, or those with educational skills, may also be employed by other tax-supported agencies. They would be involved with categorical programs, such as AIDS, cardiovascular health, and child health. Typically, such agencies have local, state, and federal levels that approximate those described earlier for health departments. The educational specialists in such agencies function approximately the same as those in health departments. Although no comprehensive listing or description of other tax-supported agencies that employ health educators is included here, examples of such agencies are the Department of Education, the Department of Agriculture, the Department of Defense, and the Indian Health Service. Again, civil service examinations, previous work experience, and advanced degrees are usually, but not always, required.

HEALTHY COMMUNITIES 2000

As noted earlier, federal agencies have charged state public health agencies with the "establishment of statewide health objectives, delegating power to localities as appropriate, and holding them accountable." States are further charged to support "local service capacity." Among the methods suggested are subsidies and technical assistance. However, *Healthy Communities 2000* "reaffirmed local public health agencies as the final delivery point for all public health efforts."[2]

The reports emphasize that units of government are the "Residual Guarantor" of health services and noted that every locale should be served by a unit of government that takes a leadership role in ensuring the public's health. The reports noted that the agency responsible for any single standard may vary:

> In most cases, the government unit is likely to be the health department. . . . Government at the local level has the responsibility for ensuring that a health problem is monitored and that services to correct them are available . . . and that the official health agency serving the community normally will have the primary responsibility for ensuring that the standards are met.[3]

Thus, health educators who work in health departments must of necessity work with the model standards as proposed in *Healthy Communities 2000*.

IN CONCLUSION

A number of rewarding career opportunities exist for health educators who work for the government as it carries out its mandate to protect the health of the people. Programs, populations, and functions vary, depending on the agency and the level.

On the other hand, government mandates, political appointments, the size of the bureaucracy, and the slowness of the bureaucratic process often combine to bring a degree of frustration to those who are employed in this setting. As in most jobs, some people are more effective in such settings than are others. More important, individuals in any position need to determine the demands of the job and fulfill them to the best of their ability or search for a position that more nearly matches their aspirations and skills.

Working in local, state, or federal health agencies remains the cornerstone of public health practice. The variety of health problems and organizational issues make health departments challenging places to practice health education. Kreuter quoted Hod Ogden, first director of the Division of Health Education at the Centers for Disease Control, as saying, "Bureaucracies are bureaucracies. . . . Nevertheless, we have a real chance to influence the health status of not just a few, but thousands upon thousands of citizens through the improvement and the expansion of health education. . . . It isn't easy but it is very possible."[4]

***

Suggested Learning Activities

1. Discuss with a health department representative the program, budget, and staffing of his or her department.
2. Prepare a list of health education–related activities described in a local health department services brochure or annual report.

NOTES

1. B.S. Collins and S.H. Custis, Health Promotion in a Shrinking Military, *Military Medicine*, 158 (1993): 386.

2. *Healthy Communities 2000: Model Standards.* (Washington, D.C.: U.S. Government Printing Office, 1991), 443.

3. Ibid., xviii.

4. M.W. Kreuter, Health Promotion: The Public Health Role in the Community of Free Exchange, in *Health Promotion Monographs* (New York: Teachers College, Columbia University, Monograph no. 4, 1984), 20.

SUGGESTED READING

Bates, I.J., and Winder, A.E. 1984. *Introduction to health education.* Mountain View, Calif.: Mayfield Publishing Co.

Freudenberg, N. 1984. *Not in our backyards! Community action for health and environment.* New York: Monthly Review Press.

Green, L., and Anderson, C.L. 1982. *Community health.* St. Louis: C.V. Mosby Co.

Lazes, P.M., Kaplan, L.H., and Gordon, K.A., eds. 1987. *The handbook of health education.* 2nd ed. Gaithersburg, Md: Aspen Publishers, Inc.

Pickett, G., and Hanlon, J.J. 1990. *Public health administration and practice.* St. Louis: C.V. Mosby. (See especially Chapters 6 and 7.)

Chapter 7

Working in Traditional and Emerging Voluntary Health Agencies

Voluntary health agencies are characterized primarily by the extensive use of volunteers. Well-known examples of such agencies are the American Cancer Society, the American Lung Association, and the American Heart Association. These three organizations have a long and distinguished history. More recent examples of voluntary health agencies include the National Women's Health Network, Mothers of AIDS Patients, and Mothers Against Drunk Drivers.

Voluntary health agencies are not unique to the United States, but they play a larger role in community health in the United States than in most other countries. They are expressions of the independent spirit that characterized the early days of the establishment of America, of self-help, of people helping people, and of limited roles for government.

Organizations developed to meet needs that government was not meeting, such as the National Tuberculosis Association in the early 1900s. Many such organizations are created to meet a perceived need and are dissolved when the need has been met or people no longer are concerned about it. Other organizations simply shift focus to other problems, such as the polio groups shifting to crippled children after the polio problem was largely solved. As a result of these factors, there have always been both traditional and emerging voluntary health agencies, and probably always will be.

As problems such as AIDS are used to mobilize the resources of people to help people in need, there will be a need for health educators in voluntary agencies, because a major task of such organizations is educating the people about the threatening situation. Yet working in a voluntary agency as a health educator is different, primarily because of the instability of the organizations themselves. The organization needs to establish stability and credibility in order to marshal both volunteers and funds. The base of the organization needs to be broadened, and the organization needs to continuously justify its existence in the early years of being. Large numbers of people need to be convinced that there is a serious problem, that there are things people can do to help, and that the organization is legitimate.

Of particular concern are fund-raising costs and use of donated money. Too many organizations have come into existence, raised a lot of money, and have had most of it go to either the fund-raisers or the salaries/expenses of its officers. People now are skeptical of new organizations and need to be convinced of their legitimacy.

Subsequent chapters in this book focus on using community organization skills and community fund-raising. These two functions are important to anyone working in a voluntary health agency but are essential to anyone working in emerging voluntary health agencies. The perceived image must be one of legitimacy, credibility, stability, and altruism. Of course, affiliation with state and national groups helps significantly. A local group with a local problem can work, but it usually needs a community group with an established reputation to give it legitimacy. If these characteristics are not widely established through education, the organization will usually not be effective.

Many agencies, such as the American Cancer Society, focus on a specific disease. Others, such as the American Heart Association or the American Lung Association, focus on an organ and its disorders. Others, such as the right-to-life organizations, are associated with a problem, such as abortion. Still others, such as the American Medical Association, are professional organizations, which are created to provide more effective service to the communities that they serve. The professional organizations believe that what best serves the public is in the best interest of the organization.

Educational activities usually consist of public education and professional inservice education. There has been an increased trend toward voluntary organizations joining forces with health departments, universities, hospitals, and even other voluntary health agencies in education programs. *Healthy Communities 2000* encourages such coalitions.

ORGANIZATIONAL STRUCTURE

Large, well-known voluntary health agencies are divided into national, state, and local levels. Although different terms may be used for these divisions, and although there may be regional or area subdivisions at either or both the national and state levels, the essence of the organizational structure is the same.

Volunteers are selected to be members of the boards and committees that make organizational decisions. While board and position titles vary from agency to agency, they typically vest actual agency control in volunteers. Therefore, care is taken to choose volunteers who have the experience and ability to function in the agency's best interest. Those appointed to state and national boards usually have had experience serving at the local level, with appropriate indoctrination. Also, specialized volunteers, such as physicians, attorneys, bankers, professors, and media specialists are recruited for these boards.

Paid staff are most likely to exist at the national and state levels, although they may be assigned to a region of the state or a large metropolitan area. They also usually have had work experience at lower levels before moving into the upper levels of the organization.

WORKING IN A VOLUNTARY HEALTH AGENCY

The general philosophy of voluntary agencies is that volunteer boards and committees make the decisions and generally run the agency. The function of the staff is to assist the boards and committees and to implement the policies and programs. Obviously, staff are able to influence many of the decisions that are made through preparation of background material and recommendations and through informal contacts with individual board or committee members.

Staff must be careful, in their relationships with volunteers, to influence decisions discreetly and to help boards and committees make decisions within agency policy. They must also be careful not to dominate or alienate volunteers, lest they cease to volunteer.

At national and state levels, staff often have specialized functions and may be assigned full-time job responsibility to work with single committees. Such positions may be in public education, public information, professional education, and fund-raising. Executive directors, or their equivalents, have more generalized responsibilities that involve coordinating the work of all the committees and providing leadership for the agency as a whole.

Health educators are likely to enter a voluntary agency at the area or regional level and be responsible for a group of counties or local units. Each of the counties will have active organizations composed solely of volunteers. The organization will typically include a president, vice-president, secretary, treasurer, and a committee structure. Standing committees include fund-raising, public relations, public education, professional education, and public service—or some variation of them.

As an agency staff member, the health educator will be responsible for the operation of the volunteer boards in each of the counties. The staff member must interpret national and state policy to local boards and must assist them to implement programs consistent with organizational policy.

Regional directors, field staff, and those with equivalent titles working in voluntary agencies are primarily administrators. They are often located in small offices in remote locations and may even work out of their homes. They may have a part-time secretary or office manager or may simply have a telephone-answering service.

The work often involves extensive travel, especially if the territory covers several counties that are spread out. The job is not primarily an office job but rather involves working with local volunteers in their units. Such regional administrators have budgets to manage, reports to prepare, and, sometimes, responsibility for hiring and supervising support staff. Additionally, they are responsible for the programs and problems of the local boards in the area. Although administrative, managerial, and supervisory skills are important, human relations skills must be dominant when working with volunteers.

Given the nature of the work, management courses combined into a minor or cognate are useful supplements to a major in health education or health promotion. Field experience in a voluntary agency is also useful, as well as related courses in chronic disease, anatomy, and physiology.

The most pervasive task of a staff member is to work effectively with volunteers to implement agency programs. Many problems and dilemmas confront staff within this general responsibility. The problems vary from unit to unit and from time to time and usually involve personalities.

RECRUITING VOLUNTEERS

A major problem of voluntary agencies is the lack of sufficient volunteers to implement the program effectively. In the past, volunteers have more often been women than men, as women engaged in such community activities to occupy their time. Increasingly, women have entered the work force as the economy dictates and now they have little time available for volunteer work. Women with full-time jobs usually also have responsibility for managing a household. If they have children at home, the demands on their time are even greater. Today, males often have more discretionary time than do their female counterparts.

This condition results in the necessity for active recruitment of volunteers. Both men and women still do volunteer work for a variety of reasons. For many, it is a sense of personal commitment because of the experiences of a family member with the problem being emphasized by that agency. For others, it may be an opportunity to do challenging work that involves more or different skills than their daily work experiences do. Opportunities to develop skills, to grow and develop as a person, and to acquire work experience in new areas are also important reasons. Involvement with people is an important motivator as well, inasmuch as retirees may want social contact; and attorneys, accountants, and others who provide professional services may want to get to know people who are potential clients. But the overriding reason for community involvement seems to be the sense of personal satisfaction, combined with public recognition, that people experience from being involved in community programs.

Literally thousands of hours of staff time are donated by members of every community, with the potential for thousands of additional donated hours if members are recruited effectively.

The most effective way to recruit volunteers is by personal contact and invitation. Brainstorming for names of new members at a meeting of the current membership is a useful technique, with the invitation being extended by a friend or an acquaintance. People respond well to requests to do specific tasks that are within their areas of expertise, inasmuch as to be needed is a common desire.

The media can also be used to recruit volunteers. Special programs of community interest can be conducted, with the public invited to attend. These contacts can then be used with appropriate follow-up to recruit volunteers.

Groups of volunteers can also be recruited for special tasks. Service clubs, church groups, senior citizens, youth groups, and sororities or fraternities are all potential sources of volunteers. Welcome Wagon, New Comers, and other sources of names of people who have recently moved to a community are often useful for volunteer recruitment.

TRAINING VOLUNTEERS

If volunteers are to receive a sense of satisfaction from their work, they must be effective in it. Staff members and other volunteers must work to help ensure that the volunteer experience is a good one, or the volunteer—and perhaps others in the community—will be lost to the group.

Volunteers need to understand the goals and objectives of the organization and to feel that what the organization is doing has real purpose, that it contributes to human welfare. They need to see what part their particular assignment plays. They need responsibilities that are challenging, yet within their range of abilities and interests. They need a clear description in enough detail of what is expected and, specifically, what flexibility or limitations exist. They need to have confidence in others in the organization and to be kept informed of progress.

The need for this information dictates some training of volunteers. Training varies according to numbers, previous experience, and so on. It can be done individually or in a group or some combination of the two. It can be accomplished through written materials, films, speakers, or conversation. The important thing is that volunteers need to have a better-than-average chance of being successful, for the good of the agency, the volunteer, and the community.

SUPERVISING VOLUNTEERS

Volunteers need clearly stated job descriptions (preferably in writing), deadlines, and enough support to be effective within that time frame. People usually want to know how they are doing, and they deserve such feedback. They may need encouragement, knowledge, advice, or technical assistance. Their performance needs to be monitored carefully and discreetly by staff. Capable people do not usually appreciate others pushing them unnecessarily to do tasks that have been delegated to them. Communication is critical, but unless it is carried out in the right spirit it can be detrimental. Volunteers need to know exactly what will be expected of them.

The quality of volunteers is improving. More and more, those who are becoming involved have professional training and work experience. They expect and deserve to be treated as professionals. This is especially true in the case of retirees from business or professional backgrounds. Supervising volunteers is best done in a business-like manner, but with warmth, caring, and personal concern.

RECOGNIZING VOLUNTEERS

As noted earlier, people volunteer for different reasons. Everyone has a reason for volunteering, a need that must be met, and it is an important function of the staff to be sure the goals of the volunteer are being accomplished. Sometimes the need is not clear in the mind of the volunteer, and he or she could not articulate it even if asked. Yet staff should attempt to discern those needs and to sense which form of recognition would be most meaningful. Recognition is a basic human need and should not be underestimated.

An appropriate form of recognition may be a thank-you letter. If work time or skills were used, it may be appropriate for a copy of the letter to go to an individual's supervisor. In some instances a thank-you note in the Letters to the Editor column of the local newspaper can be the most effective method. A recognition breakfast or luncheon with press coverage is a common practice. The presentation of awards is also common and effective. Regardless of the method used, it is important for volunteers to feel that their efforts have been noted and appreciated.

IN CONCLUSION

There are many voluntary agencies, and considerable opportunity for employment exists. The work can be extremely satisfying, and ample opportunity exists for relocation to other areas and for upward mobility. Working with and through volunteers requires both human relations and management skills, yet staff efforts and talents can be magnified many times over through effective utilization of volunteers.

***

Suggested Learning Activities

1. List the voluntary agencies serving your hometown.
2. Visit one of the agencies and determine the kind of activities in which that organization is involved.

3. Visit another agency and discuss the organizational structure, policies, and relationships of state and national units. If possible, attend a board meeting.
4. Interview volunteers asking them how they got involved, why they continue to volunteer, and what personal satisfaction they get from volunteering.
5. Volunteer to participate in a local voluntary agency activity.

SUGGESTED READING

Drucker, P. 1990. *Managing the non-profit organization: Principles and practices.* New York: Harper Collins Publishers.

Ilsley, P.J. 1990. *Enhancing the volunteer experience: New insights on strengthening volunteer participation, learning and commitment.* San Francisco: Jossey-Bass, Inc., Publishers.

Chapter 8

Working in a Hospital, Health Maintenance Organization, or Profit-Making Organization

Health education in the health care delivery setting has undergone rapid and dramatic change in the past decade. Health care in the United States continues to evolve. Health care reform is again a matter of urgency, due to escalating costs. Health educators need to follow the movement carefully. Some change has been gradual, even evolutionary. Some change has been rapid, even revolutionary. Individuals who work for health care providers must understand the changes that have occurred to meet existing and emerging organizational needs.

AN OVERVIEW OF HEALTH CARE

The use of the term *health care provider* in this edition as contrasted to *hospital* in the first edition indicates some of the change that has occurred. In the past health care was almost exclusively provided in physicians' offices and clinics, hospitals, and long-term care facilities typified by the nursing home.

Now, a plethora of agencies exist, such as (but not limited to) free-standing medical care clinics that provide a wide range of routine and emergency care services; home health agencies that provide in-home services to preclude or delay the need for hospitalization; and physician organizations such as health maintenance organizations (HMOs), preferred provider organizations (PPOs), or other forms of managed health care. In addition, there are a large number of "for profit" commercial organizations such as health spas, sports medicine clinics, and weight loss clinics. Ironically, many of these changes in the health care delivery system came about as a result of cost-containment efforts.

Health care costs have increased faster than inflation over several decades, and numerous measures have been used in an attempt to control cost, with varying degrees of success. Limiting the number of new hospital beds and reducing the number of existing beds had limited impact. More impact has occurred as a result of prospective reimbursement measures by the federal government and other third-party payers.

Hospitals previously billed third-party payers for services provided and had little incentive to hold down cost. Prospective reimbursement established categories of diagnoses and predetermined how much a hospital would be paid to care for patients with the same diagnosis. If hospital expenses exceeded the limit, the hospital had to absorb the bill. If the hospital treated the patient for less money, the hospital kept the money saved. Of course, physicians are the ones who admit and discharge patients, and reducing length of stay became a major emphasis.

Prospective reimbursement requires more emphasis on programs that shorten the length of hospitalization or that provide services on an outpatient basis. Programs that stress self-care or education to enable family members to care for a patient are being promoted. Programs that permit outpatient procedures are encouraged. Programs that minimize readmissions are important. Similarly, programs dealing with disorders that affect large numbers of patients, such as diabetes and stroke, are being stressed. Programs that can be done inexpensively with existing staff or cooperatively with other agencies, such as with coronary heart disease, are being stressed even more. The development of programs that can be delivered on an outpatient basis, through either preadmission or post discharge, is becoming more important. In general, programs that can demonstrate cost savings are being given priority. Program evaluation skills are becoming imperative. Communication of the effects of patient education on total hospital costs and/or revenue is becoming important to program viability.

Physicians recognized that patient education could reduce length of stay. Physicians and nurses always answered questions and did some patient teaching, but increased emphasis was placed on patient education because it became a means of providing cost-effective service. Support groups for patients (and their families) with chronic disease also became commonplace. Education in hospitals was reorganized so as to be more orderly, more effective, more integrated into health care delivery, and more documented.

Concurrent with cost-containment measures, health education shifted emphasis to health promotion, with health promotion specialists seeing education as one of several emphases. Moreover, the "wellness" movement gave more emphasis to promoting higher levels of wellness for apparently healthy people. Weight reduction, cessation of smoking, aerobic exercise, and other programs came into prominence. Many people demanded such services and health care providers responded to this consumer demand.

To respond to the economic and social changes, hospitals looked to health promotion as one strategy to generate revenue and lower costs over time. They redefined health care to include care for well consumers and established new health care services, including health clubs, pools, sports fitness centers, and eating disorders centers. This strategy worked for some hospitals and not for others, depending on the administration, the health promotion staff, and the community.

Community health education programs became somewhat commonplace when hospitals shifted from solely emphasizing acute care and chronic care to also emphasizing prevention. Many health educators were hired to deliver such prevention services. However, many of these programs subsequently have been eliminated because of severely escalative needs for cost containment.

More recently, health care providers have grouped together to form regional or national consortia. By using purchasing economies of scale, they are able to contain their costs somewhat. More important, groups of health care providers (typically including hospitals, physicians, and related health service providers) enter into contracts with large employers and their insurance companies to provide health care at lower costs. The lower rates are guaranteed if employees use the physicians and hospitals that are part of the network. Such arrangements provide steady caseloads for the physicians and bed occupancy rates for the hospitals. However, the network also provides greater opportunity to "manage" health care by determining what services will be provided as "necessary" and "covered" services, and what services will be considered unnecessary or optional and therefore will not be covered.

The role of health educators in managed health care programs is similar to their role in health maintenance programs, in that emphasis is on efficient use of health care and on traditional patient education. However, because of cost-containment strategies, health educators may need to set up patient education protocols and train the health care staff to implement them.

Some managed health care consortia may have contracts with employers to provide employee wellness programming. In such cases, the role of health educators may approximate that of health educators in worksite programs.

Because health care reform is progressing rapidly, the role of health education is fluid. Clearly, however, considerable opportunity exists to impact the cost of providing health care by providing more prevention programming. Also clear is the increasing demand for health-related services.

As consumers became more health conscious, the marketplace developed a variety of programs of varying quality and advertised them heavily. Health spas and weight loss clinics are most widely available, with dozens of organizations and plans, several with state and national affiliations.

Commercial, profit-making organizations exist primarily, if not only, to make a profit. They are not obligated to provide services, and they are not motivated by altruism. They exist to provide needed or wanted services in exchange for fees, which are used to pay expenses and provide a reasonable return on investment.

Such organizations are competitive, striving to increase their share of the market, however large the market might be. Convenience of location, cost, facilities, equipment, and staffing are key factors usually stressed in marketing. Professionally trained staff are often hired, inasmuch as discriminating "buyers" of such services may be very sophisticated and may demand the best.

Employers have demanded lower health care costs. Physicians and hospitals responded by offering HMOs and PPOs as cost-containment measures. Hospitals also responded by providing health promotion programs specific to the working populations and employee assistance programs, both of which had strong health education programs. Worksite programs are discussed in detail in Chapter 9.

HMOs and PPOs, of course, emphasize shorter lengths of stay by providing outpatient services, primary intervention, and primary prevention, all using health education and health promotion strategies. These movements opened opportunities for health education within business and industry. Moreover, relationships with business and industry opened the door to educational intervention in workers' compensation settings. Employees injured on the job can be rehabilitated more quickly through education, which can be offered in a cost-effective manner.

As prospective reimbursement and other economic factors began to increase their budgetary impact, many programs have been changed or discontinued. Allied health personnel have been forced to assume responsibility in some cases. In others, consumers have been forced to become more knowledgeable and to take more responsibility for their own health promotion.

In many health care settings at present, existing health care staff teach patients as dictated by their diagnosis, but other forms of health education and health promotion have begun to appear. One health problem, AIDS, is rapidly impacting health education in health care settings. Unless a cure or vaccine can be developed, these changes will intensify.

The increasing prevalence of human immunodeficiency virus (HIV) in the population increases the risk that health care workers will be exposed to blood from patients infected with HIV, especially if precautions on handling blood and body fluids are not followed with all patients.[1] Therefore, many employee inservice education and wellness programs for health care staff include basic information not only on AIDS as a disease to diagnose and treat but also on how staff should routinely protect themselves without raising unnecessary concern or actions. The Centers for Disease Control has issued "Recommendations for Prevention of HIV Transmission in Health Care Settings," which covers many areas of concern from surgery and laboratory work to dentistry.[2,3] Recent actions by the Occupational Safety and Health Administration have placed more emphasis on AIDS precautions for health care workers.[4]

AIDS has of course provided new areas of program development in patient education. Patients in such areas as surgery, transplants, dialysis, and obstetrics will have special educational needs due to blood-related issues. Some hospitals may be sites for blood banks or even AIDS counseling and/or testing sites. The increasing concern with substance abuse and AIDS has also led to more education counseling and outreach in hospitals with special substance abuse units.

Hospitals and HMOs have also joined with other community-based organizations to conduct community awareness programs, patient support networks, and professional education initiatives regarding AIDS.

WORKING IN HEALTH CARE SETTINGS

Opportunities for health educators and health promotion specialists to be employed in health care settings have grown tremendously as agencies have proliferated. Admittedly, many programs have opened and closed. Some have grown rapidly. Some health care organizations are still spending millions to develop full-service health education programs.

Health education specialists who work in hospitals in a full-service health education program are likely to be employed as directors, managers, or coordinators of the program. Various titles and job descriptions are used, but the position is often primarily administrative, rather than educative. Hospitals usually espouse the team approach to patient education. Physicians, nurses, therapists, dietitians, pharmacists, technologists, and other specialists are all part of the team. Health educators join the team as education specialists, occasionally as team leaders. Medical specialists on the team usually do the actual patient teaching. The education specialists more often play a major role in planning, implementing, and evaluating programs. Heavy emphasis is placed on curriculum development and revisions, selection of methods and materials, and staff training. Program management includes coordination of teaching assignments and materials, needs assessment and program evaluation, budgeting, and reporting.

Health educators working in such a setting need to develop management skills. Emphasis on administration in course selection and work experience do much to prepare people to move into such positions. Additionally, human relations skills are critical when educators must rely largely on others to implement a program as it was designed. The importance of "politics and personalities" cannot be overstressed. Working with people involves anticipating and meeting resistance, building support, and reinforcing good teaching. It involves carefully selecting the programs to be implemented, giving credit to others whenever possible, and, in general, understanding the realities of the situation and working effectively within or around any given set of restraints.

Programs that have survived and expanded have usually done so because a better than average health educator was involved. Health educators must be prepared to address management, in their language, and document their claims. Such successful educational specialists indeed function as program managers. A basic premise is that educators in health care thoroughly understand the motivations for the agency to do educational programming, whether financial or not, and provide appropriate data to decision makers. Moreover, educators must understand reimbursement mechanisms and must see health education in that context. It is also imperative that the best possible program is created and delivered uniformly. Administrative support must always be cultivated.

Health educators must be prepared to design a wide variety of programs in a wide variety of health settings. Programs may now be hospital based but involve or serve employers, physicians' offices, and so on. Health educators must also be prepared to help physical therapists, respiratory therapists, and others design and/or improve the educational component of their service. In some instances, a health educator who wishes to specialize in patient education may find it necessary to complete a nursing program or some other medical specialty as a means of gaining entry into the field.

Health educators in health care must also be prepared to integrate their services with educational specialists in community or worksite settings to maximize use of scarce resources.

Depending on the size of the hospital, educational specialists may also be responsible for staff development activities. In large hospitals this task is often assigned to a separate department or individual. In small hospitals time has to be divided among planning, implementing, and evaluating both patient education and staff continuing-education programs.

In commercial health agencies, a client-centered service provider emphasis is mandatory. Clients should be known by name and encouraged and assisted to maximize continued participation. Commercial agencies focus on the bottom line— profit. A reasonable profit margin requires that the number of participants be stable or increasing and that the expenses be constant or decreasing. While managers and others balance the budget, all professional staff need to work within the context of "revenue minus expenses equals profit."

It should be noted that many agencies are doing very well and have high-quality programs. Others compromise program quality in order to maintain a reasonable profit margin, or even to survive the cost-intensive start-up phase.

Community health educators should be familiar with the various spas and clinics, with the nature and quality of services, and with fee structures. For people who can afford the fees, it may be the best referral for weight loss, cessation of smoking, exercise programs, and so on. However, the community health educator's credibility can suffer if the program is not of the anticipated quality. At the minimum, fraudulent clinics and practices need to be avoided.

HEALTH CARE REFORM

Someone is always talking about reforming the nation's health care system. Often, budgets are simply adjusted upward or downward to respond to political pressure. Thus it will always be.

Politics are the art of compromise and there is never enough money to do everything people want done. It follows then that health educators need to seek opportunities to advocate for prevention, especially using educational methodologies. The prevention agenda needs to be inserted into the discussion each time health care reform occurs. If cuts in Medicare or Medicaid are proposed, health educators can advocate the value of prevention programs to minimize the effect of the cuts on clients. If health care programs are being cut, they can point out the value of preventive health and advocate for its retention. Similarly, in periods of growth, health education needs to be advocated. If proposed or existing programs impact on prevention, health educators should support them. For example, Head Start programs, Food Stamp programs, and numerous others have opportunities for health educators. New federal initiatives, such as services for AIDS clients, also provide health education opportunities.

Health educators need to be conversant with proposals for health care reform and need to recognize opportunities to advance the health education and health promotion agenda.

IN CONCLUSION

Working in a health care setting is exciting and challenging because of the changing nature of programming. Of course, the fact that health education and health promotion specialists help save lives is never more apparent than it is in health care settings. Also, in such settings, innovative, progressive health educators are given a chance to see what they can do with a minimal amount of supervision and guidance. Health care is a good setting in which creative, flexible personnel can function.

***

Suggested Learning Activities

1. Prepare a list of behaviors needed to prevent a heart attack. Develop a list of related programs that hospitals could implement.
2. Interview a practicing hospital health educator regarding past, present, and planned programs.
3. Write a job description for a hospital or an HMO health educator, including education, experience, skills, and functions. Indicate what differences occur because of the setting.
4. Compare the emphasis on prevention provided by retrospective and prospective reimbursement.
5. Interview a hospital administrator to determine what he or she sees as the benefits of health promotion to the organization.
6. Describe what a nurse health educator can do.
7. Develop a list of important segments in the community. Identify the top three health problems of each segment. List health promotion programs or services for each.

NOTES

1. Centers for Disease Control, Recommendations for Prevention of HIV Transmission in Health Care Settings, *Morbidity and Mortality Weekly Report* 36 (August 21, 1987): 15–185.

2. Ibid.

3. Centers for Disease Control, Update: Universal Precautions for Prevention of Transmission of HIV, Hepatitis B Virus and Other Bloodborne Pathogens in Health Care Settings, *Morbidity and Mortality Weekly Report* 37 (June 24, 1988): 377–388.

4. OSHA To Enforce AIDS Protection in Hospitals, *U.S. Medicine* 24 (October 1988): 1.

SUGGESTED READING

Behrens, R., and Longe, M. 1986. *Hospital-based health promotion programs for children and youth.* Chicago: American Hospital Association.

Jonas, S. 1991. *An introduction to the U.S. health care system.* New York: Springer Publishing Co., Inc.

Longe, M.E., and Wolfe, A. 1984. *Promoting community health through innovative hospital-based programs.* Chicago: American Hospital Association.

Murray, R., and Zentader, J. 1993. *Nursing assessment and health promotion strategies through the life span.* Norwalk, Conn.: Appleton & Lange.

Patient Educator's Resource Guide: Organizational and print resources for program development. 1985. Chicago: American Hospital Association.

Programming ideas for target populations. 1984. Chicago: American Hospital Association.

Snook, D. 1992. *Hospitals: What they are and how they work.* Gaithersburg, Md.: Aspen Publishers, Inc.

Teaching patients with acute conditions. 1992. Buffalo, N.Y.: Springhouse Publishing Company.

Tedesco, J., and Longe, M. 1984. *Health promotion and wellness.* Chicago: American Hospital Association.

Chapter 9

Worksite Health Promotion and Employee Assistance Programs

A large number of health education programs are developing in business and industry. They are not usually labeled as health education programs, and staff working with them may not be called health educators. Nonetheless, such programs are among the most important for health education today.

Worksite health promotion and employee assistance programs grew out of the older industrial medicine and industrial hygiene programs that were concerned with first aid and medical care; with environmental hazards, such as toxic components and noise; and with safety programs that stressed accident prevention.

The occupational safety and health programs expanded in scope and evolved in focus. The modern worksite program is not limited to medical care, precautionary measures connected with the use of toxic components, or employee safety. One typical expansion is to provide programs that improve the level of wellness. Another is concerned with problems at work, home, and play. A third changing emphasis is to provide programs for workers' families. A fourth emphasis is employee assistance programs. As these changes occur, more opportunities for health educators exist.

THE NATURE OF PROGRAMS

Such terms as *worksite health promotion, employee wellness programs,* and *employee assistance programs* can and do mean different things to different people. Some overlapping occurs, causing confusion. The more widely accepted term in business and industry is *employee health promotion*, whereas the more typical term in hospitals is *employee wellness*. The term we prefer is *worksite health promotion*. Employee assistance programs may be part of such a structure or separate from it.

Worksite health promotion is a combination of educational, organizational, and environmental activities designed to support behavior conducive to the health of employees.[1] Examples are shown in Table 9-1.

Table 9–1 Worksite Health Promotion Activities

Educational Activities	Organizational Activities	Environmental Activities
• Self-care, first aid, CPR	• Risk assessment	• Jogging trails
• Nutrition, weight control	• Smoke-free areas	• Nutritional items in
• Smoking cessation	• Screening program	vending machines
• Stress management	• Physical examinations,	• Low-salt/low-calorie
• Cancer risk awareness	newsletter	foods in cafeteria
• AIDS prevention	• Support groups	• Displays, posters
• Fitness	• Lending libraries	• Health fairs
	• Counseling hotlines	

Not all programs will have all the elements listed in Table 9-1, and some will have still other elements. The size of the corporation, the size of the health promotion project, the number of staff combined with their interests, the needs and interests of the employees, and the dictates of top management all influence program emphasis to varying degrees.

There will be worksites that are unable for economic or policy reasons to implement a comprehensive worksite health promotion program. However, employers may be willing to sponsor health education programs with proven track records.[2] This is an opportunity for health promotion planning of initial programs that can be evaluated, such as smoking cessation or weight loss projects.

The motivation to provide worksite health promotion programs falls primarily into three categories. First and foremost, a financial incentive exists, which is a primary motivating factor for most profit-making organizations.

A major study conducted by Control Data Corporation analyzed excess health care costs generated by employees who are at risk due to lifestyle factors.[3] For example, employees who smoke have 18 percent higher medical claims costs than those who do not smoke; employees who do not wear seat belts have 54 percent more hospital days than those who do wear seat belts, and so forth. With well-designed and well-managed programs, businesses can reduce the number of sick days taken by employees and therefore the cost of health insurance and disability payments. Other studies have shown that health risks are also linked to significant excess in absenteeism due to illness.[4]

The major economic benefit of health promotion to the company lies in improved productivity mediated through a lower rate of turnover and absenteeism. Effects on health care expense alone are often relatively small, as are gains from reduction in employee mortality or retiree health expenses.[5]

A 1992 national survey of worksite health promotion programs found a significant increase in such program activities and noted "substantial progress toward achievement of many worksite-related health objectives for the year 2000."[6] The survey found that 81 percent of the worksites offered at least one health promotion activity, with nutrition, weight control, physical fitness, high blood pressure, and stress management activities being most prevalent. There was also a substantial increase in the number of worksites that prohibit or severely restrict smoking at the workplace.

These factors lead to the second major reason companies support worksite health promotion programs—employee morale. Most employees value health and appreciate efforts made by companies to protect and even improve their health and that of their families. They also appreciate the convenience of such programs. Although employee morale is difficult to measure, experience suggests to employers that it is important and that it can be improved through health promotion programs.

There is also a recent trend for companies to increase involvement in community-based or public health issues that either directly impact on company image or relate to the other factors listed above. This includes the growing concern over AIDS prevention education for employees, smoke-free work environments, and the linking of health promotion programs with traditional employee assistance programs such as substance abuse counseling and referral.[7]

Employee assistance programs are usually problem centered and are designed to help employees cope with problems. Such programs have, to date, focused on alcohol and substance abuse problems but are expanding to help employees deal with depression, marital problems, chronic disease, financial problems, and grief over unexpected death and to aid in preventing suicide.

There are three keys to effective employee assistance programs. A good referral system is a must, and it must be tied to an effective staff and absolute confidentiality.

Referral networks are usually tied to adequate publicity in newsletters, employee handbooks, and closed-circuit television. These networks will, of course, promote self-referrals. Referrals are also facilitated by focused training of supervisory staff. Supervisors need to know symptoms, services provided, protocol required, and so on. Health educators may be asked to provide such training. A major concern for all trainers is to discourage supervisors from diagnosing, labeling, or discussing referrals. Items that should usually be reported include excessive absenteeism or tardiness, poor work habits, increased accidents or near misses, decreased productivity, fights, or other abnormal behaviors such as drug or alcohol use on the job or being under the influence of such substances regardless of when they were ingested. Referrals to professionals allow the experts to determine what diagnosis and treatment, if any, is appropriate.

Employee assistance programs may provide prevention services as well, depending on the structure and organization and on what other services are available at the site. Regardless, there are always prevention roles in employee assistance programs. Primary prevention suggests activities to prevent problems from ever occurring. Primary intervention suggests activities to help people with problems solve their problems as well as develop coping behaviors that will minimize the likelihood of the problems from recurring. Regardless, the health educator needs to understand the etiology of the problem, the nature of treatment, and the requisite coping skills. These obviously will vary from problem to problem.

PROGRAMMING SKILLS

Two very different levels of work may exist in a health promotion or employee assistance program. One is a managerial position, with responsibility for planning, implementing, and evaluating programs. People in this position must have strong administrative skills and a co-requisite amount of confidence in their skills and programs. They must be able to conceptualize an overall view of the program being developed and then, in a systems approach, be able to implement it element by element. A "vision of the future" should be at once both idealistic and realistic. Programs must be bold and imaginative enough to generate support from decision makers yet feasible within the constraints of reality. Group process and educational assessment skills are important. Programs should be planned with management and employee involvement in setting goals and priorities.

Health educators working at this level must be able to function in terms of organizational development and policy change. Planning for long-term programs requires a familiarity with job descriptions, organizational charts, and budgets. "People skills" are also critical, as support needs to be generated from higher level management, unions, and employees. Similarly, participation in health education programs needs to be stimulated among executives, blue-collar workers, and other employees. A positive "sales approach" needs to be combined with good programs to sell, to maximize effectiveness.

At the same time the program manager must be a good detail person. Budgets must be developed and managed effectively. Checklists must be developed so that deadlines are met. Evaluation skills are important, since stockholders and administrators want to know the costs, savings, and differential. Quality assurance must be maintained, and all the above must be monitored and the results communicated effectively and regularly to appropriate individuals and groups. Designing, implementing, and evaluating a program or managing an existing one is a responsible position in which an individual must produce positive results or be held accountable.

Another level of functioning in health promotion programs is the implementation of specific components. Rather than administer the program, some individuals function as staff health educators and conduct classes or clinics. People who work at this level use behavior change skills and should have a solid foundation in adult learning theory. They should be able to motivate individuals and groups to participate in programs and to be successful while participating.

Health educators working in such programs must be content specialists as well. They must be able to respond quickly to a multitude of questions on stress, minor injuries occurring during exercise, hypertension, nutrition, and so forth. Although health educators in these and other settings must be specialists, they must be expert in several areas. They need to be willing and able to develop expertise in new areas, such as, for example, developing a stop-smoking program.

Other health education skills are also important in worksite programs. Materials need to be developed, newsletter copy prepared, reports prepared, curricula developed, staff development provided, films selected, records kept, and agreements negotiated with voluntary agencies. Worksite health promotion programs can offer diverse, exciting opportunities for creative health educators.

OTHER SETTINGS

Health educators should also be aware that many commercial organizations are providing health education services and that health educators are trained in the skills needed to work in or manage such programs. Health spas, aerobic dance programs, Weight Watchers, Smoke Enders, and YMCAs are a few examples. Staff members in such agencies are not likely to be called health educators, but the roles are the same. Opportunities exist for employment and for vertical mobility. Occasionally, part-time employment can occur at the undergraduate level, as specialized skills are more important than credentials in such settings. Although special interests, such as aerobic dancing, are important, general skills, such as marketing and motivation, are also critical.

Many other organizations, such as health departments, HMOs, hospitals, and universities, are contracting with business and industry to conduct worksite program planning and assessment. One example can be found with Blue Cross and Blue Shield plans across the United States. A 1986 survey indicated over half of the plans offered health promotion programs to employer groups.[8]

IN CONCLUSION

Worksite programs have emerged as important opportunities for health education. A growing percentage of the population is part of the work force. Employees spend nearly a third of their day at work. Work is essential to survival in most cases and yet can be adversely affected by what happens to the employee both on the job and off. Employers are finding that it is cost effective to promote good health. Healthy employees make healthy corporations, and healthy corporations are good business for stockholders, employees, and health educators.

***

Suggested Learning Activities

1. Visit the health and safety programs of a nearby industrial plant to discover health needs as seen by management and employees.
2. Outline an ideal employee wellness program.
3. Inquire of a voluntary agency regarding training programs for facilitators of stop-smoking and breast self-examination programs and their relationship with local industry.

NOTES

1. R.S. Parkinson, *Managing Health Promotion in the Workplace: Guidelines for Implementation and Evaluation* (Mountain View, Calif.: Mayfield Publishing Co., 1982), 8.

2. R. Pruitt, Economics of Health Promotion, *Nursing Economics* May-June (1987):17.

3. *Health Risks and Behavior: The Impact on Medical Costs* (Brookfield, Wis.: Milliman and Robertson, 1987).

4. W.S. Joge and D.R. Anderson, Control Data: The Stay Well Program, *Corporate Commentary* Winter (1986): 1–13.

5. J.P. Patton, Worksite health promotion: An economic model, *Journal of Occupational Medicine* August (1991), 868.

6. *1992 National Survey of Worksite Health Promotion Activities* (Washington, D.C.:U.S. Government Printing Office, 1992).

7. B.G. Ware, Work Place Health Promotion: Issues for the Future, in *Health Link* (New York: Center for Health Education, February 1987), 5.

8. J.F. Riedel, Employee Health Promotion: Blue Cross and Blue Shield Activities, *American Journal of Health Promotion* March (1987): 28–31.

SUGGESTED READING

Association for Fitness in Business. 1992. *Guidelines for employee health promotion programs.* Champaign, Ill.: Human Kinetics Publishers.

National Health Information Clearinghouse. 1982. *Worksite health promotion: A bibliography of selected books and resources.* Rosslyn, Va.

O'Donnell, M., ed. 1993. *Health promotion in the workplace.* Albany, N.Y.: Delmar.

Office of Disease and Health Promotion. *Worksite health promotion: Some questions and answers to help you get started.* Washington, D.C.: U.S. Department of Health and Human Services, 93.

Opatz, J. 1993. *Economic impact of worksite health promotion.* Champaign, Ill.: Human Kinetics Publishers.

Parkinson, R.S. 1982. *Managing health promotion in the workplace: Guidelines for implementation and evaluation.* Palo Alto, Calif.: Mayfield Publishing Co.

Wendel, S., ed. 1993. *Healthy, wealthy and wise: Fundamentals of workplace health promotion.* Omaha: WelCOA.

Chapter 10

Working in a School Health Setting

School health education began about 100 years ago, although its precursors extend even farther into antiquity. Much of school health education started as a result of the temperance movement. Advocates of abstinence wanted that point of view taught and developed state laws that mandated it.

Early state laws also mandated schools to teach about communicable diseases and ways of preventing them. The 1800s were years of frightening epidemics of cholera, tuberculosis, diphtheria, whooping cough, typhoid, and other diseases.

The state laws were usually not enforced, and the programs that did exist varied in effectiveness. Many of these mandatory state laws are still in effect and are being overlooked. Moreover, school health education has often been forced to be faddish, responding to the crisis of the day, be it drugs, teenage pregnancy, venereal diseases, or AIDS. At long last, this seems to be changing, and comprehensive school health education programming is occurring.

School health educators typically are teachers who have a major or minor in health education. Of course, given the state of school financing, many teachers with certification in other fields are assigned to teach health education classes. In some instances, they receive inservice training, while in other instances they simply learn by doing. Under these circumstances, the quality of the program is often compromised.

School health education is an applied field of study, one that draws heavily from public health, family life, childhood growth and development, nutrition, psychology, and other disciplines. Moreover, there is opportunity for teachers of biology, home economics, psychology, sociology, government, history, and physical education to integrate into their course materials a focus on health education topics. Similarly, in preschool and elementary school, the classroom teacher has ample opportunity to teach health topics and to develop or reinforce positive health-related behaviors.

These circumstances, along with others, combine to dictate that community health educators should be actively involved in promoting school health education as a significant part of their community health education programming. Health behaviors are learned at an early stage of life. If children develop good health behaviors and practice them throughout their lives, their morbidity and mortality will be changed significantly. Promoting school health education programs is a significant opportunity to improve the health of a community and should not be overlooked.

Three-fourths of all youths now live in urban areas, one-half live with only one parent, one-half use illegal drugs, more than one-half use alcohol, about one-fourth use tobacco products, and one-half engage in premarital sexual intercourse before they are 18 years old.[1] These data also suggest that there are many complicating factors that make effective school health education difficult. A quality school health education program cannot be effectively accomplished by a single course or by the schools alone. Education of school-aged youth should be part of the responsibility of every community health educator, at least to understand and support efforts underway by the schools, and preferably to stimulate improvement and expansion of such programming. It is this belief that prompts inclusion of a chapter on school health education in a book on community health education.

Admittedly, in this chapter material will be repeated from course work that some health educators have had or will have. However, the lines are sufficiently distinct between school health education and community health education that many community health educators do not get course work in school health education and many school health educators do not get course work in community health education. Fortunately, this is changing.

There was an initiative in the Role Delineation Project to produce a "generic" health educator, who could function effectively in either setting, and at a few colleges moves have been made in this direction. However, the requirements of teacher certification and the required skills of community health education usually preclude providing both in a baccalaureate program. Many colleges and universities fear that producing "a jack of all trades" will result in that person being "a master of none," without additional graduate training.

At present, the community health educator is not usually certified to teach and the school health educator is not usually trained in sufficient depth to be chosen as an agency health educator. Clearly, however, significant overlap does occur and both educators should work closely together.

AN OVERVIEW OF A COMPREHENSIVE SCHOOL HEALTH PROGRAM

The school health program has long been thought to have three components: school health environment, school health services, and school health instruction. More recently, other dimensions have been added, but an understanding of these first three is crucial.

School health environment obviously includes a safe school plant. It includes safe playgrounds for elementary schools and safe parking lots and science laboratories. It includes clean restrooms, locker rooms, swimming pools, and food preparation and serving areas. It includes adequate classroom lighting, ventilation, humidity, and noise control. It includes protection against radiation and asbestos and adequate control and disposal of toxic wastes. It includes a smoke-free, drug-free, and alcohol-free setting and freedom from crime and violence. It includes emotional and social conditions that keep stress in control and that generate a positive self-concept.

Obviously, the healthy environment is the basis for all else that occurs in the school health program, as well as in other parts of the school system. The school must be a healthy place to be, in order for teaching and learning to have maximum effect, regardless of the subject matter being taught.

School health services include an array of screening clinics to promote early case finding, a prerequisite to primary intervention. Clinics might provide screening for hypertension, sickle cell anemia, or many other conditions.

School health services include first aid and services for those who become ill during school or for those who must cope with a chronic disease or disorder. These services may include weight loss clinics, smoke-stopping clinics, and clinics that provide family planning information. They may include support groups for children of alcoholics and often include immunization programs and other disease prevention practices. While the services vary according to the problems and the beliefs from area to area, some school health services are an important part of a school health program.

School health instruction is usually visualized as beginning in preschool and becoming a K–12 planned, sequential program. Motivation and behavior change are emphasized, as are coping with peer pressure and decision making. Typically, ten content areas are emphasized:

1. Community health
2. Consumer health
3. Environmental health
4. Family life
5. Growth and development
6. Nutrition
7. Personal health
8. Disease prevention and control
9. Safety and accident prevention
10. Substance use and abuse.

Allensworth and Kolbe[2] illustrated eight components (see Figure 10-1). The figure diagrams the interrelationship of these components with student and faculty

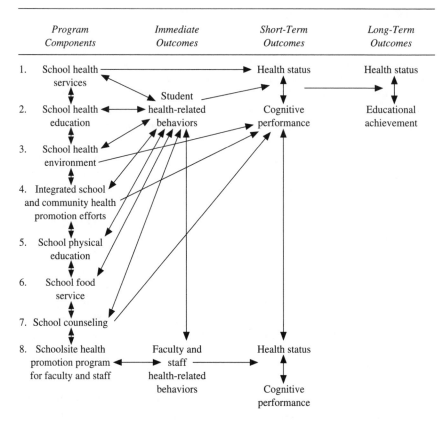

Figure 10–1 School Health Promotion Components and Outcomes. *Source:* Allensworth, D.D., and Kolbe, L.J., The Comprehensive School Health Program: Exploring an Expanded Concept, *Journal of School Health*, Vol. 57, No. 10, December 1987, p. 410. Reprinted with permission of the American School Health Association, © 1987.

health-related behaviors. Moreover, it depicts the interrelatedness to health status, cognitive performance, and educational achievement.

The work of Allensworth and Kolbe expanded the concept of a school health program to include physical education, food service, and other related components. It is readily apparent that if these components were all coordinated, with a primary purpose of health promotion and meeting the year 2000 objectives, considerable progress could be made. The Centers for Disease Control is currently funding several statewide demonstration centers to implement such programs.

Health instruction also can and should occur within the health services and health environment.[3]

Health instruction, to be effective, selects instructional methods appropriate to behavior change. It is outcome oriented and is a complex and difficult subject to teach well. While anyone can teach health education, only a few do it well, selecting methods appropriate to the age group, the subject matter, and the desired outcomes—good health behaviors.

Certainly, it is necessary to teach more than content. Cognitive, affective, and psychomotor objectives permeate all content areas. Affective objectives predominate in behavior change theory. An old adage describes the essence of this concept: "What you know is important, but what you believe is more important, because it determines what you do about what you know." Theoretical constructs recommended for behavior change focus on attitudes and beliefs. Most people know what good health practices they need to adopt, be it weight loss, cessation of smoking, more exercise, and so on. Another useful example is substance abuse. Drug users usually know more of the risks associated with drug use than do nonusers, but they still use drugs. Attitudes and beliefs are the critical factors in most prevention programs. They must be addressed in instructional programs.

SCHOOL HEALTH PROMOTION COMPONENTS

With the emergence of health promotion concepts, the contemporary model school health program expanded to add five other components.[4] Some earlier theorists included several of these as subcomponents of the previous three items. First, school physical education certainly has cardiovascular fitness emphasis and self-expression and social development. Emphasis on fitness and lifelong recreational activities are important to health. Second, food service programs may previously have been part of a health service or environment. Certainly, nutrition is central to health, and using this opportunity to color-code lunch menus to indicate best choices for low-calorie, low-cholesterol, or low-sodium diets is an important feature of a good program. Elimination of "junk" food from the menu and from vending machines is yet another opportunity. Third, school counseling can and should cope with stress, substance abuse, suicide prevention, rebellion, loss of self-esteem, assertiveness training, and referral, as appropriate. Fourth, integrated school and community health promotion efforts such as health fairs, afterschool hallway exercise programs, and parenting workshops provide still another arena for programming.

The last component also was considered part of health instruction and health environment by earlier theorists but has been isolated and elevated in status for emphasis—faculty and staff health promotion programs. Faculty and staff are visible role models to the extent that they exercise regularly, control weight, and do not smoke or misuse other drugs. Teachers who adopt health promotion activities send a powerful message to students.

It must be noted that the eight components of a school health program have synergistic effects. Concepts and practices that are emphasized and reinforced in several segments of the program are more likely to be practiced.

WORKING IN AND WITH SCHOOL HEALTH PROGRAMS

Community health educators are not normally employed in school health settings. Teachers who are certified to teach in that state and licensed and registered nurses are the most common employees. Community health educators will normally serve as curriculum consultants, subject matter experts, guest lecturers, resource brokers, initiators, and coordinators.

Often, community health educators will be the best-trained health educators in the area. As such, they are in a position to suggest, advise, initiate, or coordinate. However, the methods will vary from place to place.

Certainly, the community health educator should understand and have ready access to the specialized literature on school health programs, some of which is suggested at the end of this chapter. Politics and personalities then tend to dominate the process, trying to assess where and when to exert influence.

Active involvement in parent–teacher organizations may be a starting place. Monitoring school-related news events can also provide an opening, as can inquiring of teachers or students as to what health education is occurring. Inquiring at the local health department will often provide useful information, because health department nurses and environmental specialists are frequently involved in schools.

Inquiry of a building principal can be made informally by a parent of a student in that school and more formally if one is not. Intermediate school districts frequently are in a position to know what is happening in a school and sometimes employ health curriculum consultants. Major voluntary agencies such as the American Lung Association, American Heart Association, and American Cancer Society have school health materials and programs. They may be able to describe what is happening and who is doing it, and/or they may be willing to work with the health educator in upgrading existing programs. A coalition of health agencies is often the most effective means of improving school health programs.

Politics being what they are, some thought should be given to approaching the superintendent of schools or the school board. Consider involving the agency head in such an approach.

IN CONCLUSION

A comprehensive school health education program represents a significant part of any community health education program. If it is in place, it can be an important feature. If it is not in place, it represents a significant opportunity. Community health educators need to know and understand what comprehensive programming is like and need to be committed to implementing it.

***

Suggested Learning Activities

1. Interview a teacher or administrator about the nature and the amount of health education in the curriculum.
2. Informally survey your classmates about the nature and the amount of health education they experienced.
3. Interview a health educator or a public health nurse about health services provided to the public schools.
4. Contact a school health education specialist at your college or university and ascertain what state laws exist regarding school health programs.

NOTES

1. American Association of School Administrators, *Why School Health*, Arlington, Va.: 1987.

2. D.D. Allensworth and L. Kolbe, The Comprehensive School Health Program: Exploring an Expanded Concept, *Journal of School Health* 57, no. 10 (1987): 409–412.

3. D.K. Lohrmans, R.S. Gould, and W. Jubb, School Health Education: A Foundation for School Health Programs, *Journal of School Health* 57, no. 10 (1987): 420–425.

4. Allensworth and Kolbe, The Comprehensive School Health Program.

SUGGESTED READING

Ames, E. 1992. *Designing school health curricula.* Madison, Wis.: Brown & Benchmark.

Cohen, W., et al. 1992. Health, schools, healthy children, healthy futures: The role of the federal government in promoting health through the schools. *Journal of School Health* 62, no. 4:126–127.

Creswell, W., and Newman, I. 1989. *School health practice.* St. Louis: Times Mirror/Mosby College Publishing Division.

Miller, D., and Telljohan, S. 1992. *Health education in the elementary school.* Madison, Wis.: Brown & Benchmark.

World Health Organization. 1992. *School health education to prevent AIDS and sexually transmitted diseases.* Albany, N.Y.

Chapter 11

Working in Colleges, Universities, and Professional Organizations

Employment in a college, university, or professional organization is not usually an entry-level position but rather a position that experienced health educators obtain. Maturity, a wide range of experiences, and advanced degrees are the usual prerequisites for such appointments. The advanced degree will vary, but either a master's degree in health education or a doctorate in public health, health education, or a related field is usually preferred. Although opportunities exist for recent graduates without significant work experience to enter such fields, the integration of knowledge that comes primarily through maturation and work experience is important to prospective employers.

WORKING IN A COLLEGE OR UNIVERSITY SETTING

Health educators working in a college or university are usually not faculty members but may often teach as guest lecturers. Colleges often employ health educators to work with the student body. They may be employed in a college health service and have responsibilities that approximate those of a hospital health educator. Part of their workload is patient education, in that they provide educational services to college students who present themselves to health care providers and who are assessed as having both medical and educational needs. Part of their workload is similar to that of a health educator in a health maintenance organization, with students being the subscribers to the service. Preventive programs are provided in the health center, in dormitory settings, in classrooms, in student organizations, and in the campus media in an effort to upgrade the health of the student body. Health educators may also provide wellness programs for the student body and have job responsibilities as described in the previous chapters.

Since most colleges and universities have emphasized improved relations with the communities around them, health educators in student health services or as faculty have become increasingly involved in networking with other health-related agencies not on the campus. Many of the skills and functions used by health educators in health departments or voluntary agencies would apply here. Joint campus–community programs regarding AIDS, smoking, cholesterol, and even immunizations have become common. Health educators will use their planning and consulting skills while working on such programs.

When most people think of a health educator working in a college or university setting, they think of an instructor, stereotypically, a professor. Both imply teaching responsibility, with the difference being in rank. Entry-level positions are usually labeled *instructor*, with promotion being to an assistant professor, associate professor, and finally, professor. Promotion is based on teaching experience and ability, university service through its committee systems, community service, professional involvement, and writing for publication. Traditionally, excellence in teaching is stressed in early promotions; research and publications are stressed in later promotions.

Regardless of rank, those involved in instruction at the college level must be able to organize material sequentially, select methods appropriate for college students, and present the material in an interesting manner. The method selected will vary from course to course and instructor to instructor. Lectures may be the most appropriate method in some instances; group activities may be preferable in others. Illustrations, examples, and practical experiences are important teaching tools that are seldom overused. The instructor's "bag of tricks" should include a series of questions that cannot be answered "yes" or "no," to encourage critical thinking. Variety, application, and creativity are the keys to successful teaching.

Evaluation of student learning, one of the most difficult parts of teaching, is usually traumatic. It is not feasible to discuss this topic in detail here; indeed, several books have been written on the topic. Suffice it to say that instructors should work hard on evaluation techniques. The techniques should relate to course objectives, be flexible, be presented at the beginning of the course, and be reasonable requirements. Ideally, they should also be a learning experience for both the students and the instructor.

Faculty members also do a considerable amount of advising, and both directive and nondirective counseling skills are important. On one hand, advising on graduation requirements is often quite directive, in that advisors are expected to know the requirements and assist students in meeting them. On the other hand, selection of a career emphasis, a major and minor, elective courses, field training sites, or research topics are areas in which nondirective counseling skills are important. Being available, being personable, and being supportive are attributes that should be stressed. Faculty advisors should also be prepared to do personal counseling, since college students face problems having to do with, for example, grades, sexuality issues, substance abuse, family, and finances. Often attentive listening as a student talks about these problems is therapeutic. Faculty members do need to recognize their limitations, however, and refer to expert counselors when appropriate. They may get involved in significant helping relationships if they choose to do so and are the kind of people students turn to for help.

Another important faculty role involves course and curriculum revision, so that what students learn is not outdated before they even graduate. Indeed, college professors often influence the state of the art as they compare theory and practice, develop new theory, and stimulate new practice. Being on the cutting edge is a personality trait, just as creativity is a personality trait. Using the same lecture notes to teach the same material is easier than thinking about "what is," "what ought to be," and "how do we get there?" For example, community health education methods courses should now include discussion on appropriate use of cable television, videodiscs, and computer managed instruction.

A key element in the struggle to stay current is maintaining regular contacts with practicing professionals. This can be done in and through a field training program and through a professional organization (like the local chapter of the Society for Public Health Education), or in and through personal relationships of a continuing nature. Faculty need to avoid the "ivory tower syndrome" in their personal teaching and in the courses and curricula. Guest lecturers and adjunct faculty from agencies are also important tools that can be used in this task.

College faculty usually only teach three or four courses a week, with in-class time often being restricted to approximately 12 hours a week. Extensive reading, course preparation, grading of papers, and advising are also required functions. In addition, faculty are expected to be involved in the committee system. Most faculties pride themselves on a collegial system of governance that requires committee decisions. Such committees affect programs, budgets, course offerings, faculty composition, and nearly everything else about a university. Faculty need to be politically sensitive in all such matters, to select committees in which vested interests exist, and to prepare adequately so as to affect the outcome. Because faculty often need to consult with agency personnel, consultation skills are also important. College faculty are also being hired as consultants for health education projects at the local or state level. Of particular interest is using the resources and skills from academia in evaluating projects conducted in the field. Most community agencies lack the staffing to conduct proper evaluative studies of their programs.

WORKING IN PROFESSIONAL ORGANIZATIONS

Professional organizations exist primarily to upgrade the profession. They represent the profession in programming and, on occasion, speak on behalf of the profession. They also serve the professionals who are members. Many such organizations are staffed only by elected officers, who function on a part-time, volunteer basis. A large organization may employ an executive officer to facilitate the work of the elected officers and to conduct the affairs of the organization between board meetings. Although only a few such positions are available, this is a setting in which health educators sometimes function.

Most of the positions are with national organizations, but large state organizations also employ staff. Organizations that involve more than one discipline are also more likely to employ staff members. Examples of such positions are at the American Medical Association, the American Hospital Association, the American Public Health Association, and their affiliated chapters or state agencies.

Job descriptions vary from organization to organization but usually involve some routine matters associated with office management and service to the membership. A significant part of the job description is often in planning and conducting conferences and in consulting with the membership or with agencies that are contemplating programming change. The position may also require the health educator to plan and coordinate special health education pilot projects funded by the association. Planning and conducting conferences are discussed in Chapter 19. However, inasmuch as consultation is an integral part of the work of agency staff members, it is discussed in this chapter. This is not to suggest that all consultation is done by personnel in colleges, universities, and professional organizations, but that consultation skills may be an important component of a job in such an institution or agency.

There are many definitions of an expert; most of the commonly cited ones are derisive. It seems appropriate, therefore, to begin a discussion of consultation by indicating that consultation does not necessarily connote the image of an expert. In fact, when an expert comes into an agency, he or she may very well be viewed as threatening by personnel within that agency.

A consultant can come into an agency in a variety of roles: as a resource person to be used at the discretion of the agency; as a process consultant to assist agency personnel to develop a method to solve a problem; and as a training consultant to help assess the need for, plan, and perhaps conduct training activities. What is important is that differing expectations should be clarified before the actual consultation.

Consultants should ask a lot of questions about what led to the call for help. Knowing the sequence of events, the personalities, and the politics of the situation can help to identify the problem.

The consultation process is essentially a problem-solving process, and as always, problem definition is an important early task. This diagnostic step often coincides with information gathering.

Consultation that minimizes the image of an expert involves working with people at all stages of the process. But nowhere is it more important than in problem definition. Various perceptions of the problem are, in fact, part of the problem and part of the solution. Confusion in problem identification is important to establish and clarify.

Consultants should be careful to work on the problem they were asked to work on or to shift focus with the consent of group members. People may not recognize that the problem is larger or different than they thought and may need to be helped to shift their focus. On the other hand, consultants should not downgrade a problem because they see larger ones. Conversely, they should not overreact to problems but rather accept them as tasks that need to be addressed. The larger tasks or more difficult problems should simply be presented as tasks that need to be addressed over time.

When the group has arrived at some consensus of what the problem is and has gathered and analyzed whatever data are available, the identification of alternative solutions is possible, as is selecting and testing those judged most feasible. The process used to do this varies from situation to situation and with consultants. It may involve primarily individual appointments and interviews, a compiling of impressions and perceptions, and a discussion of recommendations. Conversely, it may involve group process in which agency personnel, with help from the consultant, attempt to arrive at a consensus of the nature of the problem, the alternative solutions, the selection of the most feasible solution, and a list of other problems that should be addressed. Many combinations of the two approaches are possible.

In either scenario, consultants must use good human relations skills. It is critical to establish rapport and trust and to build these into an atmosphere in which cooperation can occur. Team-building activities can be helpful, as can the theories of organizational development. Communication skills are important, as is careful listening. Listing possibilities, suggesting factors, and in other ways being nondirective is generally recommended. Also, an important skill is the ability to conceptualize complex problems and complex solutions. Often a diagram or agenda may help others to visualize a problem or a solution and to focus on the same issue long enough to resolve it. Finally, consultants should emphasize that there are no quick and easy solutions to longstanding, complex problems. Complete resolution may take a long time, continuous effort, and commitment from all.

IN CONCLUSION

Working in a college, university, or professional organization can be an exciting and rewarding challenge. It can involve working with the health problems of teens and young adults and helping people in different situations. It can involve helping such young adults make lifestyle changes that will benefit them.

It can involve helping individuals do self-appraisals, make satisfying career decisions, and plan college careers. It can involve establishing lifelong relationships with members of each generation of practicing professionals. It can involve influencing the state of the art of professional practice through research, inservice sessions, graduate seminars, writing for publication, and consultation.

As the profession matures, more opportunities exist for employment in college, university, or professional organization settings. Working in such settings is not open to all, nor do all health educators possess the necessary prerequisites. However, it can be a most satisfying career and is one to which many aspire.

***

Suggested Learning Activities

1. Visit a college or university health service and review current and projected health education programs, budgets, and staff.
2. Interview professors on the rewarding and nonrewarding aspects of being a faculty member.
3. Prepare a list of desirable attributes, skills, and qualities of a good college teacher.

Chapter 12

Choosing a Setting, Entering the Profession, and Being Mobile

Because health educators have skills that are adaptable to many settings, they have considerable flexibility when seeking or changing employment. For instance, they may be employed in health departments, voluntary agencies, hospitals, industry, programs for the aged or the young, pharmaceutical firms, or planning agencies. The clients in many agencies and firms need to be informed and motivated regarding health.

Early in collegiate training for the profession, serious consideration should be given to choosing a setting in which to work—although changes can and often will be made several times throughout one's career. Some job seekers allow such factors as geographical area, salary, timing of job openings, and travel time to play a large part in determining the kind of health agency in which they will work. Others systematically consider such factors and go to the job of their choosing, rather than take a job primarily because of its convenience.

CONSIDERATIONS WHEN CHOOSING

Health educators share a common need and interest in working with people. They work with various kinds of people in a variety of roles. Although it is true that job descriptions are affected largely by the individual doing the job, it is also true that job expectations vary significantly. Examples of what some positions involve are listed below:

- Administrative tasks
- Working with the mass media
- Concentration on schools
- Production of health education materials
- Work with the disadvantaged

- Fund-raising
- Client contact
- Contact with volunteers
- Working with a specific disease or disorder
- Familiarity with a variety of diseases or disorders
- Working with a special interest group
- Involvement with many and varied interest groups

Such a listing could continue, but this one is long enough to show the diversity that is possible. It also demonstrates that a "perfect fit" is usually impossible.

If, however, an individual is interested in administrative matters or is not interested in fund-raising, the scope of desirable jobs is narrowed considerably. Similarly, a strong interest in the natural sciences or the social sciences can suggest certain kinds of positions. Such issues are best discussed with faculty advisors and practicing professionals.

PREPARING FOR A CHOSEN CAREER

A person may choose a specific academic minor in order to prepare for a desired position. Additionally, choice of electives within a major or minor are important job-related factors. Someone wishing to work in a substance abuse agency should take as many substance abuse–related courses as possible and should plan to do a practicum or internship in such an agency. Similarly, someone wishing to work in the area of cardiovascular disease should emphasize courses in fitness, stress reduction, cessation of cigarette smoking, first aid that includes cardiopulmonary resuscitation, community fund-raising, and, obviously, course work directly related to understanding the cardiovascular and pulmonary systems. Such course work in a major, supplemented by an internship and a management minor, would make an individual a strong candidate for a position in the American Heart Association or in an employee wellness program.

Some might argue that in a diverse field such as health education it is better to be a generalist. Such an argument is especially crucial for individuals who are not too mobile. However, others might argue that in an era of oversupply, available jobs will go to those who are best trained for the positions. There is always room in a profession for "the best," so it is imperative that job seekers be well trained for and experienced in some subspecialty. Excellence is an easily recognized and widely respected commodity. People who have excelled in one area usually have the personality, attributes, and skills to excel in others. Therefore, they may be hired in areas other than those in which they have excelled. We strongly endorse the philosophy that individuals should select an area of job preference by the start of their junior year and begin to specialize. Specialization can continue or shift focus in graduate work.

The question of how individuals trained as health educators can get the necessary experience to break into the field always arises—usually after the fact. Practicums, internships, and field experiences for credit are three ways this can be done. It is important for interns to excel in such experiences so as to obtain a strong evaluation and subsequent job recommendation.

Volunteer work is another source of work experience. Such work may be an extension of field experience in an agency after the university's requirements have been met. It can also be in voluntary agencies in the college community or in the student's hometown. Similarly, it can be in on-campus student organizations. Any opportunities to practice leadership skills should be seized. Such volunteer work experience can then be highlighted, or at least summarized, in a résumé.

DISCOVERING THE JOB MARKET

College or university placement offices provide only one of several ways of locating job openings. Another is through informal or unprinted sources. Developing a good working relationship with a professor who is in touch with agencies is useful, because agency people may contact a professor directly for the names of two or three good prospects. Similarly, maintaining contact with field training supervisors is important, since they, too, may know of openings that have developed or, more important, are about to develop.

Being active in professional organizations, such as the Society for Public Health Education and the American Public Health Association, is also part of networking in a job search. Personal contacts in such settings can be the key to successful searching. Additionally, professional organizations usually provide a placement service at annual meetings, a job bank, or a list of job openings in their journals and newsletters. Placement services normally require that an application form be completed before the meeting. The form should be typed neatly and accurately. Inasmuch as this form is usually a one-page summary, it is advisable to take several copies of a résumé.

PREPARING PLACEMENT PAPERS

College students should file placement papers with their institutions and become familiar with the services offered. Although it is true that many job announcements bypass the placement office and are sent directly to a professor, it is also true that others routinely are sent only to placement offices.

College placement offices assist job seekers by conducting conferences and by providing materials on writing résumés and preparing for interviews. They also have a variety of job bulletins available. Although a student may not need or want assistance in obtaining a job at that time, years later his or her placement papers may be important. An inactive file can be reactivated and updated; one that has never been started cannot.

Placement papers vary in format but usually include an autobiography. This serves a dual purpose: It allows a prospective employer to get acquainted with the candidate's background and to see a sample of the candidate's writing. Placement papers should be grammatically correct and neatly typed. Lasting and significant impressions are often formed from such documents.

Recommendations from two or three professors, preferably in a major and minor field of study, are important. Students should get acquainted with professors early in a course and develop a good working relationship with some of them. Faculty recommendations and field supervisor recommendations are often critical. Indeed, a prospective employer may call a professor, describe a position, and ask to be sent résumés of "three of your best."

Although faculty letters of recommendation are often written for the placement file, this is not always the case. Letters of recommendation can be written for each job application, thus stressing factors relevant for that particular position. This approach is more important for upper-level positions.

Similarly, references are often requested as part of a job application. Prospective employers may simply want a name, title, and telephone number. Telephone inquiries permit the prospective employer to formulate the questions, and a reference is often requested to be more candid when a written record is not involved. They also permit the strengths of candidates to be compared when more than one candidate is known to the reference.

PREPARING A RÉSUMÉ

A résumé is usually included with the placement papers. Résumé preparation is an important skill for health educators. A current résumé is helpful to have and may serve many purposes other than job application. For example, it can be forwarded as background material to those presiding over conferences or seminars or can be appended to a grant application.

A résumé should be easy to read and eye-catching. Usually, résumés are done on a computer using a laser printer or professionally typeset. Good-quality paper, spacing, headings, and so on help make a résumé stand out and help get a candidate selected from among the many applicants as one of the few who will be interviewed. The résumé is not necessarily a detailed life story but rather should emphasize what makes the person a good prospect. It often is appropriate to have more than one résumé, and, for example, use one to stress experience important to voluntary agencies and another to stress experience important to a tax-supported agency.

A good way to begin a résumé is to list, by category, relevant factual information. Not all this information may be required in a résumé, but it may be helpful at a job interview.

Such an inventory should include an address and complete telephone number at which the applicant currently can be reached, as well as a permanent address and telephone number. Age, sex, marital status, and race are not required.

Past employers should be listed with complete addresses. The dates of employment, positions held, and perhaps any noteworthy accomplishments should be listed. Usually, previous employment is categorized as either full time or part time and listed in chronological order, with the current position listed first.

Education and special training should be detailed, including degrees, institutions attended, and major fields of study. Agency work experience completed for college credit should be described. It is also appropriate to note military training and licenses or certificates earned.

A cover letter should be prepared for each application (Exhibit 12-1). The best impression results from an original, typed, business-format letter that is hand signed. The letter should be on quality bond stationery and, whenever possible, should be addressed to an individual. The position and the source of information concerning the opening should be identified. The letter should explain why the applicant is interested in working for the particular organization. Related experiences and achievements in the field should be identified, with reference to the attached résumé. The letter should address areas of particular interest to the employer. A careful reading of the job description or contact with people who are familiar with the agency should facilitate preparing a cover letter that matches candidate strengths with job demands. The letter may conclude with an expression of desire for a personal interview and of flexibility as to time and place with a "thank you for your consideration."

Writing letters of inquiry or interest to agencies that do not currently have jobs available is sometimes appropriate. Such letters may inquire about anticipated openings in health education or related fields or simply request that a résumé be kept on file. Letters of inquiry are usually used when an individual has geographical limitations that restrict employment to a specific area. Care should be taken that the letter of inquiry is not phrased as a letter of application for a nonexistent position. It should be grammatically correct, properly paragraphed and punctuated, and attractive in appearance in order to make a good first impression.

When a position has been offered, one should accept or reject the contract in writing and if the position was not accepted, tell why it was rejected. Rejections should be submitted as soon as possible, usually within a few days, but always within the agreed-on time frame.

Exhibit 12-1 Guidelines for Application Letter

---

221 Popular Street
Missoula, Montana 59801
June 18, 1993

Mr. John P. Jensen, Administrator
District Health Department
555 Tamarack Drive
Petoskey, MI

First Paragraph: In your initial paragraph, state the reason for the letter, the specific position or type of work for which you are applying, and indicate from which resource (placement center, news media, friend, employment service) you learned of the opening.

Second Paragraph: Indicate why you are interested in the position, the agency, and its services—above all, what you can do for the employer. If you are a recent graduate, explain how your academic background makes you a qualified candidate for the position. If you had some practical work experience, point out your specific achievements or unique qualifications. Try not to repeat the same information the reader will find in the résumé.

Third Paragraph: Refer the reader to the enclosed résumé or application blank, which summarizes your qualifications and experiences.

Final Paragraph: In the closing paragraph, indicate your desire for a personal interview and your flexibility as to the time and place. Repeat your phone number in the letter and offer any assistance to help in a speedy response. Finally, close your letter with a statement or question which will encourage a response. For example, state that you will be in the city where the company is located on a certain date to set up an interview. Or, ask if the company will be recruiting in your area or if it desires additional information or references.

Sincerely yours,

Thomas L. Smith

Source: Adapted with permission from *Marketing Yourself as a Health Educator: Choosing a Setting, Entering the Profession, and Being Mobile,* by D.J. Breckon, Center for Health Related Studies, Central Michigan University, 1985.

EMPLOYMENT INTERVIEWS

The employment interview is a two-way communication process. The employer is attempting to obtain information about a prospective employee. The applicant, likewise, is attempting to obtain information about the prospective employer.

The applicant should try to gather as much information as possible before the interview so that informed questions can be asked.

Another important aspect of preparing for an interview is the applicant's personal appearance. The applicant should be professional-looking and conservative in hairstyle, makeup, and clothing.

The applicant should anticipate being asked certain questions and should prepare and rehearse responses to such questions. Commonly asked questions include "What are your major strengths?" "What are your major weaknesses?" "How is your previous work experience applicable to the work we do here?" "Where do you see yourself ten years from now?" "What kind of compensation are you looking for?" Typical interview questions and suggested responses are listed in Exhibit 12-2.

Exhibit 12-2 Typical Interview Questions and Suggestions To Use in Response

Tell me about yourself.

> Stress only positives.
> Key your comments to the job.
> Keep your response brief.

What are your major strengths?

> Emphasize strengths that relate to the job.
> Provide examples of how they've been useful.

What are your major weaknesses?

> Be ready to mention one or two.
> Key your response to a lack of experience or some plan for converting it to a strength.

Why do you want to leave your present job?

> Be ready to mention an acceptable reason, for example, that it is an opportunity for more challenging work.
> Be positive about the old job.

What is it about this job that interests you most?

> Do some investigation about the community and the agency so you can answer with something other than the salary.
> Tie your response to commitment to areas of mutual interest when possible.

What do you see yourself doing five years from now?

> Be honest! Have career goals in mind. Don't be afraid to express alternatives.
> If you envision a long stay at that agency, stress commitment to the community and an expectation that the needs are large enough that you expect the job demands to expand and provide you with continuing challenges.

continues

Exhibit 12-2 continued

What sort of salary are you looking for?

Indicate, if you can honestly do so, that salary isn't the overriding issue and that you can fit into the agency's salary schedule.

If salary is critical, be candid about current salary or that of other positions you are considering.

Gather salary data to use as opportunity presents.

You've had quite a few jobs haven't you?

Be prepared to explain the reason for job mobility.

Stress positive aspects of learning from each position. If a positive response will be forthcoming, offer to provide references from previous positions.

You've been unemployed for quite a long time, haven't you?

Be ready to explain, when possible, such as continuing course work or research, inability to relocate, etc.

Employers may ask illegal questions (see Exhibit 12-3). You may choose not to answer them. If you choose to answer them anyway, use special care in your responses. Some examples follow.

Who will take care of your children?

If I'm selected, you can be assured I can take care of my responsibilities at home.

How does your spouse feel about moving?

Let me assure you that I'm free to make my own decison in this matter.

How old are you?

If you mean am I over 18, yes I am.

How shall I address you? Miss, Ms., or Mrs.?

By my first name will be fine.

Source: Reprinted with permission from *Marketing Yourself as a Health Educator: Choosing a Setting, Entering the Profession, and Being Mobile,* by D.J. Breckon, Center for Health Related Studies, Central Michigan University, 1985.

Planning for the first three to five minutes is important. Within two minutes the applicant should be able to meet an interviewer and build rapport. He or she should begin with a strong handshake and eye contact and should use the interviewer's name, such as "I'm happy to meet you, Mr. Gray." The applicant should be friendly, positive, and assertive. Nonverbal communication is also important. Self-confidence needs to be expressed in posture, tone of voice, speech patterns, and eye contact. Questions should be answered in a conversational manner and seldom with simply a "yes" or "no." Special care needs to be directed to answering illegal questions. Examples of lawful and unlawful inquiries are presented in Exhibit 12-3.

Exhibit 12-3 Legal and Illegal Inquiries on Application Forms or in Interviews

Subject	Lawful Inquiries	Unlawful Inquiries
Name	Applicant's full name? Have you ever worked for this agency under a different name?	Original name of applicant whose name has been changed by court order
Birthplace		Birthplace of applicant or applicant's parents Requirement that applicant submit birth certificate or naturalization record
Age	Are you 18 years of age or older?	How old are you? What is your date of birth?
Religion or Creed		Religion preference Holidays observed
Race/Color		Complexion or color of skin
Height or Weight		Inquiry regarding applicant's height or weight
Sex		Ability to reproduce Advocacy of any form of birth control Sexual preferences
Photograph		Requirement that an applicant offer a photograph
Marital Status		Single or married Number of children Child-care arrangements Employment of spouse
Health	Do you have any impairment that would hinder your ability to do the job for which you have applied?	Do you have a disability or handicap? Have you ever been treated for any of the following diseases?
Citizenship	Are you a citizen of the U.S.? If not, do you intend to become one? If not, do you have the legal right to remain permanently in the U.S.?	Of what country are you naturalized?
National Origin	Inquiry into languages applicant speaks and writes fluently	Inquiry into applicant's ancestry, or nationality of parents or spouse

continues

Exhibit 12-3 continued

Arrest	Have you ever been convicted of a crime? If so, when, where, and nature of offense? Are any felony charges currently pending?	Inquiry regarding arrests
Relatives	Names of relatives already employed by the agency	Address of any relative other than address of parents, spouse, and minor dependent children
Organization	Inquiry into organizations, excluding those that indicate race, color, religion, or ancestry	List all clubs, societies, and lodges to which you belong

Source: Reprinted with permission from *Marketing Yourself as a Health Educator: Choosing a Setting, Entering the Profession, and Being Mobile,* by D.J. Breckon, Center for Health Related Studies, Central Michigan University, 1985. (Adapted from Pre-Employment Inquiry Guide, Michigan Department of Civil Rights.)

Many good books and articles have been written on the subject of the job interview. It is a significant evaluative tool for both the applicant and the hiring official.

Many employers look for negative points in an applicant. The best way to improve is not by emulating others but by dropping bad habits. Study the list presented in Table 12-1.

At the interview the applicant should receive responses to any questions he or she may have and be given a timetable of the selection process. A follow-up letter thanking the interviewers for their consideration and expressing continued interest and availability is appropriate.

OTHER SOURCES OF JOB INFORMATION

The help-wanted section of major newspapers is a good source of job information, because funding or administration preference may favor local candidates. Journals such as the *American Journal of Public Health* and *The Nation's Health* also list job openings. When scanning such publications, job seekers should look in related fields for openings. Some key words that may identify potential jobs for health educators are *administrator, assistant, communications, community, consumer, continuing education, coordinator, director, editor, evaluator, executive director, field representative, marketing, program director, public affairs, representative, trainer,* and *writer.*

Table 12–1 Interview Impressions

Positives	Negatives	
• Researched the organization	• Shoes unshined	• Staring out the window
• Positive responses	• Excessive talking	• Chewing gum
• Knew what he/she wanted	• Criticized previous employer	• Looking at the floor
• Self-confident	• Dressed incorrectly	• Asked about retirement plan
• Was straightforward and honest	• Would not relocate	• Was late
• Good conversational ability	• Hair not neatly groomed	• Wore sport clothes
• Good scholastic record	• Overstressed money	• Sloppy in completing application
• Good general appearance	• Fingernails dirty	• Never smiled
• Asked good questions	• Used "yeh" instead of "yes"	• Smoked during interviews
• Was a good listener	• Answered too briefly	• Lied
• Projected responsibility	• Wasn't enthusiastic	• Brought up money
• Successful work record	• Weak handshake	• Acted discouraged
• Would travel if asked	• Was evasive	• Felt he/she was superior
• Not a job-hopper	• Only interested in security	• Poor poise, diction, grammar
• Ambitious	• Didn't answer questions directly	• No purpose or goals
• Showed initiative	• No projection	• Lacked tact, maturity, courtesy
• Excellent personality	• Wasn't professional	• What-can-you-do-for-me attitude
• Self-motivated	• Became offensive	• Not prepared for interview
• Very alert and understanding	• No eye contact	• Overweight
• Would relocate with promotion	• Hand over mouth when talking	• Spoke indistinctly
	• Slouching	• Bad first impression
	• Fidgeting	• Didn't ask for the job

Sources to use in locating available health education positions are listed in Exhibit 12-4, and practical suggestions for those seeking jobs are presented in Exhibit 12-5.

ENTERING THE PROFESSION

Once a contract has been signed or a letter of appointment has been received, a period of self-doubt is typical. Reservations may arise regarding the adequacy of training and abilities. The enormity of job expectations, the unfamiliar people who are encountered, and the tasks that people want done can be overwhelming and are a form of "reality shock." A new employee needs to be clear on the job description, so that expectations can be tempered within reasonable constraints. In large agencies an announcement or introduction in a newsletter or staff meeting is useful.

Additionally, it is important to "settle into" a job. Specifically, a new employee needs to get to know other employees and their positions and responsibilities, to learn procedure and protocol, and to learn "how we do things here." It is important to develop some programs quickly, if visibility is important, but to plan other programs deliberately and carefully, because new employees are usually going to be watched carefully for a while and viewed with suspicion. Good working rela-

Exhibit 12-4 Sources To Use in Locating Available Health Education Positions

SOPHE job banks associated with various chapters
Sunday newspapers from metropolitan areas
University placement bulletins and bulletin boards
Health education faculty at schools that train health educators
APHA Annual Meeting Placement Service
The Nation's Health
The American Journal of Public Health
SOPHE chapter newsletters
Unemployment agencies
Government job bulletins (civil service)
Area health education centers
Field training contacts
Practicing health educators
Agencies that hire health educators (health departments, voluntary agencies, HMOs,
    hospitals, governmental agencies)
Health education workshops, seminars, meetings

Source: Reprinted with permission from *Marketing Yourself as a Health Educator: Choosing a Setting, Entering the Profession, and Being Mobile,* by D.J. Breckon, Center for Health Related Studies, Central Michigan University, 1985.

tionships with other staff are usually essential to the effective function of health educators and should be cultivated.

PROACTIVE STRATEGIES

Health education positions come with a variety of titles and job descriptions. Many are less than ideal. The positions usually are a direct result of the personalities and politics of the agency.

While it may be appropriate for an individual to accept a poorly designed position with an inappropriate title, it is usually not necessary to retain it. However, strategies to upgrade a position need to be carefully planned and timed.

A place to begin is to study the personalities and politics of the agency. Who makes most of the decisions? Who influences these decisions most? Who is in the inner circle? What kind of data are used in decision making? Are equivalent titles used for equivalent positions? Who has "breaks" or lunch with whom? Who visits which office most often? Observations such as these can begin to provide an assessment of the political climate.

It is then important to develop positive relationships with influential personnel. Similarly, it is important not to antagonize the opinion leaders and decision makers. Most important, the health educator must learn the staff's existing preferences and expectations regarding health education and do such preferred programs early on. Obviously, such programs must be done well, and appropriate people must be kept informed.

Exhibit 12-5 Practical Suggestions for Job Seekers

1. Work every day at finding a job.
2. Plan the job search carefully. Develop goals, strategies, timetables, contacts.
3. File or reactivate placement at the college or university placement office. Visit occasionally and study the placement bulletins they receive from other colleges.
4. Remain positive and optimistic about yourself, the job market, and the profession.
5. Be energetic and enthusiastic.
6. Be honest with yourself and others, but don't emphasize negative attributes.
7. Emphasize self-directedness and ability to work as part of a team.
8. Have evidence or examples of work available as backup.
9. Be prepared for interviews. Do research on the agency. Arrange for informational interviews with people in that agency or in similar positions.
10. Register at a local unemployment agency. Consider professional job placement agencies that assist candidates for a percentage of the first year's salary.
11. Take civil service examinations that qualify candidates for state and federal government work.
12. Participate in whatever job banks are available in your area.
13. Develop an employment search notebook to keep materials organized and readily available.
14. Evaluate your communication skills, perhaps with someone else. Focus on oral, written, and nonverbal communication.
15. Be polite and courteous at all times, especially when others are rude or ask inappropriate or illegal questions.
16. Be professional in appearance, confidence, and conversation. Be careful what you say about other people and programs.
17. Attend available workshops on résumé writing and interviewing, and read widely on these topics.
18. Have your résumé critiqued by a faculty member or colleague. Be certain it has professional quality in its appearance.
19. Develop a mentor relationship with someone who has an interest in your success and is willing to invest time and energy to assist you.
20. Attend health education meetings, workshops, seminars, etc. Make contacts; stay current; network!
21. Do volunteer work for the kind of agency in which you'd like to work.
22. Consider additional degrees, especially if the previous degree is weak or old and if the graduate degree involves a graduate assistantship or internship that provides work experience.
23. Read current issues of journals in health education, like *The Health Education Quarterly* or *Health Education*, and current books to provide an overview of the field.

Source: Reprinted with permission from *Marketing Yourself as a Health Educator: Choosing a Setting, Entering the Profession, and Being Mobile,* by D.J. Breckon, Center for Health Related Studies, Central Michigan University, 1985.

It is also important to begin educating decision makers regarding health education and health promotion. A useful strategy is to gather job titles, job descriptions, and reporting relationships from similar agencies. Selection of successful, progressive agencies as the standard of comparison is wise.

It may also be productive to look at typical job descriptions and recommended titles available from state health departments or from state or national professional organizations. A health educator may need to sell his or her services and profession to an employer. Successfully doing so is important to the clients, the agency, the profession, and, of course, the individual health educator.

While all of health education is not a power struggle, some of it is. Most often, supportive administrators have been "sold" by other health educators. Each generation of health education specialists should accept the challenge of broadening the base of administrative support for the health education profession.

IN CONCLUSION

Mobility is influenced by various factors. It involves knowing the options and how to develop them, capitalizing on opportunities, and changing career aspirations that come with work experience and with the developmental stages of adulthood. It involves dreaming big, working hard, and continuing education and work experience so as to make the dream a reality. Mobility is more a state of mind than an imposed limitation. Although there may be security in staying in a comfortable position, there is also challenge in changing positions or assuming new responsibilities. Health educators constantly face new frontiers professionally. Their task involves being a change agent. Yet they too need to struggle with changes in their lives. Job satisfaction is an important aspect of satisfaction with life. Health educators need to choose wisely the settings in which they will work, acquire skills to obtain the kind of position they aspire to, and be able to deal effectively with changing aspirations.

***

Suggested Learning Activities

1. Discuss with a placement counselor the techniques of job hunting.
2. Discuss with an employer the qualities he or she looks for in an employee. Also discuss personnel policies, salary ranges, fringe packages, and so on.
3. Talk with currently employed students about how they got their jobs and how they feel about them.
4. Review samples of good and poor résumés. Prepare your own résumé and have it critiqued.
5. Write letters of reference for other students. Discuss apparent attributes.
6. Review and list at least six health education positions currently available.

SUGGESTED READING

Asher, D. 1992. *From college to career.* Berkeley, Calif.: Ten Speed Press.

Dayhoff, S. *Get the job you want.* 1991. Acton, Mass.: Brickhouse Publishing Company.

Ellis, D., et al. 1990. *Career planning.* Rapid City, S.D.: College Survival.

Professional Skills and Practice

What do health educators do all day? What skills are needed in day-to-day work? This topic is discussed at length in Part III. It is apparent that many of the needed skills have been borrowed and applied to health problems. These skills often become unique when viewed within the context of health.

In this section, several skills are emphasized, with illustrations of their application to health settings. They constitute the major portion of what a health educator does in professional practice.

Each chapter necessarily begins with an overview. Readers should consider each chapter an introduction to, or a review of, the topic and are encouraged to consult the suggested references for a full treatment of the topic.

Moreover, health educators rarely are in situations where only one skill is needed. A combination of skills blend together in practice settings. However, they are separated in this section to permit focus and comprehension.

Chapter 13

Planning Educational Programs

Program planning occupies a large portion of time for many health educators. All health educators must engage in planning, but as promotions occur and as more and more responsibility is assumed, time spent in planning increases. Planning an effective program is more difficult than implementing it. Planning, implementing, and evaluating programs are all interrelated, but good planning skills are prerequisite to programs worthy of evaluation.

A plan is "a method for achieving an end, . . . a detailed formulation of a program of action."[1] To *plan* is to engage in a process or a procedure to develop a method of achieving an end. Green and colleagues used a widely quoted definition of planning and state that it is the "process of establishing priorities, diagnosing causes of problems, and allocating resources to achieve objectives."[2] Although use of the term as a noun or verb has similar connotations, planning as a process is stressed in this chapter.

GENERAL PRINCIPLES OF PLANNING

People have always schemed, designed, outlined, diagrammed, contemplated, conspired, or otherwise planned. Health educators, being no exception, have always planned programs to accomplish desirable ends.

Planning has become more sophisticated. Because much of the early planning failed to take into consideration a variety of important factors, it has become more systematized and, as a result, more effective. Various planning models have been developed and have enjoyed periods of popularity, but there is still no perfect model—and probably never will be—because of the accumulative nature of knowledge. Existing models are being revised continually to provide for perceived deficiencies. However, the similarities outnumber the differences. Several general principles of planning permeate all the models.

Principle One

Plan the process. It may seem like a play on words to suggest that the planning process needs to be carefully planned, but such is the case. A successful program begins as an idea that is shaped and molded through a process that is preplanned. Those who are in charge need to give thought to who should be involved, when the best time is to plan such a program, what data are needed, where the planning should occur, what resistance can be expected, and, generally, what will enhance the success of the project. Failure to take such factors into account can result in the inability to mount a good program that will meet existing needs.

A timetable needs to be developed. Many good planners use variations of the Program Evaluation and Review Techniques (PERT). To use PERT, it is necessary to state the goal of the planning process briefly and then list in sequence all the steps or activities needed to accomplish the goal. A target date for program implementation is established, and a timetable for each phase of the process is developed. The PERT process also recommends diagramming, so that planners can determine quickly what stage of the process they are in and whether they are on schedule. A typical PERT chart is shown in Exhibit 13-1.

Principle Two

Plan with people. Health educators have learned, through experience, the importance of involving clients in the planning process and the necessity of involving other principal parties to the problem or project.

Health educators, administrators, and others who are directly or indirectly affected should be involved in planning or should be consulted. Most notably, those who will be the recipients or consumers of the program and those who will be providing or delivering the service should be involved or at least consulted, preferably in the early planning stages. This action is necessary in order to develop a sense of ownership and concomitant pride. It is also necessary because those who are directly involved as participants are the ones most likely to understand the subtleties of problems and planning for this target group that are essential for success. Another reason for planning with people is the principle behind brainstorming: more ideas are likely to be generated and evaluated, with the best ones being selected for implementation. A planning committee is imperative for effective programming.

Principle Three

Plan with data. Many programs have failed because the necessary data on which to base sound decisions were not sought out. Data on diseases, disorders,

Exhibit 13–1 Patient Education PERT Chart

Tasks	Date To Be Accomplished
12 Implementation of a postcardiac education program	1-2-95
11 Staff training, internal publicity	12-94
10 Pretest and revise accordingly	11-94
9 Physician review and suggested revision	10-94
8 ICU staff review and subsequent revision	10-94
7 Pharmacy staff review	10-94
6 Respiratory therapy review	10-94
5 Developments of goals and objectives, activities, evaluation, record keeping	9-94
4 Development of patient/family information packet	9-94
3 Visitation of one or more postcardiac education programs	8-94
2 Library research, literature research	8-94
1 Visitation of American Heart Association unit	8-94

first month	second month	third month	fourth month	fifth month	sixth month

Source: Adapted from *Hospital Health Education: A Guide to Program Development* by D.J. Breckon, p. 40, Aspen Publishers, Inc., © 1982.

and other vital statistics should be gathered and analyzed by age, sex, and ethnic or cultural origin. Data on existing programs should be gathered to avoid unneeded duplication of services and to facilitate joint programming. Data on previous programs should be gathered so that credit can be given and the new program can benefit from the experiences of the previous program. In recent years, data on existing social and environmental support systems for health programs have become important (e.g., smoking laws).

The planning committee may identify other needed data, but knowledge of the community's problems, people, and programs is important baseline information for health educators. Hospitals, health departments, social and marketing research organizations, and the National Center for Health Statistics are good sources of data. Most libraries contain U.S. Bureau of the Census data. Chambers of commerce often have data on services available.

A review of data offers a perspective of the context in which institutional or agency planning should occur. Such a review is most helpful if described briefly and discussed by the planning team for meaning. It is important to be able to condense and synthesize large amounts of data and still be able to discuss segments of the data in detail, if necessary, for ramifications for local planners. Another consideration is identifying both qualitative and quantitative data needs and sources.

Principle Four

Plan for performance. Although some programs are planned on a one-time-only basis, the majority are or should be planned on an ongoing basis. Most of the problems addressed by health educators are never ultimately solved. Even diseases such as polio, tuberculosis, and syphilis still warrant attention, even though the tools for eradication exist. As new generations come along, new people are at risk and need to be educated. Health educators need to engage in long-range planning.

Staff time is usually the most expensive ingredient in the planning process. Cost efficiency dictates that programs should be planned for permanence. Budget considerations should reflect a three-year projection. Similarly, staffing should reflect long-range commitment rather than expedient means. Program planners should develop job descriptions, policy statements, and promotional documents as if planning for permanence. Advisory committees should plan for staggered terms, a system of rotating chairs, and an ongoing budget. To fail to do so is to waste valuable planning time. A sense of continuity tied into the ability to do long-range planning is necessary to both cost efficiency and cost effectiveness.

Principle Five

Plan for priorities. Because staff time is the most valuable resource expended in planning, it needs to be used wisely. Staff time should be spent developing programs that have the highest need and the greatest opportunity to make an impact. Even though a great need may be evident, the necessary resources or support may not be present to enable successful programming. In other instances, although an impact can be made, the same resources can carry greater impact in another aspect of community life.

Health educators should plan comprehensively, that is, be aware of most, if not all, of the needs and opportunities within a community or institution. A list of such needs should be kept and revised periodically. It should include the need to improve or expand existing programs as well as to add new programs. Prioritization of such a list can easily be transformed into either goals for the year or longer-range goals.

Planning for priorities implies an overall assessment of community needs and agency opportunities and a conscious decision as to which programs to develop. It avoids letting others make the decision by simply demanding services.

Principle Six

Plan for measurable outcomes in acceptable formats. Healthy People 2000 goals are to (1) increase the span of healthy life for Americans, (2) reduce health disparities among Americans, and (3) achieve access to preventive services for all Americans.[3]

Obviously, as goals, these are intentionally general and broad in scope. Objectives are more specific. *Healthy People 2000* uses three types of objectives: health status objectives, risk reduction objectives, and service and protection objectives.

In order to measure whether the three goals are being met, baseline data on the current health status of the targeted population need to be provided, along with the new health status objective. For example, Health Status Objective 18.1, regarding HIV infection, is "confine annual incidents of diagnosed AIDS cases to no more than 98,000 cases. (Baseline: An estimated 44,000 to 50,000 diagnosed cases in 1989.)"[4] Health Status Objective 18.2 reads "confine the prevalence of HIV infection to no more than 800 per 100,000 people. (Baseline: An estimated 400 per 100,000 in 1989.)"[5]

Obviously, these objectives can be applied to various target groups and to the nation as a whole. It is one way that Goal 2, to reduce health disparities among Americans, can be measured.

Yet, to reduce the incidence and prevalence of AIDS, risk reduction objectives need to be in place.

Risk Reduction Objective 18.3 for AIDS is as follows:

> Reduce the proportion of adolescents who have engaged in sexual intercourse to no more than 15% by age 15 and no more than 40% by age 17. (Baseline: 27% of girls and 33% of boys by age 15; 50% of girls and 66% of boys by age 17.)[6]

Risk Reduction Objective 18.4 states the following:

> Increase to at least 50 percent the proportion of sexually active, unmarried people who used a condom at last sexual intercourse. (Baseline: 19 percent of sexually active, unmarried women aged 15 through 44 reported that their partners used a condom at last sexual intercourse in 1988.)[7]

Healthy People 2000 also lists services and protection objectives. They are a way of measuring what services are provided and what impact they are having on protecting the public. For example, Services and Protection Objective 18.10 is as follows:

Increase to at least 95 percent the proportion of schools that have age-appropriate HIV education curricula for students in 4th through 12th grade, preferably as part of quality school health education. (Baseline: 66% of school districts required HIV education but only 5 percent required HIV education in each year for 7th through 12th grade in 1989.)[8]

Services and Protection Objective 18.13 states the following:

Increase to at least 50 percent the proportion of family planning clinics, maternal and child health clinics, sexually transmitted disease clinics, tuberculosis clinics, drug treatment centers, and primary care clinics that screen, diagnose, treat, counsel and provide (or refer for) partner notification services for HIV infection and bacterial sexually transmitted diseases in 1989.)[9]

It is believed that most of the effort of health educators will focus on risk reduction objectives, so the Risk Reduction Objectives are reprinted in their entirety in Appendix B of this book. Readers may also wish to study the health status objectives and the services and protection objectives in *Healthy People 2000* on one or more topical areas. Certainly, students will want to use localized variations of the risk reduction objectives in class projects and must be able to write objectives in that format.

Principle Seven

Plan for evaluation. Evaluation should be built into the program design. It should be a continuous process in the sense that even the planning process is evaluated. Such questions as "Do we have the right people planning?" "Do we have the necessary data for planning?" "Is this the right time for planning this program?" should be discussed periodically by a team of planners.

Even outcome or impact evaluation needs to be planned early. A determination of when such evaluation should occur and who should do it is basic. Perhaps even more important is the question of what data should be gathered. Data are usually the very essence of evaluation. Record-keeping systems and evaluation instruments need to be developed so that needed data are available for the evaluators' use. (For a discussion of evaluation, see Chapter 25, "Evaluating Health Education Programs.")

POPULAR PLANNING MODELS

Theories are relatively abstract concepts, whereas models (as used here) are attempts to diagram or otherwise pictorially represent the theories to facilitate their use. In this chapter the terms are used more or less interchangeably.

Health education is a multidisciplinary field of study and so are its theories. Moreover, the multidisciplinary nature of practice almost mandates using multiple theories.[10] Theories can focus on the individual, on the organization, on the community, on the communications process, or on public policy. A few attempt to encompass most of these theories and provide specific application to health education practice.

The PRECEDE Model (Predisposing, Reinforcing, and Enabling Causes in Educational Diagnosis and Evaluation) and the PROCEED Model (Policy, Regulatory, Organizational Constructs for Educational and Environmental Development) are the two most popular models at this time. They work in tandem, providing a continuous series of steps or phases in the planning, implementation, and evaluation process. Their authors state that "PRECEDE-PROCEED is not offered as the exclusive road to quality health promotion—there are other models of health behavior, health education, and health promotion and procedures for planning."[11]

PRECEDE-PROCEED is presented in this book because it is widely used, it is relatively comprehensive, and "it has served as a successful model in a number of rigorously evaluated, randomized clinics and field trials."[12]

PATCH (Planned Approach To Community Health) emerged from the Centers for Disease Control and has a proven track record for "facilitating collaborative community-based programs."[13] Federal dollars are sometimes available to test it in various community settings.

Other theories exist and are being successfully utilized in planning and implementing programs. Yet other models will emerge in the next decade and become popular, and all will have elements that can be used by program planners. All represent tools that can help the health educator, if used appropriately, even if used on a "mix or match" basis. In academic research settings, or in funded projects where funding sources demand that the single model be used, more or less pure theoretical applications occur. In practice, however, intervention strategies are often selected "based on . . . perception of fit within the organization and acceptability to the community."[14] Of course, what fits and what is acceptable is conditioned by familiarity, by personalities, and by organizational politics.

Familiarity is appealing because it is generally easier to keep doing what has been done. (However, it should also be recognized that if an agency keeps doing what it has done, it will keep getting what it has gotten.) Using elements of models and theories enhances the probability of improving results. Personalities and politics within an organization will also affect which theories or models are acceptable. Dominant personalities in supervisory roles may inhibit or facilitate changing policy, regulatory, or organizational constructs as called for in the PROCEED model. When such organizational change is perceived as difficult or impossible, health educators would do well to use theoretical models for institutionalization of health promotion programs. Steckler and Goodman developed such a model and have advocated its use in numerous forums.[15] Likewise, health educators who believe it advantageous to change policies are encouraged to use policy advocacy roles.[16]

With the understanding that health education practice does not often use only one model at a time, and with the understanding that the model elements can be mixed or matched depending on what fits or is acceptable, PRECEDE, PRO-CEED, and PATCH are discussed in the following as examples of comprehensive planning models that have been implemented successfully in a wide variety of settings. Results of evaluative studies of these models have been published.

The PRECEDE Model

The planning model widely used and preferred by theoreticians and practitioners in the early 1990s is the PRECEDE model, developed by Green and colleagues[17] and shown in Figure 13-1. The title was chosen partly to emphasize "the necessity of asking what behavior precedes each health benefit and what causes precede each health behavior."[18]

The PRECEDE model places heavy emphasis on diagnostic activities. The first two phases postulated by the model are epidemiological and social diagnoses, which are designed to determine which problems need to be addressed. In order to make these diagnoses, an examination of what factors adversely affect the quality of life in a community is required. The examination sorts out the health problems and prioritizes those that will, if resolved, contribute most to the quality of life.

Phase three is a behavioral diagnosis of the health problems selected in phase two. This diagnosis requires an identification of what behaviors cause and contribute to the health problem. These behaviors become the objective of change, the outcomes of a program.

Phase four is an educational diagnosis, in which the causes of the key behaviors identified in phase three are described. The causes are categorized in three groups. The first group are those factors that predispose or make people want to engage in a specific behavior. The second category comprises those factors that enable people to respond appropriately. They may want to be screened and treated for syphilis but may not be able to afford the costs involved. Establishing low-cost clinics in the locality may enable a client to engage in a behavior he or she was predisposed to practice. The third category in the educational diagnosis is reinforcing factors, the positive factors that are anticipated as a consequence of a behavior. If planning can provide reinforcement of behaviors that people are motivated and enabled to do, then the behaviors are likely to be continued and the desired impact achieved.

Phase five is a diagnosis of effective strategies. It requires consideration of resources, time constraints, and so on, as well as the selection of the right combination of interventions to predispose, enable, and reinforce desirable health habits.

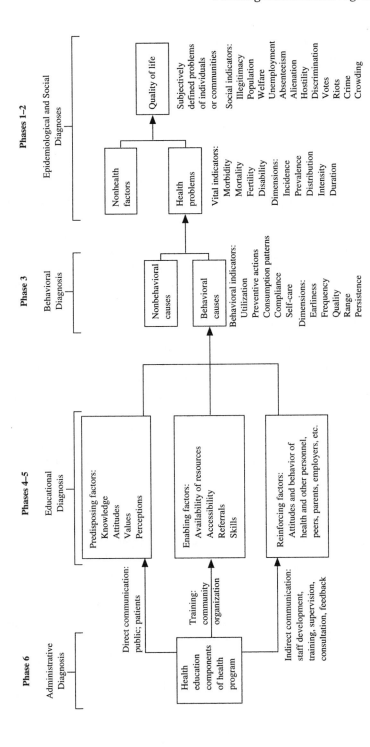

Figure 13-1 Diagram of PRECEDE Model. *Source:* Reprinted from *Theory and Practice in Health Education* by H.S. Ross and P.R. Mico, p. 207, with permission of Mayfield Publishing Company, © 1980. (Originally adapted from *Health Education Today and the PRECEDE Framework* by L. Green. p.15, Mayfield Publishing Company, © 1979.)

Phase six is an administrative diagnosis, which is the actual development and implementation of a program within the constraints of administrative problems and resources.

The PRECEDE model is a useful framework in which to approach planning. Its most important asset is the diagnostic function, which permeates all phases of the planning process and increases the probability that the programs will focus on the right issues.

From the PRECEDE Model to the PROCEED Model

As noted in Chapter 1, the health promotion movement has focused attention on social, political, economic, organizational, policy, and regulatory issues as being at least as important to health education as strictly educational interventions. Green and Kreuter led much of this discussion, at least in the textbooks of the profession.

Green is the primary author of the PRECEDE model, and Green and Kreuter are the experts on PROCEED. Currently, the best single volume on this planning model is *Health Promotion Planning: An Educational and Environmental Approach.*

The planning model called PROCEED has additional diagnostic steps, including "an assessment of the budgetary and staff resources needed . . . , an assessment of barriers to be overcome . . . and an assessment of policies that can be used to support your program or that need to be changed to enable the program to proceed."[19]

This step allows the health educator to develop a timetable, assign resources and responsibilities, and develop a budget. The authors noted that program planning is not complete without health education interventions and that policies have to be in place or be developed and necessary resources have to be marshalled. Without planning these implementation stages carefully, the educational intervention is unlikely to be successful.

> All of these policy, regulatory and organizational (the PRO in PRO-CEED) initiatives may be seen as enabling constructs for educational and environmental development (the CEED in PROCEED) that will support actions and living conditions conducive to health.[20]

Green and Kreuter also stressed that the evaluation plan needs to be described in the planning document.

Green and Kreuter thoroughly explained PROCEED in their book, but perhaps of more interest, they included a number of case studies detailing PROCEED's application to community settings, occupational settings, school settings, and health care settings. It should also be noted that a software package is being developed to facilitate use of this model in planning. The PROCEED model is shown in Figure 13-2.

PRECEDE

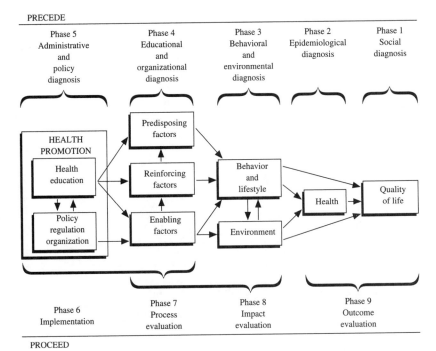

Figure 13–2 From PRECEDE to PROCEED. *Source:* Reprinted from *Health Promotion Planning: An Educational and Environmental Approach* by Lawrence W. Green and Marshall W. Kreuter, with permission of Mayfield Publishing Company, © 1991.

Patch

As discussed in Chapter 2, the Centers for Disease Control and Prevention staff have developed a planning model called PATCH (planned approach to community health). The model has been successfully used in a variety of settings and the evaluation studies indicate that it is an effective model.

PATCH is essentially a networking model of planning, as advocated by the Healthy Communities 2000 project. Both vertical and horizontal networks are encouraged. Vertical networks include local, state, and national levels of government and nongovernmental agencies. Horizontal networks operate at local, state, and national levels as well, and they also cut across the broad spectrum of agencies concerned with the target population. A key concept is local ownership, but with a sense of partnership with and support by other organizations. Figure 13-3 presents the CDC's planned approach to health education.

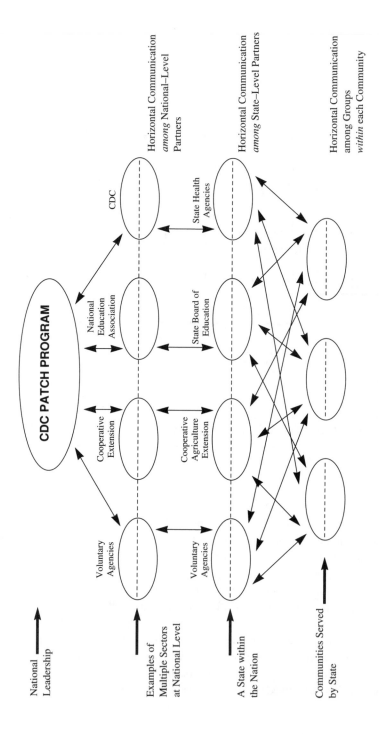

Figure 13–3 PATCH: Mobilizing Vertical and Horizontal Communications and Support among the National, Regional, and Community Levels.

PATCH and PRECEDE–PROCEED are compatible, accroding to Green and Kreuter. In fact, several of the concepts of PATCH were incorporated into the PROCEED model, so as to address the limitations of the PRECEDE model.[21]

IN CONCLUSION

Few things a health educator does are more important or occupy more time than program planning. There is no single process or single format. Models currently in favor will be revised with the passage of time. But regardless of the steps or the format used, time and energy devoted to developing planning skills will pay huge dividends to practicing professionals.

***

Suggested Learning Activities

1. Develop a PERT chart for beginning a community-based smoking cessation program.
2. Use the PRECEDE model to prepare an Educational Diagnosis of a major cause of death in your state or hometown.
3. Read current literature on "futurism" and identify implications for health planning.
4. Utilize one of the databases listed in Appendix F.

NOTES

1. *Webster's New Collegiate Dictionary* (Springfield, Mass.: G. & C. Merriam Co., 1981), 870.

2. L.W. Green, et al., *Health Education Planning: A Diagnostic Approach* (Mountain View, Calif.: Mayfield Publishing Co., 1980), xv.

3. *Healthy People 2000: National Health Promotion and Disease Prevention Objectives* (Washington, D.C.: U.S. Government Printing Office, 1991), 6.

4. Ibid., 482.

5. Ibid., 483.

6. Ibid.

7. Ibid., 485.

8. Ibid., 488.

9. Ibid., 490.

10. K. Beck, Editorial, *Health Education Research: Theory and Practice*, 6, no. 4 (1992):399.

11. L.W. Green and M.W. Kreuter, *Health Promotion Planning: An Educational and Environmental Approach* (Mountain View, Calif.: Mayfield Publishing Co., 1991), 24.

12. Ibid.

13. Preface, *Journal of Health Education,* Special issue, 23 (1992): 132.

14. K. McLeroy, APHA, *Public Health Education and Health Promotion Newsletter*, August (1993):7.

15. A. Steckler and R.M. Goodman, How To Institutionalize Health Promotion Programs, *American Journal of Health Promotion*, 3, no. 4 (1989): 34.

16. A. Steckler, et al., Policy Advocacy: Three Emerging Roles for Health Education, in *Advances in Health Education and Promotion*. Vol. 2, ed. W.B. Ward (Greenwich, Conn.: JAI Press, 1987), 5.

17. L.W. Green, et al., *Health Education Planning*.

18. Ibid., 306.

19. L.W. Green and M.W. Kreuter, *Health Promotion Planning*, 189.

20. Ibid.

21. L.W. Green and M.W. Kreuter, CDC's Planned Approach to Community Health as an Application of PRECEDE and an Inspiration for PROCEED, *Journal of Health Education*, April (1992):40.

SUGGESTED READING

Green, L.W., and Kreuter, M.W. 1991. *Health promotion planning: An environmental and educational approach*. Mountain View, Calif.: Mayfield Publishing Co.

McKenzie, J.F., and Jurs, J.L. 1993. *Planning, implementing and evaluating health promotion programs*. New York: Macmillan Publishing Co.

Chapter 14

Understanding and Applying Learning Theory Principles

How learning occurs was first studied seriously in the 1920s, albeit from a study of laboratory animals. Generalizations were made to people, and soon human learning was itself a field of study. Many educational psychologists have studied and continue to study this matter. This chapter will provide an introduction to some widely accepted principles of learning.

GENERAL PRINCIPLES OF LEARNING

There is no single theory or principle of learning that applies to all people in all situations. Rather, a series of principles and theories should be understood, so as to be able to use theories appropriate for given situations. It is generally understood that it is difficult to teach someone who does not want to learn. Attention should rather be focused on facilitating learning and on motivation. The probability that learning will occur is enhanced when the following principles are used:

1. Learning is facilitated if several of the senses are used. People retain approximately 10 percent of what they read, 20 percent of what they hear, 30 percent of what they see, 50 percent of what they see and hear, 70 percent of what they say, and 90 percent of what they do and say. Methods that stimulate the widest variety of senses will generally be most effective.
2. Learning is facilitated if the client is actively involved in the process, rather than a passive recipient. Methods that engage and elicit responses from the learner are generally more effective than when the learner is passive. Discussion is basic, and other participative methods usually enhance learning.
3. Learning is facilitated if the client is not distracted by discomfort or extraneous events. Attention to establishing an appropriate learning environment is an important step to take in facilitating learning.

4. Learning is facilitated if the learner is ready to learn. Physical and emotional factors influence readiness. An assessment of readiness makes timing of learning possible and enhances learning.
5. Learning is facilitated if that which is to be learned is relevant to the learner and if that relevance is perceived by the learner. Endeavoring to sense the readiness of the learning and making the connection to existing needs and interests of the client enhances learning.
6. Learning is facilitated if repetition is used. Reviewing and reinforcing basic concepts several times in a variety of ways enhances learning.
7. Learning is facilitated if the learning encounter is pleasant, if progress occurs that is recognizable by the client, and if that learning is recognized and encouraged. Frequent, positive feedback is important to enhancing learning.
8. Learning is facilitated if material to be learned starts with what is known and proceeds to the unknown, while concurrently moving from simple to complex concepts. Material to be learned must be organized in ways that make sense to the learner.
9. Learning is facilitated if application of concepts to several settings occurs, to facilitate generalization.
10. Learning is facilitated if it is paced appropriately for the client. Self-pacing of a motivated learner is usually preferable. Attention to the learner's feeling that the pace is too fast or slow will usually enhance learning.

Much learning is based on the above principles. However, there are groups in which special considerations or emphases are required.

ANDRAGOGICAL APPROACH

Andragogy is the theory and practice of educating adults, as contrasted to pedagogy, which is concerned with the education of children. Inasmuch as most of the clients in a community health education program will be adults, theoretical foundations must include an understanding of the principles of educating adults. This is essential from a practical point of view since most adults have had more experience being taught as a child and tend to teach as they were taught. Although it is often appropriate to treat children as if they were adults, it is seldom appropriate to treat adults as if they were children when they are involved in the educational enterprise.

When entering into a discussion of this nature, staff need to remember the many ways that adults are different from children. Obviously, adults are physically mature and legally responsible for their behavior. But far more important to the educational process, adults have a more definite mind-set than children. Their likes and dislikes are more fixed and their attitudes are more difficult to change. Their feelings about authority are more likely to be negative, because they now consider themselves to be independent and self-directing. They are less likely to do what they are told and must see the relevance of what is being proposed quite quickly or the instruction is apt to be ignored.

Adults are capable of learning a great deal but are often unwilling to exert effort to learn that which does not meet a need for them. Adults are capable of learning at all ages as well. The rate at which learning occurs slows down somewhat as physiological changes occur during the aging process, but the ability to learn is there unless destroyed by disease or disorders.

The key to adult education, then, is helping adults see the relevance of what they need to know, so that in their self-directing way they will choose to learn about regaining or maintaining their health. Stated differently, the central purpose of health education is to bring valid knowledge to bear on the decisions that clients must make. In so doing, it is aimed at achieving the needs and goals that the individual specifies and, if possible, to satisfy the needs and goals of the community and society. The importance of a needs assessment becomes instantly apparent to those subscribing to this approach.

Health education of adults should also be situation oriented, rather than subject oriented, in order to make the relevance of it obvious and to maintain interest. Too much instruction can be as bad as none. It is not necessary to tell clients everything that might be useful. If health education focuses on present or future situations that clients will probably encounter, interest is usually easy to maintain. Other problems can be dealt with if and when they occur. Health education should be an encounter with reality. It should involve coming to grips with the world in which learners find themselves. Their new knowledge should help learners in the process of understanding and interpreting whatever they encounter.

The following principles of effective curricula development and teaching in adult education programs are adapted from Knowles' basic work *The Modern Practice of Adult Education: Andragogy versus Pedagogy.*

1. Begin with a needs assessment of the client or clients. It is critical to interest and motivation that learners feel a need to learn, and that they make the decision to learn because they see a need for it. It is important to respect adult clients as self-directing humans.

An accompanying staff role is to expose learners to new possibilities, presenting what they need to learn in order to adequately confront current or future problems. Other significant staff roles are to assist learners to diagnose their learning needs and then to decide what is to be learned and how it is to be learned. Such a cooperative relationship requires trust, which leads to the second principle.

2. Establish a learning environment that is characterized by physical comfort, mutual trust, and freedom of expression. Having an adequate physical environment is basic yet often difficult to obtain in many agencies. Whenever possible, facilities should be available that have adequate lighting, heating, and ventilation; flexible seating; and adequate audiovisual capabilities. Whenever there are interruptions, distractions, noises, uncomfortable temperature or humidity, or inadequate lighting, attention is distracted from learning.

Of even more importance, however, is the development of an emotional climate that facilitates learning. This starts with the basics of establishing rapport and accepting and respecting each person as an individual of worth with his or her own feelings and ideas. It includes establishing an atmosphere of mutual responsibility whenever possible, so that clients and staff are learning from each other.

3. *Involve the client as much as possible in the learning process.* As mentioned earlier, learners need to be assisted in setting their own learning goals and selecting learning experiences from those available to them. The educator should also help clients exploit the experience of both themselves and others while learning. The experience that adults bring to a learning encounter is another major difference between adults and children. Those who would teach adults effectively must learn to use these experiences effectively.

The client must also be involved in the learning process as much as possible so as to maximize learning. Active learning is preferable to passive learning. If students are involved in thinking, discussing, viewing, trying, and so on, learning is more likely to take place. The more of the five senses that can be involved in the learning, the more learning will occur.

4. *Learners must be kept apprised of their progress toward their goals.* The educator can do this in part by facilitating self-evaluation on the part of the learners or by monitoring progress and reporting it as perceived by the staff. Such feedback is important. Pacing is also important. If teaching is faster or slower than individual readiness, learning will be inhibited.

Another role in this process is to assist learners in rediagnosis, that is, an assessment of what has already been learned and what yet needs to be learned. Thus, the process is cyclical and should ideally lead to lifelong learning.

EDUCATING THE ELDERLY

Older adults are an important target group in the Healthy People 2000 project. Because of rapid increases in life expectancy, older adults are a growing segment of society. Equally as important, they utilize a larger percentage of health care dollars. The desire to reduce health care costs mandates more attention to programming for the elderly. Although it is commonly believed that health problems in old age are inevitable, many are in fact preventable or can be controlled.

Older adults also are a major political force. Moreover, they are already concerned about their health, and they generally welcome programs that will help them maintain their health and functional independence. Developing prevention programs for older adults can help generate funding support for prevention programs that serve other populations.

Appendix B of the book lists the risk reduction objectives from *Healthy People 2000* that target older adults. They focus on exercise, immunization, and screening. A number of other program emphases are suggested in the health status objectives and the services and protection objectives sections of *Healthy People 2000*.

When working with older adults, a number of basic principles need to be utilized. The following paragraphs discuss several such principles that have direct bearing on health education.

The concept of lifelong learning is one that is readily given lip service but all too often is not emphasized in programming. Educators often accept and act on the stereotype that the elderly cannot learn very well, if at all. Elderly persons often get labeled as senile, slow, forgetful, disinterested in the real world, and living in the past. Senility is, of course, a disease process that does occur in some elderly patients, but many nonsenile patients are labeled and treated as senile, albeit unjustly. In other words, older people can often learn as well as younger people, but for noncognitive reasons they are unable or unwilling to demonstrate what they have learned.

It has been established that older people learn more slowly. There is a slight decline in various mental abilities, but this decline is not usually of the magnitude to have much practical significance, other than that they may need more time than is usually allowed for learning. The concept of self-paced learning seems especially critical for the aged.

The relevance of the material is also critical, in that it affects motivation. When the relevance of the information is apparent, older learners are often better learners. They usually have more and better organized experiences that provide a meaningful context into which new information can be assimilated. They know themselves better and can more clearly perceive what new items of learning will be most useful to them.

Care should be taken when educating the elderly to assess and meet their mental and emotional needs. As a group, the elderly are more susceptible to loneliness and depression than other groups, especially if a person lives alone. When they are not feeling well, it becomes easy for them to believe the stereotypes about the elderly. It is also easy for them to become intimidated by the hospital environment and to withdraw within themselves.

The elderly often need simply to be with people and reenter normal social activities. Again, staff should beware of stereotypes, inasmuch as many elderly people are very social and extremely busy people. Clients who appear withdrawn or reluctant to participate in educational activities should be encouraged and supported to participate in routine hospital activities instead of being forced to do so. Group learning activities are a useful way of meeting socialization and learning needs at once.

The elderly should be treated with the same respect and dignity accorded to any other human. Educators need to treat them as individuals and work to forget the stereotypes. It is also important not to overreact and patronize elderly people.

A major concern for many older people is the loss of independence, so it is important to their well-being that staff members not be overly helpful. The elderly should be allowed and encouraged to do as much as possible for themselves. It is also well to remember not to overreact to problems that occur. Small things often become increasingly important to the elderly, and if staff members are mildly distressed, it may become a major source of distress for the elderly client.

Also important to the elderly client's sense of well-being is that lost roles be replaced with new activities so that a major gap is not created. Staff need to be alert to what roles clients can no longer do and strive to assist the client to either find new ways to do it or find a replacement activity for the lost role.

Health education programs for the elderly also need to be very practical. The practical matter of cooking for one, getting exercise in a shopping mall during bad weather, and keeping track of medications are all items that can be stressed.

Elderly clients often have hearing and vision problems that need to be compensated for, with communication problems being the result. Educators have to be certain that they are effectively communicating even though hearing and vision problems exist.

For clients who have hearing problems, it is important to speak directly to them. Some elderly patients have developed the ability to compensate by reading lips, and facial expressions help all people to comprehend more quickly. It should also be remembered to speak slowly and in lower tones. Loss of ability to hear higher tones is common in the elderly. It is usually not necessary to shout, and this is distracting to an elderly person. Speaking in normal ways is recommended, but with close attention to nonverbal feedback to ascertain if instruction is being heard, so that the volume can be adjusted as necessary. Sentences should be short and simple, with avoidance of abstractions.

Vision deficiency may also be a problem, although vision problems can often be more readily corrected than hearing ones. Nonetheless, it is important to determine that the patient or patients can see adequately. They need a direct line of vision and need to be close enough to see properly any time visual aids are used. If chalkboards or posters are being used, it is important to use big print with bright colors on a light background.

In general, it is important not to underestimate or overestimate the abilities of the elderly. If needs, interests, and abilities are properly assessed, good teaching and learning can occur that will be enormously satisfying to both the patient and the educator.

There are many excellent opportunities for health educators to work with the elderly in the community. Senior citizen housing complexes exist in most areas. Those staffing such complexes are usually very receptive to the presentation of educational activities for the residents. Ample opportunity exists for programs on nutrition, exercise, medications, emotional needs, emergency medical care, and other self-help activities.

EDUCATING CULTURALLY DIVERSE PEOPLE

As with older adults, "special populations" are also singled out for emphasis in *Healthy People 2000*. Subsections list objectives targeting people with low income, African Americans, Hispanics, Asians and Pacific Islanders, Native Americans, Native Alaskans, and people with disabilities. A review of these objectives will suggest numerous program areas that need to be developed.

When interacting with culturally diverse populations, a number of principles come into play. The following discussion describes several such areas of concern.

Program planners usually address programs being developed to the majority of the constituents they anticipate serving, and appropriately so. Minority groups, however, usually bring a different set of perceptions, needs, and interests with them to health education. Therefore, in order to maximize learning, it is sometimes necessary to adjust content or methodology to the individual needs and interests of clients. Perception of need frequently varies from group to group, and it is always appropriate to respond to these felt needs. Flexibility is an important quality for health educators to acquire.

Specific groups that have minority status will vary from urban to rural settings, from region to region, and from country to country. They usually consist of ethnic, racial, or class groups. Seldom do these factors operate independently of each other. Health problems, attitudes toward services, and attitudes toward prevention all vary with minority status and usually are interpreted negatively by health care providers.

Characteristics of lower socioeconomic whites often resemble those of lower socioeconomic ethnic or racial group members. Conversely, the health status and related behaviors of middle- and upper-class minority group members more closely resemble those of middle- or upper-class whites. It has been determined that income and education are greater factors than race or ethnicity in determining many health problems, use of health services, and attitudes toward educational services. Staff flexibility and program adaptation are usually needed for lower socioeconomic group members, regardless of racial or ethnic characteristics.

However, lower socioeconomic group members who are also part of an ethnic or racial minority are more likely to be suspicious of and reticent to participate in a health education program, generally finding such offerings unacceptable. Such responses are based partly on real or perceived lack of program relevance and partly on conflict with enculturated values, such as reliance on family members with folk remedies and suspicion of "white" medicine. Distrust, fear, anger, and ill will are not uncommon. Such attitudes also have some of their origins in past experience and in ethnic or racial pride. It is often accentuated by lessened accessibility to health care and preventive services and lower than average health status.

The lack of knowledge and understanding often combine to create a fatalistic attitude more likely to exist in minority groups, resulting in less likelihood of follow-through on programs or in inconsistent behavior. Medical sociologists have explored this topic in much detail and have produced a great deal of literature on the topic. This brief introduction to ethnic, racial, and class differences, however, suggests that special attention should be given to members of these minority groups when they participate in health education programs.

Some beginning words of caution are in order. The advice is not new but has not yet been widely implemented. Educators need to be ever alert that their own feelings and behaviors are not based on distortions, stereotypes, or prejudices. They also need to be alert for any stereotypes and prejudices that members of minority groups bring with them to the educational encounter.

As has been stressed throughout this book, it is imperative that health educators know their clientele as much as possible and that programs become individualized as much as possible so that needs and interests are met. Few people consciously act on stereotypes or prejudices, although many continue to do so unaware that such feelings interfere with the educational process.

It is helpful, though not essential, for some of the educational staff to be members of the minority group being served. It will probably be true that community health agencies serving large Asian, Hispanic or Latino, Native American, or African American populations will have members of these groups on their staff in some capacity. Programs can often be enhanced by such personnel, making it easier to establish rapport and communication.

Communication can be a critical problem, ranging from the problems of a refugee who cannot speak English to Americans who have dialects or idioms that are different from those of the staff. Some programs have experimented with employing health aides from the minority groups being served, training them to do a specific program. Some problems are circumvented with such programming, while others may be created. Whatever approach is used, it must be remembered that communication must occur before education can be effective.

Health educators need to constantly remember that the "human touch" can and does often transcend any cultural or class differences that may exist between clients and staff. The ability of staff to empathize becomes critical. Sincerity of purpose must be manifested in nonverbal ways. Staff openness increases in importance, if trust is to develop. More personal contact, personal interest in the whole person, dialogue, and support often are helpful.

Clients should not be inundated with attention just because they are members of a minority group. While it is improbable that staff can care too much, it is possible that staff can do so much for a client that it is interpreted by the client as being demeaning.

Another major area of concern is in the area of educational materials. Materials should, insofar as possible, be relevant to the real world of the client. It is often difficult for the rural poor to grasp the significance of a teaching film placed in the setting of a large metropolitan area. Dietary adjustments and other aspects of home health care must be placed in the real parameters of a client's world in order to maximize learning. Home visitations are one way to enhance this if staffing permits. Unfortunately, it often does not.

It should be noted that minority group members have many of the same learning needs as others. In general, commonalities should be accented and differences should be minimized. Minorities may have difficulty seeing the relevance or feasibility of applying the learning to their particular life setting. Staff need to be more concerned that the relevance is clear to the learner when the learner's frame of reference is different from their own. Staff should also be certain that their interest and concern in each patient is genuine and is expressed in both verbal and nonverbal manners.

EDUCATING FUNCTIONALLY ILLITERATE PEOPLE

A large number of people cannot read. This should not be equated with inability to learn. Illiteracy is very often kept hidden because of embarrassment. Educators should recognize that hostility toward education or use of excuses such as poor lighting may indicate that the client has a reading problem.

When working with such clients, some of the basics need more emphasis. Establishing rapport and trust is more important. Going from familiar to unfamiliar, some simple to complex, using many examples and visuals and audiovisuals, is basic. Obviously, it is important to keep written materials at a low grade level, and to encourage self-pacing for mastery.

SELF-DIRECTED LEARNING

Concurrently, learners must also be made aware of resources for self-directed study. Because interest and motivation is often high, referrals to books, pamphlets, and community classes will often be followed. Such self-directed learning is facilitated by awareness and ready availability of resources.

Researchers have indicated that self-directed learning is most probable when there is interest in inquiry, a sense of optimism, an adequate energy level, and a sense of power or control over life situations. Accordingly, health educators working with adults should stimulate a sense of inquiry and encourage a sense of optimism and control. Certainly there is the potential for learning about health to be lifelong. There is also the potential for far more learning to occur outside the formal learning experience than in it. Health educators should encourage self-directed learning.

HEALTH EDUCATION LEARNING THEORY

The learning theory principles described above are intentionally general and basic enough to apply to many disciplines, including, but not limited to, health education. Of course, the profession has developed or adapted a number of theories that are particularly useful.

The area of behavior theory is valuable because one goal of health education is to change behavior so as to reduce risk of disease or disorder. There are numerous behavior change theories, some of which focus on the knowledge, attitudes, or beliefs that explain why people act as they do.

Some health education theories focus on the nature of diffusion, social change theory, persuasion, and opinion leaders. Others focus on the media as important elements of general communication theory that affect why individuals respond to some messages and not to others.

Yet other theories document how groups impact the behavior of their members, while other theories focus on the environment and its effect on health behavior. Some theories focus on preventive health behaviors. Others focus on health care behaviors.

A few theories attempt to deal with most of these variables. The most notable of such theories is the PROCEED model. (In this case, a model is a pictorial representation of a theory, and the two terms are used more or less interchangeably.) It or its predecessor has stood the test of time and is still widely used today. This theory is widely used in program planning and is discussed in Chapter 13.

The confines of this book limit our discussion of the many theories. It is commonplace for entire courses to be devoted to health education theory in graduate school. For undergraduate students, an introduction to general learning theory principles and to the general theory of primary prevention and early intervention is all that is feasible. However, for serious students, the health education journals are full of case studies in which theories have been applied to specific programs and target groups, and the student may examine the results of theory applications.

In our opinion, however, the single best work done on the topic, as of this writing, is that edited by Karen Glanz, Fran Lewis, and Barbara Lewis titled *Health Behavior and Health Education: Theory, Research and Practice*. A review of this work will be useful for most health educators.

IN CONCLUSION

Theory and practice have been contrasted for years. It has also been said that there is nothing so practical as a good theory.

Health behavior is complex, with multiple causes and consequences. Rarely is a single theory sufficient to explain a situation. Yet an understanding of appropriate theories and application of them to learning situations will enhance the probability that learning will occur and that the desired behavior will subsequently evolve.

Regardless of the theories or models used, teaching will not have the desired impact in all cases. Some prospective learners simply will not respond. Others will respond, but long after they leave the program. Although it is important to evaluate the effectiveness of programs, it is also important to remember that those successes that are reported will represent minimal achievement. Unaccounted for are those who find that learning is reinforced at a later time and who respond at an appropriate time. However, using sound educational theory does increase the probability of achieving the effect that is desired.

***

Suggested Learning Activities

1. Make lists of the characteristics of adults and the characteristics of children, and compare them.
2. Identify ways that you can compensate for vision or hearing problems in older adults.
3. Contemplate the implications for educators of the following: "You can lead a horse to water but you can't make it drink. You can, however, make it thirsty."

SUGGESTED READING

Glanz, K., et al. 1990. *Health behavior and health education: Theory, research and practice.* San Francisco: Jossey-Bass, Inc., Publishers.

Shield, J., et al. 1992. *Developing health education materials for special audiences.* Chicago: American Dietetic Association.

Chapter 15

Introduction to Primary Prevention and Early Intervention Strategies

Health education and health promotion focus on prevention. Primary prevention strategies focus on preventing individuals from ever adopting health-threatening behaviors, whereas early intervention strategies focus on breaking such behaviors and substituting health promotion behaviors.

Health educators are change agents. The better health education specialists understand the theory of change, the more effective they will be. Many books have been written on change theory and on primary prevention and early intervention. This chapter presents some of the basics, the foundation on which change theories can be built. Readers are also urged to use *Health Behavior and Health Education: Theory, Research and Practice,*[1] the most definitive work on the topic at this writing. It describes in detail, with case studies and documentation, many of the theories referenced in this chapter and other sections of this book.

HISTORIC APPROACHES TO PRIMARY PREVENTION

Injury, illness, medicine, health, magic, and religion have been intertwined for centuries. As more of injury and illness have been understood, magic and religion have decreased in influence. Nonetheless, religion and health are still intertwined, as illustrated by the prohibition on use of certain foods and beverages by several prominent religions of the world.

Religions, of course, focus on God, so health measures sometimes become mandates. Not surprisingly, a *moralistic approach* is one of the oldest approaches to primary prevention. The attitude of "don't do it because God and/or the church does not want you to" was and still is advocated, as is illustrated today by religious pronouncements on intoxication, use of pork, contraception, and so on. Moreover, Christians are commanded to be temperate in *all* things.

The Temperance movement focused on alcohol and drug abuse, but the concepts of moderation and temperance have many ramifications for health.

However, the Temperance movement largely failed in attempting to prevent intoxication and subsequently evolved into prohibition. The Prohibition movement also focused largely on substance abuse, by prohibiting production and use of health-threatening substances. Laws were required to do this, giving rise to the *legalistic approach*, which has been used more broadly than just in substance abuse.

The legalistic approach to prevention was and is an attempt to regulate health behavior by laws and regulations. The laws can regulate production, as with the pure food and drug laws, or they can attempt to control consumers, for example by the many laws surrounding substance abuse. Laws requiring premarital blood tests and laws requiring tuberculosis screening or various kinds of immunizations are examples. Although many people agree that morality cannot be legislated, they also agree that many people will voluntarily do what laws require and that various methods can be used to enforce compliance with the laws. Experience has demonstrated, however, that it is hard to regulate the behavior of millions of people by passage of laws, so stiffer and stiffer penalties were developed, giving rise to the *punitive or deterrent approach*.

The punitive or deterrent approach to primary prevention purports to prevent substance abuse, sexual abuse, or illegal abortion through stronger and stronger penalties, which some think act as a deterrent. Unfortunately, despite longer and longer mandatory prison terms and even a few executions of drug dealers, the problems have not gone away. Strong law enforcement efforts have, however, demonstrated the ability to limit, if not eliminate, the supply of illegal substances and services. The punitive or deterrent approach remains an attractive option to many, and it seems to reappear as a recommended strategy in cycles.

Yet another approach to prevention is to shift to *treatment approaches*, which in reality are forms of early intervention. Screening for and treating persons with communicable diseases such as syphilis, vaccinating people and animals against communicable diseases, and screening for breast cancer while intervention is still feasible are all examples of the treatment approach to primary prevention. All are forms of rendering some "treatment" to prevent a health problem from occurring, from getting worse, or from spreading to others.

A *scientific or engineering approach* to prevention has also been used for centuries in preventing illness and promoting health. Techniques to provide a safe water supply, design of better passenger restraint devices, installation of stop signs and traffic lights, addition of iodine to salt and calcium to orange juice, addition of fluoride to water and toothpaste, and production of foods low in sodium and cholesterol are all examples of prevention using this approach.

An *educational approach* also has been used, with the basic premise being that if people know of the actual risks they are taking, they are less likely to take them. The health education movement grew out of this approach. Educational approaches to prevention have had various degrees of success, working spectacularly well in some cases and failing miserably in others. The profession has matured significantly in the past few decades, and the probability of success is much greater if the principles discussed in this textbook are followed. The rest of this chapter, and much of this book, is devoted to discussing the educational approach.

CONTEMPORARY APPROACHES TO PREVENTION THROUGH EDUCATION

Many educational theories of prevention are discussed and illustrated in various sections of this book. There are many similarities and much overlapping, as well there should be when it is realized that theories build on what is known and on attempts to account for existing weaknesses in theory. In an attempt to promote understanding, prevention approaches will be grouped and described in their simplest forms.

Cognitive prevention models are probably most widely used. Dispensing information to make people aware of health risks or the harmful effects of certain behaviors is presumed to affect behavior.

Early exploration of cognitive models focused on the advantages and disadvantages of lecturing and other authoritative approaches. The authoritarian type of lecturing often degenerates into attempts at "preaching" or "scaring" the group, with mixed results.

Lectures also tend to be one sided, presenting only the negative point of view. Carefully selected information usually only supports one point of view. However, credibility gaps frequently begin to develop, as learners become more sophisticated and begin to think for themselves.

One-sided presentations on drug abuse, herpes, AIDS, or smoking lead listeners to think about what is not being said, especially if exaggeration occurs. Individuals living in an information age often become aware of opposite points of view. If the bias of a presentation is evident, listeners then tend to dismiss the entire presentation.

Cognitive models then move to balanced presentations, where information on both sides of issues is discussed and evaluated. Emphasis in these models is on factual, unbiased presentations. Risks are presented realistically but are not exaggerated. Clients are urged to make up their minds and to accept responsibility for the results of their behavior. Of course, when dealing with young people, problems sometimes occur, especially with parents who want a firm stand on premarital sex or use of illegal drugs. Parents want health educators to validate what is taught at home and often prefer authoritative, one-sided approaches. Of course, they also do not want such education presented at too young an age "lest it stimulate illicit curiosity," despite common sense suggesting that if behavior such as illicit sex is to be prevented, appropriate information should be presented before the situation is encountered.

Of course, there are those who state that presenting information about drugs or sex or contraception stimulates curiosity and increases the undesired practice. There is research to show that it does, and research to show that it does not, which probably validates the belief that by controlling the design of the study anything can be proved and that studies frequently validate predetermined points of view.

Other aspects of the cognitive models focus on who is presenting the information. Certainly there is some basis to believing that a recovered, well-adjusted mastectomy patient can best teach present mastectomy patients or that recovered alcoholics are best fitted to work in alcoholism prevention programs. However, there are other ways of looking at the presenter. The presenter's experience, although valid, may be atypical. Health educators, nurses, and others may have learned from dozens of clients and may have more accurate, less biased information than a recovered client.

The advantage of research is that educators can learn from the experiences of hundreds of people. Stated differently, educators do not have to have had cancer to know a lot about it, and most professionals know more about the disease than a cancer patient.

Another facet of cognitive models relates to whether information should be guided or provided. Group discussions facilitate active learning, and active learning is preferable to passive learning. Group involvement, on the other hand, is encouraged with the belief that internalization and application are more likely to occur in such settings. Some claim that individuals sitting in a lecture let information "pass in one ear and out the other," summarily dismissing it if it does not agree with their point of view. Participation is preferable, but lectures do have the advantage of presenting large amounts of information to large numbers of people.

Cognitive-based models will presumably always be in vogue. No health educator would presume to educate without somehow using information. However, what information, how much to present, when to present it, how to present it, who should present it, and so on, will probably always be in question.

The shortcomings of the cognitive models led many health educators to use one of the several *affective models*. Learning theorists long have postulated that there are cognitive, affective, and psychomotor domains of learning. The affective domain focuses on attitudes, beliefs, and feelings. Critics of the cognitive theories suggest that while what is known is important, what is believed is more important, because it determines what is done about what is known. Critics also point out that knowledge alone is not enough. For example, drug addicts usually know more about the dangers of drug abuse than do nonusers. Moreover, most people know of the risks of being overweight, or of not exercising enough, yet do not act on such knowledge.

The focus will then be on attitudes, beliefs, and feelings, with information becoming a secondary, albeit still important, element. Attitudes toward ourselves, families, and health all become critical in determining behavior.

Educators can plan activities in the affective domain but often do not. It is easier to plan information dispensing. However, instructional activities can be planned to improve a client's self-concept or to clarify values or to understand beliefs. Activities in the affective domain increase the level of readiness to act.

The affective models led to the development of *peer counseling and peer support models*. This group of theories centers on the importance of peer relationships and proposes that people learn best from their peers, regardless of their age. Teens learn best from teens, if the peer educators and peer counselors are appropriately trained. Schools frequently establish clinics and other programs centered around peer counseling and peer support groups. Young mothers often learn best from other young mothers, coronary patients usually learn best from recovered coronary patients, and so on. However, as pointed out above, educators do not have to have been victims to be effective teachers. Also, there are exceptions to the peer counseling model, such as older women who present a motherly image to younger people and older people who present an authoritarian image.

Another approach is to use *decision-making models*, realizing that the individual alone ultimately will make the decision, good or bad. Being told not to do something may have the opposite of the effect intended. The person may rebel or in other ways resist authority and will do whatever he or she pleases. These models start with the premise that the individual alone makes decisions and that the best educators can hope for is to influence these decisions. Decision-making prevention models place confidence in the decision-making process, and such theorists are prepared to accept the decision and the results, if the choice is made freely. Others are not and, for example, link pro-choice with pro-abortion, instead of taking it to be a middle ground between anti-abortion and pro-abortion.

Decision-making prevention models focus on the process. They encourage thought being given to what knowledge is necessary to make good decisions, where to find it, and how to evaluate it. They focus on bias and motives and analyze who attempts to influence decisions and why. They analyze decisions and their impact on others. People are affected by most decisions, and advanced exploration and consideration of the results of various decisions are the essence of the models, along with determining the most probable consequences of decisions.

Finally, there are *alternative models* of prevention, which focus on breaking behavior patterns by presenting better options. Screening clinics are presented as an alternative to not knowing and living in fear. Providing vaccination clinics is an alternative to risking infection from measles. Providing low-cost neighborhood treatment centers is an alternative to malnourished infants. Providing teen recreation centers is believed to be an alternative to substance abuse. Providing transportation and child care so as to facilitate clinic use is an alternative to not using a clinic. Identification of barriers to health behaviors and providing ways to circumvent the barriers are part of this mode.

As presented earlier, many prevention models cut across several of the groups. All use elements of the cognitive, affective, and psychomotor domains. The psychomotor domain is sometimes seen as the goal, as the desired behavior. However, there are prevention models that focus on the *psychomotor or behavior approach* as a means to an end. Modeling good behavior as an educator is one such approach. Using peer pressure to get behaviors adopted is another such strategy. Passing laws and enforcing them forces compliance with recommended practices such as premarital blood tests, seat belt laws, and so on. Adopting employment programs on smoke-free environments or on sexual harassment is yet another strategy.

EARLY INTERVENTION STRATEGIES

Certainly, there is some overlap between primary prevention and early intervention. Many elements of the above theories are used in early intervention strategies. However, there are elements that are unique to early intervention.

Intervention strategy involves behavior change. Clients need to be helped to see that present behaviors are unacceptable, in terms of impact on themselves and their impact on others. Moreover, clients need to be helped to see that alternative behavior patterns are preferable and are feasible.

To precipitate a desire to change, clients must be helped to perceive that there is a need to change. Anything that can create a perception of a crisis will be helpful. Alcoholics Anonymous has long advocated that a client must want to change in order for the program to be effective. Formerly, Alcoholics Anonymous theorized that alcoholics had to hit "bottom" before they were willing to work with the program. Substance abuse theorists now recognize that much can be done to help a client perceive that a crisis exists, long before the client hits bottom. Employers issuing ultimatums that change is necessary to retain the job, spouses issuing ultimatums that change is necessary to maintain the marriage, doctors issuing ultimatums that change is necessary to maintain health, and courts issuing ultimatums that change is necessary to stay out of jail all create the impression of a crisis, a need for change. Staff in employee assistance programs frequently coordinate these ultimatums, so that when they all happen at once, a perception of a real crisis is created.

Intervention theory focuses on the need for change, and on consequences of behavior, so that clients are more willing to attempt change. Educators need to be well versed in the etiology of conditions such as coronary heart disease, AIDS, herpes, diabetes, and so on, in order to be effective in helping create the need to change. They should take care not to exaggerate the prognosis but rather to present conditions realistically.

Individuals need to feel dissatisfaction with the status quo. Helping clients accurately assess the present conditions and the consequences of unchanged behavior patterns is an important part of early intervention theory.

Clients should also be helped to see that there are attractive alternatives, that life does not have to continue as it is. Intervention theory emphasizes the differences between the ideal and the real. The client needs to be helped to perceive a vision of what can be.

Once an accurate perception of "what is" and "what can be" has been created, educators need to use basic principles of motivation. Educators often talk about motivation and despair at their inability to motivate learners. The problem is often rooted in inappropriate learning goals. If clients are helped to perceive a need to learn new knowledge or behaviors, motivation is easier.

Some behaviors of educators are conducive to client motivation. A dozen of these are summarized briefly below.[2]

1. Inspire confidence of clients. It is important to act professionally and to model good behavior, although professional behavior may alienate some clients. Establish a business-like atmosphere, yet one that is warm and accepting.

    The positive effect of role models is now being documented in research, but it has been known for years that a good example adds credence to good teaching. Maintaining an appropriate weight, not smoking, and adequately handling stress are three visible areas that may impact on teaching effectiveness of health education.
2. Treat each client as an individual. It is especially important to avoid stereotypes and to establish rapport with each client. Few things are a more powerful persuader than a genuine interest in a client. Try to establish a helping, supporting relationship, rather than an adversarial relationship. People tend to feel more cooperative if they feel accepted and not judged.
3. Try to establish a connection between the wants and needs of a client and the recommended course of action. It is always important to establish the relevance of the recommended behavior to the client.
4. Work with the client and try to identify incentives that might be effective for that client. Intrinsic motivations, such as feelings of achievement and self-satisfaction, are worth focusing on and are usually preferable to extrinsic motivators. However, extrinsic motivators, that is, rewards of various kinds, can be effectively worked into the educational process. The behavior modification approach emphasizes such incentives.
5. Establish client goals realistically, both in short-range and long-range terms. Be sure that the task is divided into meaningful parts that will not overwhelm the client. The objectives must be as clear as possible so that the client will know exactly what has to be done, and in what sequence.
6. Work toward getting clients to "own" their goals or plans so that behavior change is something they want to do rather than something the staff want them to do. It is appropriate to "seed ideas," including, but not limited to,

attributing ideas to the client. It is especially important to work toward a verbal contract, some sense of commitment that the client will attempt to implement the behavior change.

7. Involve people in the rationale for behavior change and in the discussion of alternatives in the decision-making process when possible. Think out loud with the client. Those who are given reasons for change are most likely to accept the change. The fullest compliance with a new procedure usually results from the fullest understanding of it.

8. Organize and present new information in a way that makes sense to the client. Relate new tasks to what is already known. Always augment ideas discussed with written instructions. Also be sure that all questions are answered, and encourage further contact if questions remain.

9. Minimize high anxiety levels and downplay failure. Maximize feelings of self-worth whenever possible. People tend to resist changes that are perceived as lowering their status. They tend to accept change that is perceived as increasing their status. Success is more motivating than failure. Mild anxiety may be motivating, but fear may inhibit an appropriate response or may even precipitate an antagonistic response.

10. When clients object or are in other ways negative, let them verbalize their negative response. Let them "blow off steam," but you must "maintain your cool." Establish that you understand what they are feeling and why. Very often clients will realize that the initial objection needs to be revised and much of the resistance will then dissipate.

11. Stimulate a sense of readiness to act that includes an understanding of the need for behavior change. Work toward a sense of immediacy. Feelings of remoteness interfere with actions. Work toward the client having a sense of a "felt need" for the behavior change.

12. Reinforce good behavior whenever possible. Recognize and praise even the smallest positive response. Likewise, review and reinforce discussions and good intentions when the opportunity is presented.

IN CONCLUSION

There are many primary prevention and early intervention theories that health educators can use alone or in varying combinations. However, all combine some elements of the cognitive, affective, and psychomotor domains of learning. All the theories also include some elements of change theory. The domains of learning and how they affect change are the foundation on which all models of prevention and intervention theory are based.

The decade of the 1990s will generate many models useful to health educators and health promotion specialists. Each will have a unique name and unique emphasis. Yet all will emphasize in varying degrees some of the elements discussed in this chapter or the preceding one. These chapters are not intended to emphasize current models but rather to present the basic elements of which all models are composed. Health educators who understand the foundations presented here will then be able to understand and use intelligently whatever models and theories are currently in vogue.

***

Suggested Learning Activities

1. Obtain materials from Alcoholics Anonymous groups or from the library, and review the Twelve Steps. Think about how each of these steps can be applied to other health problems.
2. List as many ways as possible that health information can be transmitted other than by lecturing. Identify the advantages and disadvantages of each.
3. Select a health problem such as coronary heart disease. Identify what relevant knowledge, attitudes, and behaviors might need to be changed. Identify practical strategies to change each.

NOTES

1. Glanz, K., et al. *Health behavior and health education: Theory, research and practice.* (San Francisco: Jossey-Bass, Inc., Publishers, 1990).
2. D.J. Breckon, *Hospital Health Education* (Gaithersburg, Md.: Aspen Publishers, Inc., 1982).

SUGGESTED READING

Abraham, R. 1988. *Substance abuse prevention and treatment.* New York: Chelsea House.

Derryberry, H., ed. 1988. *Educating for health, The selected papers of Mayhew Derryberry.* New York: National Center for Health Education.

Glanz, K., et al. 1990. *Health behavior and health education: Theory, research and practice.* San Francisco: Jossey-Bass, Inc., Publishers.

Katz, A. 1987. *Prevention and health: Directions for policy and practice.* New York: Haworth Press.

Matthews, B.P., ed. 1982. *The practice of health education: SOPHE heritage collection.* Oakland, Calif.: Third Party Publishing Company.

Mico, P.R., and Ross, H.S. 1975. *Health education and behavioral science.* Oakland, Calif.: Third Party Associates.

Milo, N. 1986. *Promoting health through public policy.* Ottawa, Canada: Canadian Public Health Association.

Ross, H.S., and Mico, P.R. 1980. *Theory and practice in health education.* Mountain View, Calif.: Mayfield Publishing Company.

Simonds, S.K., ed. 1982. *The philosophical, behavioral and professional bases for health education: SOPHE heritage collection,* Vol. 1. Oakland, Calif.: Third Party Publishing Company.

Chapter 16

Using Community
Organization Concepts

Health educators are like missionaries in the sense that they strongly believe in the programs they promote and are convinced that the programs will benefit others. So with evangelical zeal, health educators have, on occasion, become manipulative and have forced decisions and programs on an unprepared public. Accordingly, they were labeled do-gooders by the poor and other groups with which they were working.

As leaders in the profession recognized the image that was developing, they began to stress the concepts of community organization. This emphasis, which started in the 1960s, has continued and has resulted in increased effectiveness and an improved image. Thus, community organization skills have continued to be important skills for health educators to develop.

COMMUNITY ORGANIZATION CONCEPTS

The essence of community organization is implied in a literal analysis of the term. It involves helping a community organize for communitywide action. To fully appreciate the concept, one needs to view the term *community* as the community organizers view it. A community is a social unit that is interdependent in at least one context and is aware of that interdependence. Stated differently, it is a group of people with some things in common who are aware of those commonalities.

Such a definition of community suggests that the term might refer to the citizens living within the city limits or that it might include people outside the city limits who come to the city frequently. It also could include subgroups within the city, such as the poor, elderly, college students, and members of a minority group.

Viewed from this perspective, community organization involves helping a specific group or subgroup of people organize for action. It also becomes apparent that the concept is essentially process oriented rather than task oriented in that once the community is organized, many tasks can be accomplished and problems solved.

Accordingly, a widely accepted and time-tested definition by Ross states that community organization is "a process by which a community identifies its needs or objectives, ranks these needs or objectives, develops the confidence and will to work at these objectives, finds the resources (internal and external) and in so doing, extends and develops cooperative and collaborative attitudes and practices in the community."[1]

The definition presupposes the importance of the community in that the community decides which tasks need to be done and the order of their priority. Likewise, the community not only identifies resources and cooperatively accomplishes the task but, more important, also extends and develops collaborative attitudes and practices in the community.

The basic supposition is that communities want to and will obtain health services and facilities, both individually and collectively, but that they may need help doing so. The supposition also suggests that the most effective and lasting change comes from within a group and is largely handled internally.

Community organization skills, then, involve methods of intervention by which a community is helped to engage in planned, collective action. They are efforts to mobilize the people who are affected by a community problem. They are part of the process of strengthening a community through participation and integration of the disadvantaged and other subgroups.

The concepts of community organization also encompass the concept of consumerism. This concept supports the orientation that recipients as well as providers of health services should be involved in decision making when planning and delivering such services. It advocates early and consistent community involvement when decisions on program structure and priority are made; in fact, some boards, task forces, and committees require a consumer majority.

The extent of consumer involvement varies considerably, leading Arnstein to conclude that structures organized to facilitate community participation are, in reality, forms of manipulation, tokenism, placation, or consultation.[2] Arnstein saw partnership, delegated power, and citizen control at the other end of a continuum illustrating degrees of community participation. Community organizations are generally committed to some form of citizen control but recognize that often a partnership between members of the community and government authorities is necessary to improve the economic and social conditions of communities. This difference of perspective is illustrated in Figure 16-1.

Another tenet of community organization concepts is the orientation toward power. As suggested earlier, this principle holds that power should reside in the community and that the process is, in large part, empowering the community to act. This process requires analysis of the power structure of a community, with power being defined as the ability to either block or induce change. Many sources of power and influence exist, including political position, control of information, knowledge and expertise, social standing, and money and credit. Knowing that power may be "possessed, but not expressed," that is, used only when necessary,

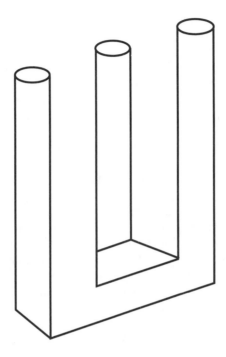

Note: Cover the bottom half of the diagram and view the exposed part of this diagram. Then cover the top part of the diagram and view the exposed part at the bottom. This illusion demonstrates the well-known fact that a community looks different when viewed from a position of power at the top as opposed to when viewed from a position of powerlessness at the bottom.

Figure 16–1 Our Community.

---

is important. If the premise is accepted that change usually produces conflict, then power struggles are inevitable. An understanding of the nature of power and of where and in what degree it exists is an important ingredient in helping a community engage in planned change.

COMMUNITY ORGANIZER ROLES

The health educator who undertakes the task of helping a community organize should understand at the outset that it is a long-term project. Different communities move at different speeds, and sensing the appropriate pace is important. This aspect is handled partly by letting the community members make the decisions. An important role of an organizer is as a catalyst or a facilitator, not as a decision maker. Care should be taken that people are encouraged and supported, not pushed into decision making.

Another essential skill is that of communication, as suggested by the common root word in *communication* and *community*. The definition of community advanced in Chapter 5 suggests an awareness of an existing interdependence. Often that awareness has been suppressed or people have been conditioned to accept a problem as an insoluble given. Communication is an important ingredient in changing those perceptions. Talking with members of a community and "seeding" ideas is useful in raising awareness levels and focusing discontent into an action organization. For example, a group of health department clients may accept as a given that services are available only between 9 A.M. and 4 P.M. in a central location. A community organization approach would suggest working with the clients, establishing rapport, and determining if the times and the place are problematic. It would propose that if enough clients suggest it, evening hours and another location may be possible. Other suggestions may be in order, such as getting a few people together to talk about it to see if there is enough interest. This approach assists the community to organize, rather than having the health educator do the task for them, with the result that other tasks may be tackled because the community has been helped to develop a simple structure to make decisions concerning its well-being. This example supports the contention that a key role of community organization is communicating with members of the group on some possibilities.

Another role suggested in the illustration given is that of assessing leadership ability and, if necessary, developing it. People with ability may lack confidence because of lack of experience. Providing practical suggestions, encouragement, and support can help develop leadership, which increases the probability of success.

Another organizer role is that of expert, or expediter. When citizen groups are working with government bureaucracies, they may need information. An organizer can determine where the information can be found and give the group a name to contact. Alternatively, if the bureaucracy is viewed as being uncooperative, if the information is complex, or if the group leadership is nonexistent, the organizer may have to function as a researcher and obtain the needed information and explain the options.

On yet other occasions, a community organizer might act as an advocate, speaking on behalf of the group in staff meetings or in other settings in which the members are not present. Occasionally, the staff member may serve as a mediator or negotiator, trying formally to resolve differences of opinion in ways that are acceptable to all parties.

STEPS IN THE COMMUNITY ORGANIZATION PROCESS

No simple prescription exists for organizing a community. One rule, however, does not change: Start where the community wants to start.

Two general approaches are often used. The first is most typical and involves starting at the grass-roots level, working with the people of the community in initiating action. The health professional can seed ideas, make suggestions, discuss options, encourage and assist leaders, and generally build support for action in a community. The concerns need to be legitimized in the eyes of the community and then be diffused so as to have a broad base of support for whatever action evolves. It can, in fact, be a health official initiating change, which is legitimized by government officials and diffused by influential people and groups, which eventually results in lay people taking action. For example, a health educator may see a need for a rape counseling center in a community. The person can look for key people who are interested and then generate a broader base of interest and support. Discussions can be held, materials disseminated, and representatives of other agencies involved, so that the idea of a rape counseling center is perceived by the community as being feasible and something that the community needs. As the proposal is developed and refined, the concept passes through the legitimization stage. Meetings, media coverage, and other techniques help get the idea through the diffusion stage, so that there is a broad base of support, which ultimately results in lay people taking action. This approach "emphasizes full reliance on community initiative, development of indigenous leadership, active participation, democratic cooperation, and educational objectives."[3]

The process can also work in reverse. Health professionals can take action, such as in an interagency attempt to provide hospice services to the elderly of a community. The concept then has to be diffused and legitimized among the citizenry. This approach emphasizes social planning using professional expertise in conducting needs assessments, in setting short-range and long-range priorities, in devising alternative strategies for action, and in designing monitoring and data feedback systems to facilitate implementation.[4]

POLITICAL ACTION STRATEGIES

An additional dimension of planned change within a community grows out of the social planning model and relies on political action. The political action may be at the local, state, national, or international level. It involves affecting change on public policy, as, for example, in funding abortions out of tax dollars or changing the laws regarding driving while intoxicated. The strategy is appropriate when the decision will be made by a legislative body and when time and money are available to influence the minds of the policy makers.

The political action process is essentially an educational task, combined with political power and influence and usually conditioned by the spirit of compromise. A well-educated public is important to the functioning of a democracy; indeed, an informed and active citizenry is the lifeblood of a democracy. Legislators are elected representatives of the people. Legislators want to know what their constituents want, and citizens want their representatives to represent them well. However, too many people never have any contact with those who represent them in government, even though their representatives' votes may decide what price the people will pay for services or what their standard of living will be. Principles of community organization can be used effectively in forming a group to lobby for or against legislation. Group effort is often more effective than individual efforts. A group is more visible, has more resources, and carries more political clout.

Community members can be organized around a specific issue of concern. Goals must be defined, tasks identified, and work shared. As with other community organization efforts, concern must be widely shared, the power structure must be analyzed, and available resources and influences must be mobilized.

Public health and health care professionals who use political action must know how the legislative system works in a particular location. They should know how a bill becomes law, what the committee system is, and which legislators deal primarily with health matters and should become personally acquainted with one or more legislators.

Preparation should be made before personally contacting a legislator. Background material on an issue should be obtained and studied. Knowing a legislator's past voting record on such matters is helpful. Telephoning for an appointment is also recommended. It is common to be given an appointment with a member of the legislator's staff. The staff member should be treated with the same respect and courtesy accorded a legislator. Staff members often summarize issues for legislators, draft copies of bills, or in other ways influence the final product. Contacts with legislative aides can be extremely beneficial to those who are engaged in political action.

The contact with a legislator should be constructive. Information or reasons for a position can be presented. Make clear at the outset who you are and what organization, if any, you are representing. Maintaining a calm, reasonable approach is important. Arguments and emotions are usually not helpful. It is appropriate to ask legislators what their views are, to listen carefully to those views, to ask questions, and to take notes. It is inappropriate to demand a commitment before an issue is decided, because the final outcome is affected significantly by amendments added during the process. It is also inappropriate to attempt to intimidate a legislator. Anger and abuse are poor and ineffective substitutes for courtesy.

Political action systems also use letter-writing campaigns. These campaigns can be facilitated in a community by a group write-in. A letter-writing kit that includes such items as addresses, samples, and issues can be distributed. The letter should be personal, brief, factual, and constructive. It should include the writer's name and address and be in proper format. Letters should be written in time to do some good and should provide reasons for positions. Key times to write a letter are when a bill is being drafted, when it has been introduced, when it is being considered in committee, and when it is on the floor of the legislative body. It is also appropriate to write the legislator a thank-you note.

As one can see, much of political action programming involves education of the citizenry and their representatives. The educational task is combined with political power and influence. But health care professionals can also exert power and influence. Community groups should remember that (1) large numbers are power, (2) coalitions are power, (3) a unified position is power, (4) members who are in credible positions are power, (5) knowledge is power, (6) voting is power, and (7) money is power. Coalition building is a common emphasis among community organizers.

SOCIAL ACTION STRATEGIES

Occasionally, health care professionals may decide that action needs to be forced and confrontation strategy is called for. Civil rights and antinuclear war demonstrations are examples of large numbers of people trying to force action.

Organization is important in such situations, since more is being risked. Issues should be clearly defined and stated in writing. A brief statement of views, beliefs, policies, or intentions can be used in gaining community support and in contact with the media. The issue should be selected carefully and the position should be defensible, with credibility. Activities, such as meetings, rallies, vigils, strikes, fasts, and release of media statements should be timed so as to build momentum, in campaign style.

When possible, working through channels is preferable. It is important to get necessary permits for rallies or parades, to know the laws pertaining to picketing, and generally to avoid lawsuits and criminal charges, which often impact on credibility.

Because social action strategies rely on publicity, planned media coverage is essential. Posters, leaflets, bumper stickers, pickets, news coverage, and radio and television coverage are crucial to success. A publicity committee, a media contact person, and an information center are critical.

When used effectively, confrontation strategies can force change to come about more quickly than it would otherwise. However, more is at stake, including a job, a reputation, fines, and even jail sentences. Other alternatives should be explored, and the decision whether to participate should be made carefully.

IN CONCLUSION

This discussion of using community organization concepts has ranged from helping people decide what they need from the system to forcing the system to adapt to demands. Although the philosophy varies, the organizational principles are essentially the same. In any case, the ability to help a community organize is a valuable one for health educators to develop.

***

Suggested Learning Activities

1. Relate the term *ecology* to the human community and to world health.
2. Visit a community meeting (i.e., city council or county commission) and do a sociogram of the meeting. Analyze the results to determine the apparent power structure.
3. Develop a priority listing of health education needs in your community. Determine what support would be necessary to implement such a program, and develop strategies for obtaining that support.
4. Develop a scrapbook of newspaper clippings on political action strategies or social action strategies in action.

NOTES

1. M. Ross, *Community Organization: Theory, Principles, and Practice* (New York: Harper & Row, 1967), 14.

2. S. Arnstein, A Ladder of Citizen Participation, *AIP Journal* July (1969): 216.

3. H. Ross and P. Mico, *Theory and Practice of Health Education* (Mountain View, Calif.: Mayfield Publishing Co., 1980), 157.

4. Ibid.

SUGGESTED READING

Bracht, N., ed. 1990. *Health promotion at the community level.* Newbury Park, Calif.: Sage Publications.

Patton, R.D., and Cissell, W.B., eds. 1988. *Community organization: Traditional principles and modern applications.* Johnson City, Tenn.: Latchpins Press.

Chapter 17

Communication Skills

Effective communication skills are imperative if health educators are to be effective. Communication of information, ideas, and concepts is a basic ingredient of most educational encounters. Much of learning involves either written or oral communication, supplemented by observation. Thus, developing communication skills to a high level of competence is critical to all fields of education, including health education.

Other ways that communication can be enhanced are suggested in other chapters. In this chapter the basic tenets of both oral and written communication skills are reviewed. Readers whose communication skills are not well developed are advised to enroll in course work where individual attention can be provided.

INFORMAL ORAL COMMUNICATION SKILLS

Often during routine, work-related tasks an opportunity occurs to talk to people. At other times talking to the people involved to gather information or to see how they feel about it is mandated. An office appointment to discuss a matter with other professionals or with clients is a commonplace occurrence for practicing professionals. It is a task that is too often taken for granted. It is a skill that most people assume they have acquired but also one that most people can improve. Most especially, entry-level health educators need to consider their own performance and work at self-improvement. Coincidentally, improved communication skills may exert a positive impact on a health educator's personal life as well.

A beginning place for improving communication is to work at establishing rapport. A smile, an introduction by the name you wish to be called, and a warm handshake can do much to set the stage for a good exchange. Small talk at the beginning is useful to allow people to relax, establish a relationship, and prepare for discussion of more serious matters.

It is usually easier to establish such communication in an informal setting. Refreshments help in such matters. Arranging the seating so that one person is not sitting behind a desk is also helpful. The desk acts as a symbol of authority and tends to inhibit exchange of information. Sitting around a table as equals tends to facilitate the exchange of information. The setting should be conducive to discussion of confidential information. Lack of privacy can easily block the free exchange of information and feelings. Similarly, freedom from interruptions is important. Phone calls or "drop-ins" can interrupt the flow of communication, which may be difficult to reestablish.

Another part of setting the stage for effective communication is to provide undivided attention and to act prepared for and interested in the exchange. If necessary materials are readily available and eye contact is established, the stage is set for effective communication. Conversely, if during the exchange the health educator is searching through a file or a stack of papers for needed information, the attention of both parties is diverted. Above all, to facilitate effective communication, the health educator needs to act interested in the individual and the topic. If it appears that he or she does not care about the individual or views the problem as insignificant or the exchange as an intrusion, real obstacles to communication must be overcome.

As the meeting progresses and rapport is established, the encounter progresses to a discussion of the problem or issue. At this juncture it is an important, but often underemphasized, part of the exchange to clarify the problem or issue. Such clarification may be a one-way or two-way process, but it is necessary to have agreement on the problem or issue and the context in which it is being examined. To be certain that both parties are focused on the same topic, it may be necessary to probe, restate, or in other ways clarify the problem.

Listening actively is another important part of communication. Hearing is a physical process in which sounds that are made are heard, getting the attention of the person hearing the sound. Listening is a mental-emotional process that involves interpretation and assignment of meaning to that which has been heard. Sometimes a person may say one thing and mean another; the intended meaning is not always obvious. Additionally, people cannot always put into words exactly what they are thinking and feeling, partly because of the limitations of language. Therefore, it is usually necessary to read between the lines to discover the intended meaning. Such a process suggests that there is an intended message to be expressed, a message that is actually expressed, and a message that the listener thinks was expressed. Given this reality, it is not surprising that poor communication is so common.

Nonverbal clues are important to watch for, as they are part of the communication process. Many times more information is communicated nonverbally than verbally. Such factors as tone of voice, loudness, pace, distance, bodily tension, posture, and eye contact all may be significant but may be easily missed or underemphasized. Yet even when such factors are noted, meaning must still be assigned and errors of interpretation can occur.

Paraphrasing is a useful technique to check the accuracy of what has been understood from both hearing and listening. It also allows the other person in the exchange to hear what he or she has said. As noted earlier, sometimes the communication problem is the inability to verbalize complex opinions or beliefs. Such feedback can be useful in clarifying what has been communicated. Clarifying the conclusions that are reached so that there is agreement on the outcome of an exchange and perhaps a next step is especially important.

Much planning for and actual dispensing of health education can and does occur in informal settings. Health educators should be able to communicate effectively under such conditions. The problem is that unless a speech or hearing impediment exists, most people take this ability for granted and assume their communication skills are well developed. To the contrary, many of the problems that health educators face would not have become problems if they enhanced their ability to communicate effectively in informal settings.

FORMAL ORAL COMMUNICATION SKILLS

Health educators have considerable opportunity for public speaking and communicating in formal settings, so these skills are also important. Effectiveness in public speaking is not primarily an inherited trait, but rather a function of training and experience. As with many other health education skills, experience is the critical ingredient. People improve through practice. However, without training or self-study, one can practice poor techniques and reinforce them and not show improvement.

As with most health education, effective communication in formal settings begins with an analysis of the target group. The composition of the prospective audience in terms of such factors as age, sex, ethnic background, work experience, and existing health knowledge is critical in determining needs and interests. It should be readily apparent that if people do not need a message, or if they are not interested in a topic even if they do need it, communication with them will be more difficult. It is usually preferable to have a group do that kind of an analysis and provide the topic. As an alternative, the suggestion of possible topics to representatives of the group should result in agreement on a topic of need or interest.

Agreement on an audience and topic allows the health educator to then prepare the speech. An early step is to state clearly the objective or objectives for the presentation, preferably in behavioral format. Behavioral format clarifies in the mind of the presenter the desirable outcomes. If the individual preparing the lecture is not sure what he or she wants the audience to know or feel or do, the presentation is likely to be ineffective.

The purposes of the presentation need to be clear, preferably stated in writing, to facilitate the selection of appropriate material. It is also necessary to know the objectives or purpose in order to identify a "residual message." Most of the details of a speech or lecture are forgotten by an audience within minutes or hours of hearing them. An effective speech writer should therefore identify in advance what he or she wants an audience to remember. This central theme, purpose, or objective can then be introduced and illustrated in different ways at different times during the presentation to reinforce it.

Once it is clear who the audience is, what the topic is, what the objectives are, and what the residual message is, it is then time to focus on what emphasis or techniques will interest the audience. Failure to interest the audience may result in all else being in vain. The audience may be interested in a current event, a practical application, a theoretical treatise, an entertaining presentation, or a chance to get questions answered. If expectations are not met, an audience may become restless.

How the audience is approached can also be important in generating interest. A lecture that is illustrated is more interesting than one that is not. The use of slides or transparencies is a good way to get the audience's attention. Similarly, using well-known current events or other media events as "launching points" or as illustrations can be useful. A key to effective public speaking is the use of an adequate number of either verbal or visual relevant examples of the point being made.

A good presentation should be well organized and tightly structured. A method of organization, such as chronological, cause and effect, or known to unknown, must be selected. Information can then be included or excluded, based on the objectives, and placed logically, based on the structure. All irrelevant information can be excluded.

A speech or lecture should be well prepared, clearly focused, and brief. It can then be stylized with a good introduction and conclusion and an effective presentation. An effective presentation is a composite. It includes a good appearance with attention paid to details such as appropriateness of dress, posture, and use of notes. It is usually extemporaneous or at least not read. A formal paper may be prepared for distribution, but the presentation itself should be a discussion of the major points. Standard practice is to distribute the paper after the presentation; to distribute it beforehand will result in people racing ahead as well as the lecturer having to contend with the distraction of pages being turned.

An outline or note cards are typical aids for an extemporaneous presentation. A paper with certain points highlighted is also commonly used. When an outline or note cards are used, the opening and closing remarks should be prepared and rehearsed. The opening remarks should be rehearsed because of the probability of being nervous and of the importance of making a good first impression. Similarly, the closing remarks should be prepared and rehearsed because they constitute the culmination of the presentation.

WRITTEN COMMUNICATION SKILLS

Health educators are required to use their written communication skills almost daily. The type of writing varies from setting to setting and job description to job description. Some writing tasks have to be performed daily, such as letter writing. Others are done infrequently, such as preparation of résumés. Some writing must be done at regular intervals, like preparation of newsletters or annual reports, whereas other writing is done at irregular intervals, for example, writing for publication. Some writing has a required format, such as a journal article, whereas other writing allows for considerable creativity, such as pamphlet preparation. Some writing is targeted for large audiences, such as newspaper readers, whereas other writing is addressed to an individual, such as a legislator or an administrator.

In all cases, however, written material is a representation of the writer and a reflection of the writer's ability. Health educators are judged, consciously and subconsciously, by what they write. A study of the qualities that help or harm one's chances of being promoted includes capacity for hard work, ability to get things done, good appearance, self-confidence, ability to make sound decisions, ambition, and the ability to communicate. Written communication is most important in large agencies, because in those settings written reports must often substitute for oral reports. It is important to improve writing style as much as possible. A writing style develops partly because of personality, past training, and personal preference and partly by default, as individuals are unaware of writing problems or preferred methods. In this chapter common problem areas are discussed and suggestions for improvement are made.

One's writing improves as a result of critical analysis and practice. Few writers make errors intentionally or fail to correct known problems, suggesting that others should be involved in a critical analysis of writing if it is to improve significantly. Although a careful review of this chapter and other publications on the topic, accompanied by a thoughtful self-analysis, may produce some improvement, more gains will usually be made through enrolling in a course or having others edit one's writing. A nondefensive analysis and discussion of editorial comments plus a sincere effort to incorporate suggestions usually result in an improved writing style.

Preparing for Writing

Good writing is more "perspiration than inspiration," more a matter of discipline than ability. Stated differently, poor writing is a matter of not taking enough time to do it well. If a letter or report is written with little advance thought, and if it is not reread and rewritten, it is apt to have areas that need improvement. Failure to prepare written materials thoughtfully and carefully is one of the most common problems faced by professionals and, fortunately, one that is relatively easy to correct.

The best place to begin improving one's writing is in a prewriting stage. It is important to have blocks of time that are free of interruption available for writing, if possible. Needed items, such as dictionaries, a thesaurus, information to be quoted or summarized, and lots of writing materials, should be gathered ahead of time. Before actual writing is done, notes or perhaps even an outline should be prepared; at the very least, thought should be given to content and sequence. Getting started is often the most difficult part of writing a report, and advance planning makes it easier to get into the flow of writing. Many authors who write daily make notes about the next section they will write to facilitate getting started again. This approach saves time not only in composition but also in rewriting sections and thus becomes useful for correspondence.

A major task during the prewriting phase is audience analysis. As in most aspects of health education, identifying the intended audience, the most likely audience, or the most important segment of a diverse audience is important. Knowing the recipient of a letter facilitates composition of the letter.

Audience analysis involves first and foremost determining what the audience wants to know. Health education is based mostly on a needs assessment; needs and interests are important predetermining factors in written communication. An assessment of what is already known is also valuable. This allows the writer to make some assumptions about the level of writing, the amount of detail that is required, how much background must be given, what terms are appropriate, and what will be unknown jargon. This type of audience analysis provides a context in which composition can occur. When corresponding with known individuals, much of this analysis is done automatically or subconsciously. When preparing manuscripts for diverse audiences, the analysis should be done consciously. A thoughtful audience analysis serves as a useful guide when preparing or revising a draft copy. For example, material on a family-planning project that is prepared for physicians can be different than material that is prepared for clients. Similarly, the annual report an agency prepares for its board of directors might have different emphasis than the report the agency prepares for taxpayers. The difference centers primarily in answers to two questions: "What do they want to know?" and "What do they already know?"

In this prewriting stage it is important to clarify the tone that will be conveyed. A letter or memo can convey interest and be convincing, vague, noncommittal, optimistic, pessimistic, angry, caring, forceful, gentle, and so on. The tone of the letter is approximately equivalent to the tone of voice. Just as supervisors can shout "no," they can write a strongly worded memo that carries the same expression. Such a tone is conveyed by such factors as choice of words, sequence, and length of sentences. Just as emotions sometimes enter a conversation unintended, so the tone of a letter may not be planned and may in fact be regretted later. A commonly used strategy is to write a letter one day and not send it until it is read on a subsequent day. This strategy helps ensure that the overall message carried by the letter is close to what is intended.

The Composition Phase

When materials and thoughts have been gathered, the intended audience analyzed, and a desired tone or overall emphasis identified, effective writing can begin. These tasks must be accomplished at some point. Doing them ahead of actual composition rather than integrating them in composition allows the flow of thought to get started more easily and to flow more smoothly. Much of good writing involves developing an appropriate stream of consciousness and not interrupting it.

When actually composing copy it is important to be clear in what is conveyed. The purpose of a communication should be clear in the mind of the writer and should be conveyed clearly to the reader. Unless vagueness is deliberate, a reader should understand what he or she has just read. Clarity is an essential ingredient of communication. If sentences are too long, if too much jargon is used, if the writer does not understand the issue well enough to state it clearly, or if examples or other techniques are not used to clarify material, the communication may confuse rather than clarify.

Written materials should also be coherent. An organizational structure should be determined for reports based on the internal logic of the material or discipline, chronology, going from the known to the unknown, or other structures that fit the material and the situation. Some combination of organizational patterns can be used as long as it is conceptually sound and consistent. This task is often difficult. Once an organizational framework has been conceptualized and an outline prepared, the actual composition becomes somewhat mechanical. Writing that is clear and coherent is more apt to be persuasive.

Written material should also be concise. Conciseness is a matter of judgment. As pointed out earlier, audience analysis partly determines what is known and what is wanted. Yet verbosity or brevity is partly an attribute of personality or at least a matter of personal preference. Some individuals use more detail than do others. How much detail is enough is a matter of judgment. The tendency to err is on the side of being verbose. Most inexperienced writers can eliminate or combine many words and phrases to condense the overall report without losing meaning. In fact, editing a report or memo to be more concise usually enhances clarity.

A fourth factor to remember when composing copy is correct construction. This factor is often believed to be the most important, but in reality it pales in significance when compared with other factors. A letter may be grammatically correct yet convey an inappropriate tone. A letter may have a good appearance but lack clarity. A report may be grammatically correct and look good but be rambling, poorly organized, and unconvincing. Notwithstanding, a letter, a proposal, or a report with spelling or typographical errors, problems with sentence structure, punctuation errors, poor paragraph construction, or overall poor appearance usually fails to convey the intended message. At minimum, it will convey a message that the writer would prefer not to convey. Exhibit 17-1 illustrates common grammatical problems.

Exhibit 17–1 Rules of English.

This anonymous list of rules, although humorous, can help writers identify common writing problems. If you do not understand or see how the point is illustrated while it is being made, perhaps you are apt to make that mistake.

1. Don't use no double negatives.
2. Make each pronoun agree with their antecedent.
3. Join clauses good, like a conjunction should.
4. About them sentence fragments.
5. When dangling, watch them participles.
6. Verbs has to agree with their subject.
7. Just between you and I, case is important, too.
8. Don't write run-on sentences they are hard to read.
9. Don't use commas, which are not necessary.
10. Try to not ever split infinitives.
11. Its important to use your apostrophe's correctly.
12. Proofread your writing to see if you any words out.

Again, individuals seldom deliberately leave mistakes in a report. The problem is usually a matter of not looking for such mistakes or not being able to spot them. Therefore, having work edited as necessary by secretarial staff or others is desirable. The use of a spelling checker in a word processing program should be considered routine. The judgment of others regarding clarity, coherence, conciseness, and correctness can avoid embarrassment later.

Editing and Rewriting

As indicated, two keys of effective writing are adequate preparation and being clear, coherent, concise, and correct during composition. The third key factor is in the rewriting stages.

During composition many writers let the stream of consciousness flow and commit ideas to paper as quickly as possible. Ideas are produced faster than they can be written, typed or entered, or even articulated orally. Taking time to state concepts in correct format results in ideas being lost. Capturing ideas quickly does, however, place more emphasis on editing and rewriting.

As noted earlier, a letter or report should be reread on a subsequent day. Many writers find it helpful to read aloud what they have written so that they can see and hear concurrently. Using sight and sound in editing helps to identify trouble spots that need additional work for clarity.

Also as noted earlier, having the opinions of more than one person helps. Various individuals are alert to certain kinds of problems. Often, however, editorial comments are a matter of personal preference and must be viewed by the writer as suggestions that can be selected or rejected.

Some sections may need to be rewritten several times, and rewriting one section may dictate rewriting another. Clear writing requires clear thinking. If an issue was not thought through clearly in the prewriting phase, the lack of consistency or clarity may be apparent when putting it in writing. Writing helps to clarify thinking and vice versa.

The document should be read from beginning to end without interruption, if possible. This permits a check on the document's flow. Some sections may be too detailed; others may require a little more elaboration. The need to add some new points or illustrations may become apparent from such a reading. Finally, the document should be proofread for typographical and other minor errors that may not have been corrected earlier.

HEALTH COMMUNICATION THEORY

Oral and written communication skills are essential for community health educators. Every opportunity should be seized to improve such skills (including additional writing and public speaking college courses). However, although good communication skills are imperative, they are not enough. Because communication in health education involves matters of life and death, attention needs to be focused on theoretical considerations.

The burden of communication is usually on the person responsible for doing the teaching. Therefore, dissemination of concepts should be carefully planned so as to enhance the probability that a message is actually received and used. One useful way of looking at the communication process is demonstrated in the model shown in Figure 17-1.

The target group to be educated should be carefully selected to be homogeneous and as narrowly defined as possible. This process usually identifies more than one target group in a program. Pragmatically, the process often means adapting a given program to more than one group.

The educational messages needed should then be identified. Once the group and the messages have been identified, the educator should select the most effective senders and channels to deliver the messages to the target group and implement a process of feedback to ensure that the messages are received.

A given educational program will often involve several target groups. It may be necessary to reach the client, those caring for the client, and personnel in community agencies. Different messages may be appropriate for the differing groups, though all may need some common information as well. Once all the target groups and messages have been identified, the most credible senders and the most appropriate communication channels need to be located for each group.

There is often great disparity in the credibility of senders from group to group, and senders need to be selected with a great deal of care. Credibility involves per-

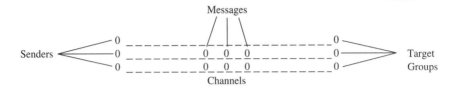

Figure 17–1 Communication Process.

ception of expertise and trustworthiness. Effective educators must know what they are talking about and must be trusted to present information without bias. Generally, senders need to be credible with the target group before the message is sent or the message is likely to be ignored.

The communication channel is likewise important, and messages should be fed into channels already used by the target group whenever possible. If, for example, a community program for mothers of young children is the goal, midmorning radio spots by the president of the Parent-Teacher Association might be an effective way of reaching them.

Research has established that low-income families benefit from face-to-face communication more than from mass media. For individuals of lower socioeconomic status, telephone contacts or other personal invitations would be more likely to succeed.

Basic planning of communication is important to all health educators. It is appropriate for health educators trying to reach people in the community, but is equally applicable to those doing staff development work. In each case, it is important to consider (1) the individuals who constitute the target group, (2) what messages they need, (3) what senders of information they believe, and (4) what channels they use to receive messages.

The communication theory described above applies to many aspects of human interaction. When applied to health communication, it takes on extra importance because it deals with matters of life and death. Accordingly, the Centers for Disease Control and Prevention convened a work group who defined health communications as "the crafting and promotion of consumer-based messages and strategies to contribute to the improved health and well being of individuals and communities."[1]

The CDC staff working on this project depicted the ten steps of this process in a Health Communication Wheel, which is depicted in Figure 17-2. This model is based on elements of communication theory described above. The evaluation component is much stronger than in most planned communication, perhaps only with the exception of market research on major advertising campaigns. The Health Communication Wheel is a useful reminder of the ten steps, of the importance of evaluation, and of the necessity for the consumer to be at the center of the process.

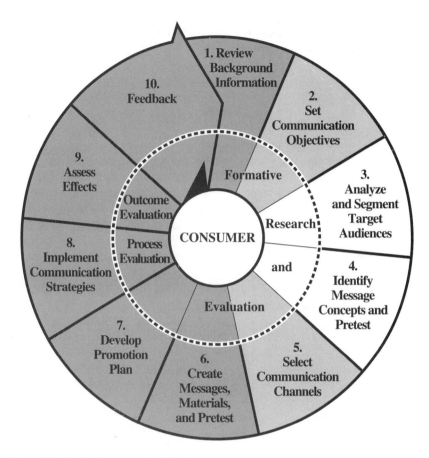

Figure 17–2 Health Communication Wheel.

IN CONCLUSION

Health educators have many opportunities to speak to individuals and groups about health habits. Being effective in these encounters is important. Effective oral communication skills undergird nearly all of health education. The ability to speak effectively will usually mean success for an educational specialist. Public speaking skills are worth developing and are a primary avenue of self-improvement.

Health educators also have to prepare many documents, such as grant proposals, program plans or reports, letters, and evaluative studies. Although the format for these writings varies, the ability to communicate well in writing is required for all. Writing comes more easily for some than for others. Those who find writing easy have a significant advantage over those who do not. However, all can be successful and all can find room for improvement.

***

Suggested Learning Activities

1. Prepare and deliver a 15-minute health topic presentation, for a specific group, such as those gathered at a senior citizen congregate food site or a Girl Scout troop.
2. Develop a short skit that illustrates good and bad communication techniques in a health education setting.
3. Prepare a letter of inquiry and a memo to volunteers in a new community health program in your state or hometown.
4. Review the rules of English listed in Exhibit 17-1 and identify those that are most problematic for you.

NOTE

1. W.L. Roper, Health Communication Takes on New Dimensions at CDC, *Public Health Reports,* 107, no. 2 (1993): 81.

SUGGESTED READING

Gregory, H. 1990. *Public speaking for college and career.* New York: McGraw-Hill, Inc.

Lucas, S. 1992. *The art of public speaking.* New York: McGraw-Hill, Inc.

Murphy, H.A. 1990. *Effective business communication.* New York: McGraw-Hill, Inc.

Chapter 18

Technology and Health Education

Change is continuous and rapid in today's world. The rate of change is increasing rapidly as the 21st century nears. Although change permeates all sectors of society and all aspects of the health education profession, nowhere is the rate of change more rapid than in technological developments. And in no areas of technological development are changes more rapid than in the area of electronic media. Behind this change is the computer, inasmuch as computer chips make most forms of electronic media possible.

Technology presents a many-sided dilemma to health educators. Among the more pressing issues are time and money. One usually needs significant blocks of time to learn to use technology effectively and efficiently, especially when the equipment is of recent origin. (Over time, use promotes "user friendly" modifications.) The learning curve is especially slow for the technologically illiterate person.

Beginners typically struggle with elementary aspects of technology, and unless they use the equipment frequently, they may never reach the stage of using it efficiently. More experienced users, however, can focus on applications that solve problems, because they know how the equipment works and can skip the "how to use it" concerns and progress to the "what else can it do for me" stage. Of course, the ease of learning to use technology will vary from equipment to equipment. All professionals have learned to use the telephone and copy machine, because of ease of use. Admittedly, many health educators have not learned to use all the features of the telephone or copy machine yet, and may never do so, because the technology changes faster than the learning rate of many users. For example, most agencies are not yet using computer-dialed phone calls to inform parents that it is time to immunize their children, or to remind AIDS patients that it is time to take their medication. Even fewer professionals have learned to program VCRs or to use a fax machine. Although not based on data, it is probable that an even smaller number of health educators can efficiently use an electronic library system, access a CD-Rom database, do desktop publishing, use microcomputers, access computer networks via modem, use E-mail, or use teleconferencing capabilities. Yet these electronic media can be of even more value to health educators than is the copy machine, if they progress beyond the basics.

It should be noted that considerable transfer of learning occurs in the electronic media field, because all of the above-mentioned technological developments use computer chips. There often are common elements. For example, the electronic library and desktop publishing capabilities use almost identical keyboards and similar commands and use of a modem (computer to telephone connection) is common to several forms of electronic media.

Perhaps most basic of all is a positive attitude toward technology, rather than fear and apprehension. A positive attitude is becoming commonplace today, perhaps because many forms of technology have been introduced in either educational or entertainment formats. However, a large number of "post–PAC MAN" people are still not comfortable using most electronic media.

Another barrier to widespread use of technology is the lack of budgeted dollars to acquire and maintain equipment and to train those who must use it. A related problem is that even if one agency can afford to stay current and does acquire the equipment, its ability to use the technology is limited because other agencies or professionals have not done so. Moreover, real efficiency on equipment requires in-home installation so that it can be used as needed, when needed. Many times, these needs or opportunities occur evenings or weekends. Of course, health educators' salaries often preclude purchasing equipment for home use.

We strongly recommend that students become familiar with microcomputers and acquire one for home use as soon as financially feasible. Similarly, complete familiarity with electronic library use, especially database searches, is fundamental. These two sets of skills will form a strong foundation on which to build skills in other existing or evolving electronic media.

MICROCOMPUTER APPLICATIONS

Microcomputers are electronic tools that have applications in many phases of health education and health promotion. Small enough to fit on a desk or lap and flexible enough to manipulate numbers or the alphabet, they are enormously useful. Microcomputers can store large amounts of information and provide access to an entire library, which can increase a health educator's efficiency. Microcomputers can produce professional-looking newsletters, charts, and graphs, increasing the effectiveness of the health educator. And when programmed appropriately, they can be teachers with infinite patience that can teach anytime and anywhere.

The heart of a microcomputer is the microprocessor, which manipulates whatever data are put into it. There are a variety of input devices, most common of which are the keyboard, electronic pen, and mouse (a rolling desktop device that moves symbols around on the screen). Some computers also respond to voice commands and touch commands, in which a variety of functions are displayed on the screen and the user chooses a function by touch.

Of course, the results of the computer's work needs to be displayed in order to be useful. Common output devices are the television screen or page printouts.

SOFTWARE TYPES

Computer programs (sets of instructions to the computer) can be used many times and are usually refined to software (hardware is the equipment).

Computer software is evolving, so categorization is difficult. However, most software packages can be placed in one of five categories[1]: instructional, word processing, filing, spreadsheets, and special purpose.

Instructional software refers to microcomputer programs that can be used to teach. It is often called computer-assisted instruction (CAI) because instructional software, like other forms of educational media, should not be used alone. This category of software is increasing rapidly because it can be used by a client wherever and whenever the technology exists, in a classroom, a clinic, a hospital, or a home. Learners can work at their own pace, and self-paced learning is usually considered ideal.

CAI is personalized in that after the user enters a name, the user is called by name throughout. Some programs ask for other personal data such as weight, so that, for example, an alcohol simulation is personalized as well. CAI is interactive, which means that the computer responds to the user with instant feedback and reinforcement on the user response.

Some CAI is a simple tutorial, where information is presented and illustrated in a logical sequential manner. Tutorials can teach any content material that can be presented in other ways. Some CAI is drill and practice. Lists can be presented for memory, after which practice exercises are presented to see if the material is remembered well enough to be applied. Learning medical terminology is a good example of this type of CAI.

Computer games are popular, both as entertainment and as instructional programs. Instructional games have many formats, with competition being against oneself or against others. Many computer games follow the format of television game shows. The content can be varied; for example, there are many games that deal with nutrition.

There are many fine instructional programs in the health field and many that are poorly designed.[2] Exhibit 18-1 is a checklist to use in evaluating microcomputer software.

The second and most frequently used category of computer software is word processing. Typing is a form of symbol manipulation at which computers excel. Once material is typed into the machine, it can be stored, corrected, changed, or

Exhibit 18-1 Worksheet Evaluating Microcomputer Instructional Software

Program title_____

Disk title_____

Subject _____ Date _____

Publisher _____

Call # _____ Purchase Price _____

Format (Check correct answer)

____ 5 ¼" Floppy Disk   ____ 8" Floppy Disk   ____3 ½" Hard Disk   ____8" Hard Disk

Brand compatibility (Check correct answer(s))

____ Apple   ____ Radio Shack   ____ IBM   ____ Other (Specify)_____

Objectives, purpose, or theme _____

_____

_____

Approximate time required to use program_____

For what group is this material appropriate? (Check all that apply)

____ Preschool   ____ Elementary   ____ Jr. High   ____ Sr. High

                        ____ Adult Males   ____ Adult Females

Specific cultural groups _____

Specific occupational groups _____

Please grade the program on the following characteristics, where A is excellent, B is above average, C is average, D is below average, and E is nonexistent or extremely poor.

	Program Content
A B C D E	Accuracy of content
A B C D E	Educational value
A B C D E	Freedom from stereotypes
A B C D E	Built in self-assessment

	Screen Format
A B C D E	Well spaced, easy to read
A B C D E	Clear directions for the next step

	Program Timing
A B C D E	Self-paced
A B C D E	Exit available at any time
A B C D E	"Cuing" to focus attention when necessary

Exhibit 18-1 continued

Graphics

A B C D E   Sound turn off available
A B C D E   Graphics serve educational value
A B C D E   Graphics technically accurate
A B C D E   Graphics well designed and useful

Program Operation

A B C D E   Ease of use
A B C D E   Little delay in loading program
A B C D E   Random generation of material
A B C D E   Free from programming errors
A B C D E   Handling of inappropriate input
A B C D E   Consistent input response

Motivation and Feedback

A B C D E   Rewards given randomly
A B C D E   "Hints" available when answer is unknown
A B C D E   Multiple attempts to answer available
A B C D E   Nonpunishing response to inaccurate answers
A B C D E   User informed if there are delays

Program Instructions

A B C D E   Clearly stated instructions presented within the program
A B C D E   Bypass of instructions available
A B C D E   Review of instructions available
A B C D E   Menu accessible anytime

Program Objectives

A B C D E   Objectives clearly stated at beginning
A B C D E   Objectives are met

Program Level

A B C D E   Appropriate for target group
A B C D E   Avoids unnecessary jargon
A B C D E   New words defined
A B C D E   Humor handled appropriately if used
A B C D E   Program is user friendly

Instructional Technique

A B C D E   Ideas presented one at a time
A B C D E   Program uses capabilities of computer
A B C D E   Program uses "branching" for difficult material
A B C D E   Input can be corrected
A B C D E   Information is logical and well organized
A B C D E   Program use can be monitored by educator

Documentation

A B C D E   Teacher's guide available
A B C D E   User's guide available
A B C D E   Printout of sample run available

continues

Exhibit 18-1 continued

A B C D E	Documentation is easy to follow
	Evaluation
A B C D E	Overall assessment of the program

Comments: _____

_____

_____

Reviewed by _____ Date _____

Source: Hospital Health Education: A Guide to Program Development by D.J. Breckon, p. 111, Aspen Publishers, Inc. © 1982; *Health Education,* p. 85, American Alliance for Health, Physical Education, Recreation, and Dance, © October 1983.

formatted several ways before being printed. Word processing can be used to develop, store, and print various forms, class materials, newsletters, and question-naires. Policy manuals and directories can be electronically stored and updated quickly.

A third type of computer software is that used to do filing. Microcomputers are capable of storing large amounts of information. Such filing systems are some-times called databases. Electronic filing systems are used to file a variety of infor-mation, such as mailing lists, inventory of pamphlets, and film usage.

A fourth type of computer software is electronic spreadsheets, which do busi-ness-type, numerical computations. Spreadsheets do not require knowledge of programming but do require some knowledge of algebra. Users can easily set up charts and tables that can be changed quickly, with the row and column totals changing with each new entry. Spreadsheets are a valuable tool for budget control and forecasting, expense accounts, and many other activities.

A fifth category of computer software is special purpose software. The four cat-egories of software discussed above can do a wide range of tasks. Special purpose software usually does only one thing but does it well and is easy to use. Special purpose software exists to publish newsletters, to print fliers, or to compute read-ability levels. Dozens of other special purpose programs exist that are useful to health educators.

Community health agencies often provide clinics for screening or other health care services. Clinics are diverse and include family planning, hypertension, maternal and child health, nutrition, immunization, breast self-examination, and so on.

It is a common practice to make educational services available to clinic partici-pants, and sometimes clients are required to complete an educational segment prior to receiving other clinic services. Literature is nearly always available in waiting rooms or is given to the client as part of the clinic visit. Microcomputers can also be used in such settings. CAI can be very effective, because it is interactive, self-paced, and personalized.

Thus, a microcomputer program on birth control could be used in a family planning clinic to present information or to promote discussion of advantages and disadvantages of various methods. Users could choose from a menu the methods they wished to study. For example, they could choose to study oral contraceptives and from a submenu could choose to study how oral contraceptives work. Other users could skip these sections and go straight to a section on associated risks of contraceptives.

Community health educators often set up health fairs or prepare displays for home shows, county fairs, and conferences. Computer programs that can be done in five or ten minutes or less can be effectively used in such settings. Such displays need to be staffed so that first-time users have a good experience. Programs such as "Test Your Temper," "Check Your Nutrition IQ," or "Viral Invaders" are appropriate, as are health-risk appraisals.

Computers excel in analyzing data. For example, client intake interviews can be done on computer, permitting a variety of reports. For example, a stop-smoking clinic could enter name, address, phone, age, sex, marital status, race, educational level, amount smoked daily, number of years of regular smoking, previous attempts to stop smoking, smoking habits of spouse, and any other desired data. Reports could then be generated after clinic conclusions as to success rate by age, sex, and educational level. Moreover, the file could be updated for smoking behavior at six-month or yearly intervals and analyzed again. Obviously, such a procedure can help analyze program effectiveness in the aggregate and by various subgroups.

Microcomputers can be very useful in managing mailing lists and in generating individualized responses to each. Record keeping and mailing labels, individualized for letters to segments of the mailing lists, are commonplace in communicating with the various groups with whom health educators interact.

Statistical packages, of course, can analyze any data. Graphics packages can convert that data to bar graphs, line graphs, and so on.

Health Risk Appraisals

A special purpose software that is widely used today is called by various names but most generally referred to as health risk appraisals (HRAs). As the name suggests, HRAs compute the health risks of individuals by comparing behaviors and current health status to those of a cross section of healthy people the same age and sex as the user. This requires storage of large amounts of morbidity and mortality data for various ages, sexes, and ethnic groups. Normal life expectancy for a person that age is stated. Then any especially healthy or especially unhealthy behaviors the user reports are factored in and a new life expectancy is reported for the user.

Most HRAs report specific health-related behaviors, along with relative life-expectancy increases, if adopted. For example, stopping smoking might increase life expectancy by 3.4 years, reducing weight to normal range might increase life expectancy by 2.7 years, and so on. Most HRAs will print the life expectancy of the user, suggested risk-reduction activities, and associated increases in life expectancy for each activity. This can be retained by the user for later use.

HRAs are primarily useful as methods to catch people's attention and to focus it on their health behaviors. HRAs can be used as tools to bring about desired behavior change by health educators, regardless of the work setting. The quantitative focus on life expectancy can be a powerful motivator, if channeled into behavior change. Referrals to specific risk-reduction programs are the desired end result.

Some HRAs have the capability of summarizing data of all participants and generating a summary report. For example, if used as part of all college student entrance physical examinations or as part of a new employee registration system, HRAs can produce summary data for that group of students or for that group of employees and prioritize needed programs. For example, a business might determine that the most needed behavior change programs were weight reduction, seat belt usage, cessation of smoking, and breast self-examination. Obviously, such data are useful for health educators planning programs, and retakes a year later can generate significant program evaluation data.

There are several kinds of HRAs and many uses for them. They can be integral parts of health education programming. A list of HRA sources is included in Appendix F.

Health Education Databases

Health educators are, of course, used to using the library, be it a university library, a city library, or an agency library. Knowing what others have thought, said, and done is an important part of program planning. Today, computers can make it easy to search the holdings of many libraries and, more important, can search more quickly than was previously possible through the information in one library.

Many libraries have simply loaded their card catalog into the computer, listing authors, titles, and subject descriptors. Such a catalog most often focuses on books. A typical health educator can walk into a library and do a computer search for books in that collection on a given topic or by an author. (With a computer and modem, it is often possible to do such searches from the home or office as well.) Some systems will also permit searching other libraries, if they have been networked. In some states, the system of state universities is networked, to facilitate serving students through interlibrary loans.

Systems typically are made user friendly, to allow the users to do the searching, rather than paid staff. Not being afraid of computers and the ability to follow simple directions are the primary requisites. Beyond that, knowing the topic and the nature of the search are critical, as is choosing descriptors that direct the computer in the search process. For example, the computer might search for disease, for chronic disease, for carcinogenic disease, for lung cancer, or for prevention of lung cancer. Many other descriptors could be entered to define the search so as to obtain needed data. The search can be refined on screen, and once the desired items are selected, a bibliography of the selected items can be printed. In some systems, the bibliography can be annotated if desired. In some libraries facsimile machines are used to transmit needed materials to the user, almost instantly.

There are several specialized databases that search groups of periodicals for magazine articles. There are also specialized databases that have journals, books, reports, pamphlets, and audiovisual materials listed in the same database. The Combined Health Information Database (CHID) is one such database and is sponsored by the United States Public Health Service. Health education databases are listed and described in Appendix E.

Users of databases should inquire in advance about rates. Some charge by the item in the bibliography; some charge by the minute of computer time. If a user is not careful, substantial charges may be incurred. Others that are subsidized may be free or very inexpensive.

Another useful feature of databases is their accessibility from the home or office, if the user has the right brand of computer and a modem. This puts the library at the disposal of the user any time, day or night.

Health education databases are important tools that can be used by practicing professionals. Computer literacy can make these databases readily available.

COMPUTER CONFERENCING

Microcomputers, or the larger mainframe computers, can be networked and used to facilitate conferencing. *HEEF Bits and Bytes* (Health Education Electronic Forum newsletter) is one such conference that is currently available. HEEF currently has eight conference categories and more than 50 specific conferences. One conference likely to be of interest to college students is "Jobs-Info."[3]

The Healthier People Network is a nonprofit organization founded in 1991 to continue health risk appraisal work of the Centers for Disease Control. The network synthesizes scientific findings relevant to the understanding of the natural history of disease, the prevention of disease, the causal factors that lead to the onset of specific disease outcomes, and the modes of intervention that can prevent disease. These findings are then disseminated to health providers and health educators so they can better inform members of the public regarding their health risks.[4]

CABLE TELEVISION

Computer technology makes cable television more usable for health educators. Of course, one opportunity is simply to have health programming on one of the channels. In some areas, many health programming channels are available. One role of the health educator can be to encourage the local cable outlet to carry health-related programs.

Cable television stations are required by federal law to provide community access stations. These represent a significant opportunity to present matters of local interest. For example, during epidemics or disasters, local programming on the health aspects of the disaster is usually appropriate. Media talk shows, another opportunity, are discussed in Chapter 22. It may also be feasible to arrange for a monthly show organized by the health educators.

The community access channel usually has studio production capability and frequently has staff who will help plan and arrange the program. However, programming can be as simple as arranging for an expert guest to be interviewed by the cable TV staff on a topic of current interest. Such programs often do not have to be precisely timed, because community access channels normally have only sporadic programming with interim time slots filled by written messages on "reader boards."

Health educators can, and probably should, prepare educational messages for these cable TV electronic bulletin boards. Normal practices used in developing written messages for bulletin boards apply to electronics bulletin boards as well. (See Chapter 23 for more discussion of these principles.)

The technology of pay-per-view cable TV has applications for health education as well. Computer technology allows a station to send a movie to a specific household, where it has been ordered. Working with cable TV personnel, educators can use the technology to send health programming into homes where it is needed. In-home education for diabetics, for mothers of newborns, for cardiac rehabilitation patients, and for many other kinds of patients is feasible and can come at a time of their choosing. This technology can also be used in retirement communities with programs for the elderly, in hospitals with programs for patients with chronic diseases, in nursing homes for the terminally ill, and so forth.

It remains for the profession to develop the numerous applications of the technology. Certainly, opportunities are present and will increase, in that cable television permeates today's society.

Videotape rental stores may become unnecessary because of the above-described technology. Viewers will be able simply to call the cable TV station and order whatever movies they want to be shown on their home television, at whatever time they specify. However, for the foreseeable future, rental stores are also a resource for health educators. Placing a series of health education videotapes for free loan in such establishments is possible, if appropriate partnerships are developed. Similarly, educational videodiscs and computer games can conceivably be distributed through commercial outlets for other users of these electronic media formats.

IN CONCLUSION

Technology does not make things happen; people do. Potential exists for innovative programming. Computers, videodiscs, and cable television can revolutionize health education, if health educators enter the process creatively. National conferences have already been held to forecast microcomputer needs for the 21st century. Networks between health education computer users enable educators to learn from and help each other. The effect of technology will continue to grow.

Health educators, then, should take course work in computers and perhaps buy one, so as to become comfortable with it. Those who do will become computer literate and will be in a position to make a major impact on the profession.

***

Suggested Learning Activities

1. Obtain a computer-assisted instruction microcomputer program and evaluate it using the worksheet in Exhibit 18-1. You might set up a demonstration for your class and evaluate the program as a group.
2. Obtain a copy of a health risk appraisal listed in Appendix F. Set up a class demonstration using "dummy" data. Discuss the appraisal's strengths and weaknesses.

NOTES

1. D.J. Breckon, *Microcomputer Applications to Health Education and Health Promotion* (Muncie, Ind.:Eta Sigma Gamma, 1986),10.

2. R.A. Sager, Microcomputer Software—The Hard Part, *Health Education* June/July (1987):54.

3. To join HEEF, send name, address, and phone/fax number to 59 Monterrey, Kenner, LA 70065-3142.

4. To join The Healthier People Network, send name, address, and phone/fax number to The Healthier People Network, Inc., 1549 Clairmont Rd., Suite 205, Decatur, GA 30033.

SUGGESTED READING

Breckon, D.J., and Pennington, R.M. 1986. Interaction videodisks: A new generation of computer-assisted instruments. *Health Values: Achieving High Level Wellness* 10, no. 6: 52–55.

Chapter 19

Planning, Conducting, and Attending Meetings

Planning, conducting, and attending meetings are important parts of the health educator's job. Meetings are held for many reasons—to communicate information, influence attitudes, deal with different points of view, solve problems, provide a learning experience, meet social needs, raise questions and issues, and even plan other meetings. Some meetings are highly successful, whereas others should never have been held or should have been planned or conducted differently so as to be more effective. Whether the event is called a meeting, a conference, or a seminar, skillful planning is important.

Health educators are often asked to present a program to a ready-made audience, such as a service club or a parents' group. On other occasions they are placed on a conference planning committee because health educators are supposed to be good at that sort of thing. Clearly, health educators need to acquire meeting-related skills.

PLANNING PROCESSES

There are many ways to plan a meeting, but the standard advice is still best: Plan a meeting with representatives of the group who will attend. A planning committee almost inevitably results and is almost always the best planning process to use. The representation should be selected carefully, so that the planning committee consists of informed, enthusiastic individuals. There is a need for positive-thinking, hardworking individuals on the committee. They should actually attend the conference and usually meet after it for an evaluation or wrapup session.

The planning committee can be large or small, depending on the size of the meeting. For a small local meeting, three or four people are enough to provide diverse inputs and carry the workload. For a regional, state, or national meeting, more representation is required to plan effectively.

The committee should be appointed with sufficient lead time to plan in an orderly fashion. The required amount of lead time varies with the size and complexity of the meeting. Planners of national conventions often need more than a year. State convention planning committees are usually appointed at the previous year's meeting to plan for next year's convention. In yet other instances, two or three months' lead time may be enough.

The organizational structure also varies. If a relatively small meeting is being planned, the committee may choose not to appoint subcommittees. Individual members may be delegated specific tasks, but the group will still function as a committee of the whole. In other instances, subcommittees are necessary. The appointment of one or more of the following committees is fairly typical: local arrangements, hospitality, registration, exhibits, public relations, and finance. Clearly stated tasks with deadlines for completion need to be assigned to each subcommittee. Some monitoring should occur to be certain the process is on schedule.

Two other early, but important, tasks are to agree on the purpose and objectives of the meeting and to develop a theme or title for the meeting. The purpose and objectives should be relevant to the world of practice for prospective attendees in order to stimulate interest. Preferably, objectives should be drawn from a needs assessment. The title or theme should be stated so as to make people want to attend.

The location and date of the meeting should be established as early as feasible. Reservation of facilities is critical, but so are travel time and the nature of the facilities. Again, a needs and interests assessment is helpful to planners, or, at the minimum, representatives who know the group should be on the committee. Some groups prefer to get away to somewhere exciting; other groups prefer to have sessions close by. Some groups prefer to be in a wooded resort in the fall, near a ski resort in the winter, near a lake in the spring and summer, or near stage productions and fine restaurants any time of the year. All the above reasons can be the determining factor in swaying a decision on whether to attend a conference.

The date, location, and theme should be publicized as early as possible. Most individuals have to choose between several such meetings, so as to make wise use of their limited time and resources. Also, calendars get full and commitments are often made months in advance. An early announcement will often result in increased attendance.

An important consideration in planning a meeting and selecting a format is the facilities available. If small-group sessions are planned, meeting rooms or at least movable chairs are required. Eye contact is important in facilitating discussions; circular, semicircular, or U-shaped arrangements help interaction.

MEETING FORMATS

There are numerous meeting formats that can be used (Figure 19-1). Some of the most common are described in the following paragraphs. The format selected

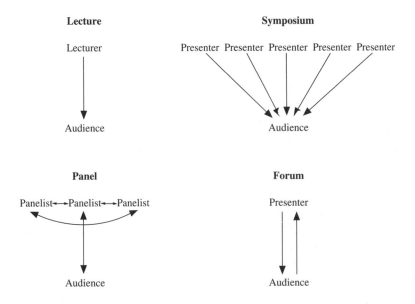

Figure 19–1 Meeting Formats.

should relate directly to the purpose of the meeting. There is much overlapping and imprecision in the use of terminology, and more than one format can be combined into a session.

Lecture

Perhaps the most commonly used meeting format is the lecture, in which a speaker is brought in to make a presentation to the group. Considerable care should be given to selecting a speaker, because if the presentation is poorly prepared or presented, a lot of time, energy, and money will have been wasted. Preferably, one or more members of the planning committee should have heard the speaker make a presentation. In lieu of this, the committee should talk to people who have heard the speaker. Effectiveness in such a situation is paramount. Ideally, speakers should be enthusiastic and knowledgeable of the topic as it relates to the audience. Good posture and eye contact, a smooth delivery, the ability to speak extemporaneously rather than read a paper, and the ability to answer questions effectively are all important attributes of a good keynote speaker. In addition, having someone with a reputation or position that is known, or who is at least viewed as important by those who will be invited to attend, is important.

Arrangements with the speaker or speakers must be clear and should be final-ized in writing. A specific title or topic should be negotiated, as should travel expenses and the honorarium. These tasks should be completed early, either in person or by telephone, and confirmed in writing.

Budgetary consideration will often dictate which speakers will agree to come. Before contacting speakers, the committee should have developed a tentative bud-get that projects such items as attendance, registration fees, and expenditures for promotion, facilities, and speakers. It is usually preferable to state up front what the budget will permit. Generally, the speaker's full expenses are paid, although some government agencies cover such expenses and do not permit their employ-ees to accept honoraria. A modest honorarium should be provided. Expenses plus an honorarium often fail to recompense a speaker fully for time, trouble, and indi-rect expenses involved. This is especially true if copies of a paper are expected for distribution or inclusion in conference proceedings.

A policy is also needed for members of a sponsoring organization who are asked to present papers. Sometimes registration fees are waived or housing and meals are provided, but no honorarium is given. Again, it is necessary for planners to be clear and consistent and to confirm whatever arrangements are made in writing.

Symposium

A symposium is a series of lectures on a specific topic, each with time limits. Usually a moderator presides over the session. The moderator introduces the speakers, keeps time, summarizes, and handles the question period, if one is scheduled. Symposia are especially effective with controversial topics, when sev-eral differing points of view can be presented. It is also an appropriate way of exploring current issues of concern to the group.

All the concerns expressed in the section dealing with lectures apply to plan-ning symposia. It is also critical to emphasize the time restriction. If 15 minutes is allowed for each of four speakers, this should be stated, as should the fact that a two-minute warning will be given and the speaker cut off at 15 minutes. If a speaker will be given time to comment on other speakers' presentations or to respond to questions, this, too, should be stated clearly.

Panel Discussion

Symposia and panel discussions are related and often confused. In a panel dis-cussion, a set of experts discuss a topic among themselves in front of a group. The session may begin with a position statement by each panel member, followed by a free-flowing discussion of the position. Obviously, a skilled moderator is needed.

As with symposia, this is a good format to use for exploring items of current concern, especially those that are controversial or poorly understood. Again, suggestions provided in previous sections of this chapter are applicable. It is particularly important to encourage panel members to discuss the topic rationally and to downplay emotional appeals.

Workshops

A working conference is a useful way to solve problems or plan strategies. This format usually involves bringing in resource people to work with the participants in a variety of ways. A resource person often is asked to present a broad overview of the issue and place it in historical context. Beyond this, the roles of the resource person may include being available to groups as a consultant and summarizing the outcome of the workshop.

Skilled group facilitators and recorders are needed. A carefully prepared and followed timetable is a must. Groups of 7 to 12 members with diverse interests often work well in such settings. A quick method for formulating such groups is necessary, as are adequate facilities to permit good discussion.

Forum

A forum is a question-and-answer period that is added to one of the formats already described. This type of exchange is important because the speaker's logic may not have been easy to follow, the material may have been difficult to comprehend, or the speaker may have assumed too much background on the part of the audience. If handled properly, a forum can be an important addition. If handled poorly, it can be anticlimactic and disrupted by participants filing out. The most common problems associated with forums are (1) no questions are asked and an embarrassing silence exists; (2) the questions are so technical as to be of interest only to a small segment of the audience; and (3) the question is really an extended comment as a member of the audience tries to seize the occasion to make a speech.

An early consideration when planning a question-and-answer period is to be certain enough time is left. A forum is often the most expendable part of the meeting and serves as a cushion for overly long speeches, late beginnings, and long announcements.

Another major consideration is to provide focus to the session. The effective forum should be a fundamental part of the meeting, not handled as if it were an afterthought. It is a way to get points clarified and to explore applications or extensions of major points. It can also be a way of assessing whether the speaker was understood, whether there was a gap in knowledge, whether there is resistance, and whether further help is needed in actually using the information.

Audiences should be prepared for the question period before the presentation. They should be encouraged to formulate questions and even instructed as to what types of questions to raise. If audience members are instructed to ask questions about points that they did not understand or about how a point would apply to a given situation, they will usually try to comply.

Another approach is to prepare listening teams. One team might ask questions requiring clarification. Another group might ask questions about areas of disagreement. A third team might ask questions about possible areas for group action. Reactor panels can be used in other ways than asking questions, but they are effective when used in this manner.

Another way of organizing a forum is to provide cards or notepads. Audience members can write down questions as they occur. The questions can then be collected and sorted quickly so that those of most interest to the audience can be answered in a logical sequence.

Yet another way to handle this part of the meeting is by forming buzz groups. Breaking up a large audience into small groups to formulate questions can help people frame better questions. Hearing questions usually helps individuals frame their own. It also is a useful way to prioritize questions, as, for example, when small groups are asked to prepare three questions they most want to ask.

It is not necessary to have a speaker answer all questions, nor is it always desirable. Again, a panel of group members can often answer application questions more effectively than a person brought in to make the presentation.

Other Meeting Formats

A *conference* is attended by interested people to discuss technical areas. It has one theme and many subjects. A *convention* is held to decide policies and plan strategy and helps people to better understand the organization to which they belong. Conventions often have conference elements built into them, and the distinction is often blurred.

A *colloquy* is held to explore a single problem. Six to eight people discuss issues that a moderator brings up. Normally, half the speakers are experts brought in, with the other half representing the audience. Obviously, there are similarities with the panel format. An *institute* consists of participants who are brought up to date on a new development in a short period of time. An institute is sometimes called a short course. A *seminar* is a group of people brought together and led by an expert to engage in in-depth discussion of a subject. A *case study* is focused on a specific case, which has been read by the audience before arrival and which is studied and discussed together. A *discussion group* consists of people who have been given information in advance, who explore the issues, identify solutions, and develop a plan of action. A *brainstorming session*, on the other hand, is used to generate a list of ideas, which are listed without discussion. The purpose of brainstorming is to generate as long a list as possible. The best ideas then are examined further.

Because there are a multitude of details to work out when planning a conference, planners usually need a checklist, such as the one shown in Exhibit 19-1. This form can be modified to fit other situations.

Exhibit 19-1 One-Day Seminar Planning Form

A. General Information
   1. Name of meeting:_____
   2. Location: _____
   3. Date:_____
   4. Seminar coordinator(s): _____
   5. Theme of meeting: _____
   6. Number of persons expected:_____
   7. Agency budget: _____Other:_____
   8. Cosponsors: _____

B. Program Planning Committee
   1. Members: _____
   _____
   _____
   _____

   2. Seminar assignments
      a. Moderator(s): _____
      b. Reactor panelists:_____

      c. Assistance to speakers (transportation, entertainment):
      _____

C. Registration
   1. Fee: Yes____ No____   Amount: _____
   2. Location (place and room): _____
   _____ Time: _____
   3. Luncheon ticket cost: _____Prepaid_____At door _____
   4. Complimentary luncheon tickets for guests and staff (names):
   _____
   5. Room reservations for staff (names):_____
   _____

D. Conference Accommodations
   1. Meeting room arrangement (sketch setup of tables, chairs, podium, etc.):

continues

Exhibit 19-1 continued

2. Agency responsibilities (audiovisual, place cards, other):
_____
_____

3. Host facility responsibilities (PA system, blackboard, other):
_____
_____

4. Location of registration desk:_____Typewriter? Yes____ No____
5. Checkout time for meeting room:_____Extendable? Yes____ No____

E.   Dining Accommodations
1. Dining room arrangement (describe setup of tables, chairs, podium, etc.):
_____
_____

2. No. of luncheons guaranteed:_____Percent allowed over/under:_____
   Serving time:_____Meal price:_____
   Menu: _____
3. Program participants staying for dinner? Yes____ No____ # staying: _____
4. Cocktail or social hour? Yes____ No____ # of guests:_____
   Serving time:_____Room: _____
   Charge to participants? Yes____ No____

F.   Exhibits
1. Coordinator of exhibits:_____
2. Location: _____
3. Kinds of equipment:_____
4. Setup time (date and hours): _____
   Takedown time (date and hours): _____
5. Exhibitors

Exhibitor	Address	Representative

6. Space allotment (including tables and chairs): _____

7. Require electrical outlets? Yes____ No____ Oxygen tanks? Yes____ No____
8. Describe exhibitor duties or procedures: _____
_____
_____

9. Agreement with exhibitors:
   a. Exhibitors to make reservations directly with hotel?
   b. Exhibitors to purchase luncheon tickets at the door?
   c. Exhibit room open afternoon and night before meeting?
   d. Coordinator to supervise exhibitors during the meeting?
   e. Is the coordinator to assist with setup and takedown of exhibits?
   f. Exhibitors' evaluation:
      (1) Arrangements satisfactory? Yes____ No____
      (2) Sufficient time to demonstrate? Yes____ No____
      (3) Meet any new prospects? Yes____ No____
      (4) Suggestions: _____
_____

Exhibit 19-1 continued

CONFIRM ARRANGEMENTS WITH EXHIBITORS ONE MONTH BEFORE SEMINAR!

G. Seminar Mailings

1. Advance flyer (mail 70 days before meeting) Date ready: _____
   a. Suggest one sheet on organization letterhead, print front and back.
      (1) Announcements to invitees, including program topics and speakers (front)
      (2) Short biographies and pictures of speakers (back)
   b. Send (bulk rate) to prospect groups, associations, and health agencies.
   c. Copy to program participants as information/confirmation of engagement.
   d. Responsibility (staff member or outside agency):
      (1) Copy: _____
      (2) Design and layout: _____
      (3) Printing: _____
      (4) Mailing: _____
2. Program invitation (mail 30–40 days before meeting) Date ready:_____
   a. Suggest one sheet of cover stock, one color, letterfold.
      (1) Announcement message (with double-barred cross), front fold; speakers' names, backside.
      (2) Complete program information on inside fold, including return registration blank.
   b. Send (bulk rate) to target groups and program speakers.
   c. Responsibility:
      (1) Copy: _____
      (2) Design and layout: _____
      (3) Printing: _____
      (4) Mailing: _____
3. "Thank you for accepting" letter to all early registrants.
   a. Enclose "in case of emergency, call . . ."card for secretary.
   b. Include a parking permit card if parking is a problem.
   c. Prepare name tags from early registrations.
4. Publicity releases to newspapers 2–3 weeks before meeting.
5. Make arrangements for favors, awards, literature for handout.

DO NOT BE LATE WITH MAILINGS!

H. Speaker Data

1. Speaker:_____From: _____
   Topic: _____
   Do we have advance copy of paper?_____Available? _____
   Hotel accommodation: Yes____ No____ Place: _____
   Photo for publicity: Yes____ No____ Biography: Yes____ No____
   Travel schedule:Plane____ Auto____ Other_____
   Arrival:_____
                             (time, date, place)
   Who will meet:_____
   Departure: _____
                             (time, date, place)
   Speaking aids requested: _____

continues

Exhibit 19-1 continued

Honorarium?____Amount:____Travel expenses: _____
Additional meetings scheduled:_____Explain: _____

_____

2. Speaker:_____From: _____
   Topic: _____
   Do we have advance copy of paper?_____Available? _____
   Hotel accommodation: Yes____ No____ Place: _____
   Photo for publicity: Yes____ No____ Biography: Yes____ No____
   Travel schedule:Plane____ Auto____ Other_____
   Arrival:_____
                              (time, date, place)
   Who will meet:_____
   Departure: _____
                              (time, date, place)
   Speaking aids requested: _____
   Honorarium?:____Amount:____Travel expenses: _____
   Additional meetings scheduled?:_____Explain: _____

_____

CONFIRM ARRANGEMENTS WITH EXHIBITORS ONE MONTH BEFORE SEMINAR!

Source: Reprinted with permission from *Public Health Education Workbook*, Central Michigan University Press, Mount Pleasant, Mich.

Teleconferencing

A meeting format of increasing importance is teleconferencing, which uses telephone and/or television technology instead of physical attendance at meetings. Traveling to and from meetings incurs travel expense and time commitments.

The simplest form of teleconferencing is to arrange a telephone conference call. Several offices or conference rooms can be linked by a secretary and/or operator, permitting conferencing to occur. If speaker phones are used, groups around a table can both hear and speak, permitting a small-, medium-, or large-sized group to confer. A nationally known expert can lecture to a group, with people who wish to pose questions using a previously designated microphone. This technique can be especially useful for committees and other small groups.

In order to ensure effectiveness, someone usually acts as the leader or moderator, sending an advanced agenda to the participants and setting locations and times for the conference call. The participants are told of their responsibilities and expected contributions to the group prior to the call. Following the meeting, the moderator sends out a memo for the record.

Another form of teleconferencing makes use of both audio and video technology, usually transmitting the conference by satellite. Such conferences are expensive to conduct, in that they require use of satellite up-link equipment, that is, the equipment required to get the signals transmitted up to the satellite. The equipment can be rented, or conferences can be scheduled in facilities equipped for that purpose. Down-link facilities are much less expensive and consist of a satellite dish, used in lieu of a television antenna in rural areas. Some hotel chains are so equipped and advertise teleconferencing capabilities. Rapid copy centers are now also offering teleconferencing to supplement their fax services.

Satellite time needs to be prearranged and publicized so that people at remote sites will know how and when to tune into what satellite. Satellite time can be rented and conference fees charged to cover the costs involved.

Such teleconferencing usually transmits video from the host site to the several or many ground sites, with transmission usually being one way. Of course, classrooms can be equipped to have two-way audio and video transmission, but the cost is often prohibitive. Far more common is using telephone connection back to the host site.

A typical teleconference would be conducted by a national organization such as the American Hospital Association, with many members around the nation. The organization would announce and publicize the meeting and arrange for facilities, distribution of materials, and collection of fees. A national host/moderator and a number of local host/moderators work together in conducting the conference. The local coordinator usually gathers written questions and forwards them as appropriate.

Teleconferencing has an advantage in that experts can share the latest information with people quickly and get some feedback from people watching. They do, however, suffer from limitations of expense, complicated organization, limited active participation by those watching, and difficulty in conducting and interpreting evaluation. Innovative health educators are working on ways to improve this type of conference with two-way video and other technological advances.

CONDUCTING MEETINGS

Health educators will often be called on to preside over meetings. This skill needs to be developed. A warm, personable atmosphere should be established whenever possible. Refreshments and name tags are important beginnings. A sincere greeting, audience introductions, if appropriate, and a description of the purpose of the meeting are all important ingredients of setting the atmosphere .

Introduction of the speaker needs to be handled properly. Usually the best way is to have someone who knows the speaker introduce him or her. The introduction should be somewhat informal, stressing what the audience wants to know. Usually an introduction is not read, but highlights are paraphrased from a résumé. It need not be long and should not be boring. It should be serious enough, however, that the speaker or audience is not embarrassed. A minute or two spent summarizing or highlighting a speaker's background or accomplishments is usually sufficient. Again, a key determining factor should be what the audience wants to hear.

Another task of the presider is keeping the meeting on time. Although this task may seem trivial, it is important and often difficult. The presider sets the tone for the meeting by starting on time and stressing to the audience the importance of remaining on time. It is helpful to give time signals to speakers or groups as they near the end of their allotted segments.

Health educators also have to preside over business meetings, ranging from small informal groups in which business is conducted by consensus to larger, more personal groups in which parliamentary procedure is critical. An important tool for the presider is an agenda that guides all involved through the meeting. The order of business in a meeting is typically as follows:

1. Call to order
2. Roll call (if needed)
3. Approval of minutes of previous meeting
4. Treasurer's report
5. Reports of officers (if needed)
6. Reports of standing committees (if needed)
7. Reports of special committees (if needed)
8. Old business (itemized)
9. New business (itemized)
10. Program
11. Adjournment

Parliamentary procedure is intended to facilitate the conducting of business, not stifle it. When in doubt on proper procedure, it is usually better to stop and discuss what procedure should be used, following whatever is agreed on. Reading a book on parliamentary procedure or taking a course is usually the best way to supplement skills in conducting a meeting. Careful observation of others in action is also a good beginning point.

Most action requires that a motion be made, seconded, and discussed. The motion can be amended informally if agreement exists with those who made and seconded it. Lacking such a "friendly amendment," a motion to amend is appropriate, which needs to be seconded and requires subsequent discussion. The amendment is voted on, after which the main motion is considered again and a vote taken.

A substitute motion is appropriate if the intent is significantly different from the original motion. It, too, needs to be seconded and requires subsequent discussion before action.

These actions will cover the majority of situations. Motions to table, close debate, and adjourn are handled differently, in that they are not debatable, meaning discussion before a vote is not appropriate.

One other situation that should be mentioned briefly is the election of officers. The floor is merely opened for nominations. No second is needed for a nomination.

Determining the outcome of a vote in a large meeting may necessitate asking individuals to serve as counters. In most instances, the outcome will be determined by the individual or issue receiving the most votes cast. Sometimes, however, bylaws may require a majority of those present, a majority of the membership, two-thirds of those voting, and so on. Obviously, it is important to know ahead of time how many votes are needed to determine the outcome of an issue.

The presider is really a nonpartisan mediator whose chief responsibility is to see that members are treated equally, regardless of personal beliefs. In some informal settings the chairperson may participate; in more structured meetings the chairperson should relinquish his or her responsibility to someone else before participating. In such an event the chairperson does not reassume responsibility until the vote is announced. The chairperson usually "recognizes" speakers, giving them permission to address the group. The chairperson should not recognize the same person twice until all others who wish to speak have had the opportunity.

Many different issues can come up in a formal business meeting. Beginners find it helpful to appoint a parliamentarian with whom to confer and on whom to rely for decision on procedure. Most meetings, however, are conducted informally. When in doubt, common sense should be used to clear up the problem and continue business. Health educators should acquire the skills to act effectively in both formal and informal settings.

A special consideration for health educators working in public agencies is compliance with state and federal "open meetings" laws. These laws require public notice of meeting times, places, and agendas. Details vary from state to state, but generally, a closed meeting can occur only to consider personnel issues, contract negotiations, land acquisition, and other matters that must remain confidential. Even so, the final action must be taken in open meetings.

Nonverbal Cues

A primary responsibility of a presider over any meeting is to be attentive to nonverbal cues and, when possible, responsive to them. In most meetings, far more is expressed nonverbally than verbally, and presiders can make the meeting more meaningful to more people by being alert to these cues.

Attention to basic nonverbal cues is essential. Are people straining so as to hear or see? Is it too warm or too cold? Is there too much outside distraction? Have people been sitting too long? Is a break needed? Such needs should, of course, be anticipated by meeting planners, with accommodations built into the schedule. It is also appropriate for someone other than the presider to be given the responsibility to monitor the meeting for such nonverbal cues, allowing that individual to make necessary adjustments.

There are yet other nonverbal cues that presiders should monitor. Are heads nodding in agreement? Does there seem to be a lot of buzzing about a controversial topic? Is the topic boring, or is it time for a change of format or a change of pace? Is the energy level running low? Are people seemingly anxious to get started on the return trip? Has the coffee arrived and begun to distract people?

Of course, noting nonverbal behavior is important, but it is only useful if the presider or presenter responds to what is being observed. The appropriate response will vary with the nonverbal cue, but often a "stand and stretch" break, an introduction of humor, or a change in delivery will suffice.

ATTENDING MEETINGS AND CONFERENCES

A health educator who attends meetings has responsibilities and opportunities. As discussed in Chapter 20, "Working with Groups in Leadership Roles," leadership responsibilities can be shared by members of the group. Not only is this helpful to the group, but it is also a useful way to develop and refine these skills.

Beyond the basic skills of summarizing, keeping the discussion on track, and encouraging participation by all, the individual attending a meeting has the responsibility to become a sound thinker. As issues are being addressed, health educators should ask questions as they come to mind so that they understand the problem that is being discussed. Likewise, they should search for prejudice, hearsay, and superstition and insist on facts. Similarly, it is important to watch for false analogies, loaded words, catchy phrases, and rationalizations. Critical thinking can add much to a meeting.

Health educators should plan carefully so as to maximize the benefits of attending a conference. An important beginning place is to review the theme, objectives, and type of people the meeting is planned for before deciding to attend. A telephone call to a committee member may help determine whether the focus or the level of the presentation makes the conference appropriate for a particular individual to attend.

Beyond that, a few notes on sessions to be sure to attend and people to be sure to meet are useful reminders. Coffee breaks, meals, and free time are often the most productive periods, since informal discussions or personal contacts occur.

Although name tags are commonly used, it is also a good idea to review the membership list so that past acquaintances can be called by name and the employer of a new acquaintance is known. Health educators should plan to attend as many receptions, open houses, and other social activities as possible so as to meet people who may be helpful to them. Possibly a committee meeting could be scheduled during a conference, en route to one, or returning from one. It may be appropriate to plan travel time so as to make an agency visitation. If the conference is held at a university, a visit to the bookstore to look at the current literature might be productive.

If exhibits are part of the conference, ample time should be set aside to visit them. When possible, materials can be mailed to the office so they do not have to be carried back. Bringing a larger-than-necessary piece of luggage to accommodate new materials and other acquisitions is also helpful.

Those who attend conferences should plan some free time to exercise, see the sights, buy gifts, socialize, or rest. It is helpful to take stamps, addresses, and telephone numbers along, as well as a good supply of business cards. On the way home the health educator should make a list of all the things he or she has agreed to do on returning to the office.

IN CONCLUSION

Planning, conducting, and attending meetings is an important part of the work of a health educator. With practice, health educators can get good at it and even come to enjoy it. Planning is the key to effective meetings. Well-planned meetings are easier to conduct and attend. In such situations the evaluations tend to be positive and everyone leaves feeling that something worthwhile has been accomplished.

***

Suggested Learning Activities

1. Prepare an agenda for a simulated or an actual meeting.
2. Collect and analyze conference promotional materials for various groups. Compare meeting formats and attempt to relate them to objectives.
3. Visit a continuing education or staff development specialist and discuss the procedures and forms he or she uses in planning and promoting programs.
4. Develop a skit demonstrating correct format and procedures for a panel discussion, symposium, lecture, forum, and listening team.
5. Attend a conference and analyze its format, procedures, and quality and identify possible areas of improvement.

SUGGESTED READING

Anderson, K. 1992. *To meet or not to meet: How to plan and conduct effective meetings.* Shawnee Mission, Kans.: National Press Publications.

Simerly, R. 1990. *Planning and marketing conferences and workshops.* San Francisco: Jossey-Bass, Inc., Publishers.

Chapter 20

Working with Groups in Leadership Roles

Health educators spend a great deal of time planning, implementing, and evaluating programs with groups. A significant percentage of a day's work is typically spent in a group, preparing for a group activity, or following up on the recommendations of a group. Group skills are the key to the success or failure of a health educator. This importance of planning programs *with* people rather than *for* people is well known. The importance of brainstorming in nearly all the activities of a health educator is accepted as fact among practicing professionals.

Health educators are invited to be members of some groups and find it appropriate to start a group in other situations. The groups may be client groups, staff groups, or interagency groups. Groups may be organized on a temporary or ad hoc basis or on a permanent basis. They may be formal or informal, large or small. Group membership may be static or changing constantly.

Group process is not always effective. Committees are the subject of many deriding comments, such as "A camel is a horse designed by a committee," or "For God so loved the world that he didn't send a committee."

If, indeed, groups are recommended highly and used frequently and effectively, yet laughed at on occasion, the key is in proper utilization. Although reading about group skills may contribute to acquiring such skills, this is an insufficient—but important—step in becoming adept in group process. Additionally, health educators need to observe and analyze critically the groups in which they function and to practice their ability to diagnose why a group is not functioning well. Likewise, they need to develop their personal skills in improving the way a group is functioning and the way the members feel about their group. Health educators who have developed these skills will generally be effective.

FOCUS GROUPS

Focus groups have become increasingly important to health education specialists, especially in needs assessment, program evaluation, and research. Focus groups are a method used in testing the perception and receptivity of a target group to an idea, by recording the reactions of a sample of eight to ten people discussing it with each other.

Focus groups are assembled for a specific purpose and usually only meet once. The focus is usually announced at the time the invitations are sent. For example, a group of patients in a cardiac rehabilitation program might be assembled to focus on ways to improve the program, that is, to evaluate present components and/or identify components that should be added. A simple list may be generated, and/or the items on the list may be prioritized. If ranked numerically, the responses can be averaged within the group or between the groups.

Another approach is to present a list to a group, focus discussion on the list, and then ask members to add or subtract from the list before prioritizing the items. This technique can generate much subjective data and, if it is desirable, provide a format for quantifying and comparing that data.

GROUP COHESIVENESS

A group can be defined as "a number of individuals assembled together or having common interests."[1] The definition suggests that, first and foremost, members are individuals who may or may not have common interests. An important first task, then, is to develop a sense of cohesiveness, so that the needs and interests of the group take precedence over the needs and interests of the individuals.

There are no guaranteed ways of establishing group cohesiveness, but an informal and conversational atmosphere is usually a good beginning. Members should be introduced to one another with enough background to be helpful but not so much as to be intimidating. Sometimes written communiques can provide details, and personal introductions can just deal with names and agencies represented.

Refreshments before and after a meeting can foster development of rapport. Name tags may be helpful if the group is large. Seating arrangements often can contribute as well. At minimum, eye contact should be permitted between all members of a group, which is achieved by a circular or semicircular seating arrangement. Members should be seated within easy reach of one another, rather than spread out in a room.

Beyond the introductory tasks, an effort should be made to describe clearly the reasons for the group's existence and to reach consensus on the group's purposes and procedures. These activities may have been formulated by another body, and the members of the group may simply need to understand the charge and agree on a procedure that will accomplish the charge. To establish the ground rules by which the group will function is also important.

When the group develops a set of procedures, or accepts those suggested by the convener, a decision has been made that strengthens the cohesiveness of the group. If the members of the group accept the need for the group to function, the purposes to be accomplished, and the procedures to be used in functioning, they are well on the way to thinking of the group as a unit, rather than as an assemblage of individuals. Similarly, when these tenets are agreed on, members are more likely to work together for the best interests of the group and to conform their interests to those of the group.

GROUP DECISION MAKING

Among the most commonly cited criticisms of group process is the fact that so much time is expended and so little is accomplished. Stated differently, an individual can usually be more productive in less time. Unfortunately, such a complaint is often valid and is a sad commentary on group leadership.

The process by which a group reaches a consensus largely approximates that of problem solving, or the more formally stated scientific method. Groups need to be helped to state the problem clearly, to gather and analyze data, to identify alternate actions, to select the most feasible solution that will alleviate the problem, and to recommend implementation strategies. Health educators can help groups accomplish these tasks in sequence.

Some problems are complex and can best be dealt with in parts. Dividing a complicated problem into components can often facilitate a group decision. Written summaries or diagrams can also facilitate discussion and comprehension of a problem and thus decision making. Use of handouts, a chalkboard, or an overhead transparency can greatly aid decision making. The ability to conceptualize, to generalize, and to summarize, either graphically or verbally, are important group skills.

Whenever possible, groups should avoid insisting that a decision be unanimous, although consensus is an important goal toward which to work. Again, an oral or written summary of the advantages and disadvantages of the various solutions may help to reduce the emotional element and increase the rational element of decision making.

Group decisions should not ordinarily be rushed or forced, but discussion should not continue indefinitely. Health educators should be sensitive to a readiness within a group to make decisions and should use the concepts discussed in this section to facilitate group decision making.

GROUP LEADERSHIP SKILLS

A variety of leadership roles are necessary for a group to function smoothly, but they need not all be performed by the same individual.

In fact, shared leadership is a goal that many groups strive toward and achieve in varying degrees. A democratically led group may take longer to be productive but tends to be more productive over time, and members feel a greater sense of satisfaction than when participating in an authoritarian led group.

Some of the needed leadership roles are implicit in earlier discussion. Groups often need help to reach agreement on their tasks and to establish a timetable for task completion, a process for approaching the task, and rules by which the group will function. These and other tasks that emerge need not all be facilitated by the same individual. One member may help to state the issues clearly, another may inquire about and clarify the timetable, and so on.

Groups do need facts to use in decision making. Some members should anticipate and supply the data that will be needed. A fact sheet, a resource person, and an inquiry or two before the meeting will all facilitate group decision making. An important group leadership role is to analyze the need for facts and arrange for them to be available when needed. If this skill is not used, a discussion may degenerate to a "pooling of ignorance."

Another leadership role is to guide the discussion toward decision making. If the group is a formal one, preparation of a written agenda will help members to see the complete list of topics to be addressed and the specific items on that list. An agenda is an important tool to use in large meetings, but it can be useful in small meetings as well.

Lacking a written agenda, a verbal summary or overview of the items to be addressed is helpful. Group members need a shared sense of direction or else the time required to reach decisions will increase.

Once agreement is reached, discussion needs to be confined to the topic under consideration. Someone may need to suggest something like, "We appear to have gotten away from the subject and should be discussing . . ."

Another often needed leadership role is that of ensuring that alternate points of view have been considered. If someone plays the "devil's advocate" and asks difficult questions, the quality of the decision will improve and the confidence level of the group will increase.

Yet another needed skill is the ability to draw out ideas from those who have difficulty expressing themselves. Paraphrasing and elaborating on answers may be necessary. Asking for other points of view or for thoughts from those who have not participated may draw some individuals into the discussion. Similarly, looking at people who have not participated may make it easier for them to enter the discussion. These techniques and others can also be used to cope with individuals who dominate a group.

The ability to deal with differences of opinions and power struggles that may exist is also part of the leadership role. Clarifying, summarizing, and consensus testing are all helpful ways of handling difficult situations. They are useful in conflict resolution and in other situations as well.

When group leadership roles are exerted as necessary, a sense of group consciousness emerges and interaction increases. Individual preferences tend to blend, and the ability of the group to act in a unified manner increases.

IN CONCLUSION

The ideas introduced in this chapter can be reduced to simpler, more useful terms by ordering them into checklist form, as presented in Exhibit 20-1. The checklist is intended to assist health educators to evaluate both the groups in which they participate and, by implication, their leadership roles. When used in a diagnostic fashion, such a checklist can be useful in deciding what group skills are needed in a particular group and what skills an individual needs to develop. Although the application of these skills will not solve the problems of all groups, it is an important step toward improving the quality of groups. Equally important is that health educators are expected to be able to use these techniques effectively.

Exhibit 20-1 Group Process Evaluation Form

Listed below are some characteristics of effective group behavior. Evaluate a group's behavior as well as your own behavior by using this checklist immediately after several group activities.
Rate whether members of the group did the following:

<u>Yes</u> <u>No</u> <u>Sometimes</u>

Yes	No	Sometimes	
—	—	—	Arranged the physical setting so as to be comfortable and so as to facilitate interaction
—	—	—	Clarified the purpose of the meeting and identified group goals
—	—	—	Helped initiate ideas and activities within the group
—	—	—	Solicited information and ideas from others
—	—	—	Called for alternate points of view
—	—	—	Helped others participate
—	—	—	Helped solve power and leadership struggles as they surfaced
—	—	—	Suggested procedures to help move the group toward a goal
—	—	—	Clarified and summarized issues
—	—	—	Helped the group reach consensus
—	—	—	Supported members of the group as needed
—	—	—	Helped to reconcile disagreement
—	—	—	Helped the group cope with tension
—	—	—	Expressed feedback honestly and openly
—	—	—	Received suggestions and disagreement without becoming defensive
—	—	—	Concluded discussion before members lost interest
—	—	—	Summarized the ideas expressed or the conclusion of the group
—	—	—	Gave positive recognition to the group for its accomplishment

204 COMMUNITY HEALTH EDUCATION

***

Suggested Learning Activities

1. Observe a community or agency meeting using the Group Process Evaluation Form (Exhibit 20-1).
2. Volunteer to lead groups whenever the opportunity presents itself so as to improve your skills.
3. Identify which aspects of group leadership you are good at and which you need to improve.

NOTE

1. *Webster's New Collegiate Dictionary* (Springfield, Mass.: G. & C. Merriam Co., 1981), 508.

SUGGESTED READING

Schopler, J.H., and Galinsky, M.J., eds. 1990. *Groups in Health Care Settings.* Binghamton, N.Y.: Haworth Press.

Chapter 21

Public Relations and Marketing

Most health educators need to master the skills associated with public relations and marketing. Those who are in the health field have had years of experience using public relations techniques. Conversely, discussions of marketing health programs have proliferated in recent years. Marketing is a more comprehensive approach to health promotion but incorporates much of public relations. In this chapter the focus is on both, beginning with public relations and evolving into a discussion of the broader, newer emphasis on marketing.

PUBLICIZING COMMUNITY HEALTH PROGRAMS

For a human service agency to receive news coverage of its demise and for many citizens not to know that the agency even existed is commonplace. For people to need health services and not know where to obtain them is also commonplace. These situations illustrate the need for a good public relations program. People need to know what services are available in order to use them. People need to become aware of a health practice before it can be adopted. Administrators and decision makers need to know about a program in order to support it financially. Visible programs are more likely to obtain participation and administrative support than are obscure ones.

To publicize a program and make it visible is, as are most tasks, more complex and difficult to achieve than would appear on first review. Good public relations is an enormously complex topic that is often treated simplistically. Yet even as it is complex, it is also extremely important. The presence or absence of public relations can make the difference between program survival and failure. It need not become an overwhelming task, however.

Many community health agencies cannot afford a press agent or a public relations director. Hospitals and state or national organizations are the major exceptions. The function can, however, be delegated to a staff member, provided that the person has the time and commitment to do it well. Most typically, the program is directed by an administrator or by a health educator who has had training in this area. Again, however, support and cooperation are required of all staff members. It is an appropriate task for a community health educator, but one that can and should involve all staff members. Health educators should at least master the basics.

There are public relations specialists who have emphasized public relations study in their college curricula. There are also many other self-trained specialists who have read the literature on the topic and have learned by doing. Health educators can do likewise. Dozens of courses and books are available for those who wish to improve their skills in this area, as well as dozens of pamphlets listing do's and don'ts for the uninitiated.

Why is good public relations so complex? Why is it so important? "The single purpose of public relations activity is to help the organization obtain and maintain a social climate in which it can prosper best. The organization exists only by public consent, and its existence is justified only in terms of its contribution to society as viewed by society."[1]

As indicated earlier, how people perceive an organization will have impact on how it is funded, as well as on whether they use its services. Such perceptions are based in part on the personal experiences people have had with an agency and on the experiences of their acquaintances. The perceptions are also affected by the availability of either accurate or inaccurate information. One principle seems to be true over time: "If correct information is not provided, misinformation will take its place."[2] Good publicity should, at minimum, provide accurate information about programs offered.

Another principle deserves attention early in this chapter: What we are speaks louder than what we say. Publicity will not produce lasting results unless the program being publicized is a quality one. Sheldon Coleman, principal owner of the Coleman Camping Equipment Company, said: "You've got to have your product right. If your product is bad, all your advertising does for you is more people find out you've got a lousy product."[3] That is obvious enough, yet it still needs emphasis for those who are looking for shortcuts. A good program must precede an effective public relations program.

The reverse side of this issue is a major focus of this section. Quality programs usually need quality public relations to survive. The world expects results. As one anonymous quote advises, "Don't tell them of your labor pains. Show them your baby!" This is in opposition to creating news for publicity value. Things done for publicity value often have little long-term impact, but programs with intrinsic worth can be turned into a newsworthy event by an astute public relations person. Stated succinctly, good public relations results from good performance publicly acknowledged and appreciated.

A good public relations program demands commitment from the chief administrator and from all levels of the staff. Inappropriate actions or lack of appropriate action from any staff member or volunteer can create negative attitudes toward the agency. These attitudes may remain unchanged and, worse yet, may spread through the rumor mills as fact. Good public relations must involve the entire organization and be consistently demanded by the administrator.

An effective public relations program demands that a single person coordinate it. The old adage, "What's everyone's business is no one's business," still applies. Someone must be held responsible and have time allocated in the job description to carry out the functions. Such coordinators must of necessity be program generalists. They must be acquainted with the programs of all divisions in order to be effective spokespersons for them and to work effectively with their staff.

Another point deserves emphasis. It is imperative that an agency speak with one voice. Even if a public relations committee exists, public stance should be agreed on before going to the media. Only one person should be authorized to contact the media, and inquiries should be referred to that person. Other staff members can go along to be interviewed or whatever, but the coordinator should be present. In order to coordinate a publicity program, the coordinator must know what other staff members are saying to the media.

An effective public relations program depends heavily on personal contact and a good working relationship with members of the media. Such a relationship develops most readily from frequent and consistent contact.

The major part of any good public relations program is an action plan. A common mistake that a busy administrator may make is to overlook this part of the process and just do whatever comes up. In so doing, the administrator loses control of the program and instead has to respond to whatever crisis arises. Failure to do a thorough job of preplanning means that many opportunities for effective public relations will be lost and that many efforts will be less effective than they could have been. A good public relations action plan should include at least the following elements:

1. *An identification and assessment of the "publics" that constitute target groups for the program.* Note the intentional use of the plural in publics and groups. To think of the public as a single group is overly simplistic and inadequate. An educational program must be group specific to have a maximum impact. The target group should be narrowly defined and as homogeneous as possible. Some assessment should be made of such factors as socioeconomic status, ethnic composition, sex ratio, and age composition. Some assessment should also be made of the group's attitudes toward and use of program services. Existing resistance should be analyzed as to cause. Some assessment of the power structure of the target group should be made. Opinion leaders and currently used channels of communication should be identified. Such preplanning will enhance the probability of an effective public relations program manyfold.

2. *An identification of the most effective senders and channels for each target group.* There is a great disparity in the credibility of senders from group to group.

Senders need to be selected with a great deal of care. Generally, they need to be credible with the target group before the message is sent or it is likely to be ignored. Effective opinion leaders are different for different target groups. Generally, opinion leaders are similar to the people they lead. They are usually of the same socioeconomic level and the same culture. The more powerful the opinion leader, the more effective he or she will be as a sender of an educational message.

The channel is likewise important. Messages should be fed into existing channels commonly used by the target group. For example, to reach mothers of the middle class, the health educator might have young children dictate radio spots in midmorning homemakers' programs, or mothers might have to be contacted at their places of employment. To reach mothers of low income, it is advisable to do telephone contact or door-to-door canvassing. (Low-income families benefit more from face-to-face communication than from mass media.)

3. *An identification of what specific messages are needed for each target group.* The message has to create awareness, interest, trial, and adoption of the recommended behavior. Research suggests that awareness and interest are achieved effectively by mass media, but the trial and adoption often require a personal touch. Group presentations can be effective and obviously suggest the importance of group dynamics. Dealing with resistance and barriers to action is best individualized as well.

Messages built around the beliefs model are more effective in producing desired behaviors than those that are not. The model suggests that the message should be verbally and visually designed to convince the intended target group members (a) that the condition will likely affect them, (b) that it will have serious consequences when it does, and (c) that the recommended action will reduce their susceptibility or the severity of the consequences. Even with such a carefully designed message, the model calls for individual attention to barriers to action and for triggers or cues designed to capitalize on the increased level of readiness.

4. *A calendar for a year-round public relations program.* Such a calendar helps ensure that each of the important target groups is reached, that each of the major programs is covered, that programs are timely, that opportunities for good public relations are not overlooked, and that there is ample time to do what needs to be done in order to have maximum impact. A file of ideas, clippings, and examples from other programs should be kept.

When planning a public relations schedule, be sure to plan for some repetition. Audiences tend to be like a parade, constantly moving by. Further, the level of readiness of individuals varies from time to time. Important messages must be repeated often.

5. *A procedure for dealing with adverse publicity.* Often little can be done except to grin and bear it, if the problem is minor. It is inadvisable for administrators not to be available to the press, since this implies guilt. To admit the shortcomings of an organization and promise to correct them may be best on occasion.

Keeping everything open expresses confidence in the programming of an agency and expresses goodwill toward the public.

If, indeed, a biased or inaccurate story has circulated, a judgment has to be made whether to reply or ask for a correction. If either of these routes is selected, the reply must be immediate to have the desired impact. Likewise, the reply must be accurate and above reproach. Overstating a case weakens an argument.

If a newspaper is consistently biased in its reporting of an agency, it may be helpful to select three to five of the top staff members or board members and go in a body to the editor to discuss the situation. A calm, reasonable approach is required, with supportive examples. Presentations must stick to facts that can be verified. Such a session requires advance arrangements and has a goal of urging the editor to seek the agency's point of view before going to press.

Once one person is appointed to coordinate public relations for your agency, and once an effective action plan is developed for the year, the public relations program should largely run itself. Considerable effort and attention to detail will still be required by all. A lot of attention must still be addressed to providing variety and to assessing the impact of the program, which leads into the planning for the next year's action plan. Above all, all phases of implementing a public relations program should involve personal contact with the media. Such an effort will result in a program that will please everyone involved. Periodic review and emphasis by the chief administrator in staff meetings should serve to remind each staff member of the program's importance.

A publicity plan and timetable is usually developed for each event to facilitate more detailed planning. A sample publicity timetable is presented in Exhibit 21-1.

PUBLIC RELATIONS AND MARKETING COMPARED

From the foregoing discussion one can see that public relations is a management tool. It reflects primarily the concerns of management and publicizes programs to potential consumers or to the public at large. Public relations is, first and foremost, concerned about images and works to improve people's opinions of programs or agencies. Marketing, on the other hand, is more concerned about programs and products than about opinions and works to determine what people want or need, rather than how people feel about a program, agency, or service. Both use data obtained from and about consumers but with differing emphases.

Both public relations and marketing emphasize programs being group specific, that is, developed for specific target groups, but for differing reasons. As was noted in the previous section, public relations specialists want to determine the best way to publicize a program to a particular group. Marketing people are more interested in determining what that market segment wants and needs and in developing such programs, rather than attempting to change people's opinions of existing programs.

Exhibit 21-1 Sample Publicity Timetable for Annual Glaucoma Clinic

---

1. One month before clinic
   a. Order posters at Buyer's Guide.
   b. Send article to senior citizens' newsletter.

2. Three weeks before clinic
   a. Send preliminary press release announcing clinic and describing glaucoma and clinic planning.
   b. Send reminder to all senior citizens' groups in area.

3. Two weeks before clinic
   a. Send out radio spots to WCEN and WBRN.
   b. Send suggested bulletin announcement to local churches.
   c. Distribute posters.
   d. Remind Buyer's Guide about ad space.

4. One week before clinic
   a. Contact newspaper photographer.
   b. Send second press release to media.

5. Day before clinic
   a. Remind photographer.
   b. Give reminder spots for the day of clinic to the radio.

6. Clinic day
   a. Put up signs at high school.
   b. Distribute glaucoma pamphlets.

7. Postclinic
   a. Get results to media.
   b. Send thank-you letters to all involved.
      (1) Possible letter to the editor
   c. Evaluate publicity.

Source: Reprinted with permission from *Public Health Education Workbook*, Central Michigan University Press, Mount Pleasant, Michigan.

Marketing emphasizes program planning and testing. In the health field it is often referred to as social marketing, inasmuch as it is social change that is being planned and implemented. Social marketing is a useful framework in which to approach health problems in society. It is a useful tool for those in health promotion. Students are encouraged to enroll in a social marketing or social psychology course and to do class projects on health-related topics. Marketing selects a market segment predisposed to use a program or product and then designs and tests a program specifically for that segment. It emphasizes development of needed programs that then tend to sell themselves.

Marketing health programs is a management tool, as is public relations. It works well in the business world and is being used successfully in health promotion programs. But differences exist between marketing a toothbrush and marketing sound dental health practices.

As Hochbaum noted, "if marketing increases sales of a product by 3 to 5 percent, the effort is considered successful."[4] Health education and health promotion programs are usually not cost effective at such levels of success. Marketing products is judged successful in terms of generating a small profit. However, the concept of profit is difficult to define or measure in health education. Health educators are usually asked to make lasting changes in people's behavior. Those who market good dental health must influence several decisions each day for a large number of people, whereas those who market toothbrushes need only to influence one or two such decisions each year. Health educators must reinforce the newly chosen behavior each day. It is also difficult to apply the principle of market segmentation to health education programs at times, because all people need good health practices. Moreover, primary target groups are often those who are least inclined to respond, rather than, as in the business world, those who are most likely to respond.

Thus the marketing model cannot be applied effectively to health education activities without some adaptation. However, the techniques can be used to improve program effectiveness. Prudent educators and administrators in the health field are applying such principles successfully. Indeed, one reason marketing is being emphasized in the health education field is that its principles coincide with recommended health education practices, albeit with differing labels and emphases.

APPLICATION OF MARKETING PRINCIPLES TO HEALTH EDUCATION

It is as difficult to reduce marketing to a few basic principles as it is to do so to public relations principles. Readers are encouraged to go beyond the simplifications and generalizations in this chapter and study the materials cited in the suggested reading.

A beginning principle is to determine the orientation of various consumer groups toward programs or products being considered for implementation and to select programs or groups for which a significant degree of success is probable. Although it is true that few health educators would intentionally design a program that they know will fail, it is also true that many health education programs have been doomed to failure from their conception because of lack of attention to this detail.

Although all people need good health practices to achieve optimum health, cost effectiveness demands that limited resources be used where they will have the most impact. Maximizing success is also important to staff morale. If audiences can be selected that are predisposed to act favorably, successful programming is more probable.

Part of the principle is inherent in the "teachable moment" concept. Sometimes the attention of individuals or groups is focused on a specific topic or issue. During an outbreak of measles may be a good time to emphasize immunizations in general, because people are already interested in communicable disease. While a person is hospitalized is usually a good time to promote general good health practices, such as weight control. Similarly, when a prominent figure has had surgery for breast cancer or has died of AIDS, interest in that topic is high, and then may be a good time to feature a breast self-examination clinic or provide AIDS education. An ideal time to introduce or expand programming is when the orientation toward the program is positive in a defined audience.

Implementing the principle of "presupposing consumer orientation" in health programming need not be difficult or expensive. In product marketing, a marketing study is done. Such studies consist of a survey of representatives of a defined audience in which interest is believed to exist. The studies can be contracted to marketing firms or can be done in-house. However, the principle can be applied without doing a formal study, and such is usually the case in health education.

The selection of potential audiences to study is made using whatever indicators of public interest exist. Such indicators include a request or demand for services, a problem to alleviate, and considerable interest in a current event. Although a single interest indicator might not warrant a program, a combination of factors may well suggest probable success.

As discussed in Chapter 16, "Using Community Organization Concepts," it is important to work closely with people in the defined audience to determine as accurately as possible what is wanted or needed. Educators make a significant distinction between wants and needs, but consumers tend to blur the boundaries between the two. The principle of presupposing community orientation suggests that more emphasis should be given to consumer wants. Community organization theory emphasizes this orientation, suggesting that the place to begin working with a community is at the point of its perceived need. This approach enhances the community's readiness to respond and helps develop a background that will increase the probability of success in later efforts. Such orientation has not always been emphasized by practicing health educators. The principle of presupposing market orientation brings the profession back to the principles of community organization.

Stated simply, if one finds out what a defined audience wants or needs and designs a program to meet those wants or needs, then the program has a high probability of succeeding. Focus groups are key marketing tools for defining audience needs and are discussed in Chapter 20. The probability of success is even higher if early emphasis is placed on consumer perception of wants and needs, rather than on provider perception of wants and needs. In evaluation designs, this type of information gathering is known as formative research. See Chapter 25 for more discussion on this topic.

Another principle of marketing is that of assessing the environment in which the program under consideration will be introduced. A major consideration in such an assessment is competition. If, for example, an agency is thinking about a weight control program, and determines that there is a predisposed audience, an important question then becomes, "Will such consumers use the proposed program, or one offered by an existing competitor?" Weight control can be pursued through a variety of options, including commercial firms, nonprofit organizations, and physicians. Doing a thorough analysis of the competition's strengths and weaknesses is as important as thoroughly analyzing the strengths and weaknesses of the proposed program. Among the factors that ought to be examined are cost, convenience, effectiveness, and prestige. An assessment needs to be made as to why participants will come to a program under consideration instead of to existing ones. If there are not enough good reasons, serious consideration ought to be given to not implementing the program, because it will probably not be cost effective, and effort and resources could be better expended on other programs. If there are enough good reasons, such reasons ought to be incorporated into the promotional activities.

Yet another principle of marketing is to develop a strategic plan for program implementation. Many good programs have been developed on paper but do not get implemented effectively because of poor strategic planning. Development of a marketing plan can help ensure that programs are implemented effectively.

A marketing plan should include, at minimum, a listing of primary and secondary audiences, the most cost-effective ways of reaching each of these audiences, the messages needed to motivate the desired behavior from each, a timetable, and a responsible person. Usually the timetable will have both short-term and long-term components. The short-term elements of the timetable will usually include a period of testing and revision of the program and product and a schedule for introducing continued promotion. The introduction of a new program or product usually involves more emphasis on publicity than does the continued promotion of the program. Long-term elements include reinforcement of earlier messages and testing to determine the extent that those messages are residual. Less effort is required to maintain one's position with respect to the competition than to increase one's percentage of the market.

A marketing plan usually contains an estimate of the costs of the marketing effort and the start-up costs of the program. Effective marketing requires a budget, which varies, depending on the intended emphasis. While free public service media is available, it is difficult to market a program effectively relying too heavily on such coverage. Although such elements may be an important part of a marketing plan, they often are inadequate to market a program to its potential.

The existence of a marketing plan builds accountability into programming and permits effective allocation of human and fiscal resources. But accountability goes further. Accountability requires evaluation. Evaluation of health programs is discussed in more detail in Chapter 25, which includes an evaluation of the planning process, the marketing plan, and the program being developed. A plan should be designed to determine if marketing had its desired impact.

IN CONCLUSION

Effective use of specific marketing techniques, such as media, is discussed in later chapters. This chapter is intended to present the overview and to stress the importance of a planned, orderly approach to program development and promotion. Such efforts will pay huge dividends.

***

Suggested Learning Activities

1. Develop a marketing plan for a new voluntary health agency program initiative.
2. Prepare an annual public relations plan for a local health department.

NOTES

1. R. Ross, *The Management of Public Relations* (New York: John Wiley & Sons, 1977), 9.

2. Ibid., 3.

3. *Detroit Free Press*, September 10, 1978.

4. G.M. Hochbaum, Application of Marketing Principles to Health Education (Paper presented at the workshop of the Texas Society for Public Health Education and the Texas Public Health Association, Austin, Texas, August , 1981).

SUGGESTED READING

Cutlip, S.M. 1990. *Effective public relations.* New York: Prentice Hall, Inc.

Keegan, G., et. al. 1992. *Marketing.* New York: Prentice Hall.

Mano, F.F., and Richard, K. 1985. *Social marketing: New imperative for public health.* Westport, Conn.: Praeger Publishers.

Peter, J.P., and Olson, J.C. 1992. *Consumer behavior in marketing strategy.* Homewood, Ill.: Irwin, Inc.

Chapter 22

Working with the Media To Achieve Maximum Impact

Current theorists are talking about "demassifying the media," narrowcasting versus broadcasting, and other related items. The intended result of such discussion is to make mass media more effective.

The media is becoming more special-interest oriented. The advent of journals that have a high interest level for a carefully defined segment of the population illustrates this phenomenon, as do cable television channels with a single emphasis. This trend will not eliminate mass media, however, or lessen its value. It is still important to reach the masses with information about health and health programs. The media most used will change periodically, and recommendations for effective use will change, but use of mass media to promote behavior change and to promote programs that will result in changes in health-related behaviors is gaining in importance, not lessening. As the population increases, the dollars for staffing decrease, and the technology improves, more mass media will be used.

Mass media has been used and misused in the past. As with computers, most problems are not the fault of the media but rather of those health educators placing materials in the media. The media is most effective in raising awareness and interest levels in a program. There are many kinds of mass media and an even larger variety of instructional media. In this chapter, emphasis is given to newspapers, radio, and television.

The effectiveness of mass media is directly a function of using it to do things it can do well. Careful matching of the media, the message, and the target group can result in significant impact. Careless use of the media can be a waste of both time and money. Criteria to consider when selecting a communication strategy to deliver a carefully prepared message to a specified target group are summarized in Table 22-1. How communication strategy is related to the stages of a simple behavior change model is shown in Table 22-2.

Media is not the only form of educational methodology. Other methods are discussed in other chapters. Table 22-3 illustrates the advantages and disadvantages of several methods when used in AIDS education.

Table 22–1 Selection Criteria When Deciding To Use Mass Media

Face-to-Face Communication	Mass Media Communication
1. When message is complex	1. When message is simple and factual
2. When behavior change is extensive	2. When change is close to present practice or directed to those already motivated to change
3. When target group has low educational levels	3. When target group has high educational levels
4. When long-term attitude and behavior change is desired	4. When desired decisions are short term

USING NEWSPAPERS EFFECTIVELY

Despite the widespread use of radio and television, people still read newspapers. They remain an important source of health information, and health educators need to be able to use them effectively. Some agencies and institutions employ public relations specialists who manage the contact with the press. In other health agencies part of the job description of a health educator is to prepare copy for the news media or to work with reporters who will prepare the copy.

In either case, a good personal working relationship with the press is important. Knowing what the reporters like and what format they prefer is helpful. It is also useful to know what deadlines are, on what days feature articles may be used, and what other options are available.

A common contact with the press is through a news release. By definition, a news release should be newsworthy. It should be current and pertain to local events or people. It is often the principal way an event or activity is promoted.

Table 22–2 Matching Communication with Simplified Behavior Change Strategy

Steps in Behavior Change	Preferred Communication Strategy
1. Create awareness of a health practice	1. Mass media methods
2. Stimulate interest in behavior change	2. Mass media methods
3. Evaluate behavior change	3. Face-to-face methods
4. Stimulate trial of new behavior	4. Face-to-face methods
5. Stimulate adoption of behavior change	5. Face-to-face methods
6. Reinforce behavior change	6. Mass media and face-to-face methods

Table 22–3 Selected Educational Methodologies for AIDS Education

Method	Target Group	Advantages	Disadvantages
Television/radio Public service announcements News coverage Feature presentations	All	Reaches the broadest segment of the target population; can direct audience to other sources of information; radio messages can reach more specific target groups.	Information may be insufficiently detailed for particular target groups.
Newspapers Feature stories News coverage Advertisements	All	Provides greater detail than radio or TV; newspapers that serve specific audiences permit targeted messages.	Does not reach as many persons in each group.
Posters Billboards Bus posters Public facilities	All	Can reach specific target populations; can direct audience to additional sources of information and complement other methodologies by reinforcing various messages.	Provides only limited amount of information.
Brochures/fliers Inserts in utility bills Health care facilities Workplace	All	Messages can be appropriately individualized, detailed, and graphic for each target group.	May be less effective for some target groups like prostitutes and IV drug abusers.
Newsletters/journals Organization newsletters AIDS update newsletter	Health workers Community leaders and risk populations	Messages can be individualized, detailed, and complex messages sent to segments of the public.	The longer the document, the less likely it is to be read.
Resource materials Guidelines Curriculum materials Reprints Resource directories	Health workers Community leaders	Provides technical information to specific target groups.	The longer the document, the less likely it is to be read.

continues

Table 22–3 continued

Method	Target Group	Advantages	Disadvantages
Presentations Community groups Health care facilities	General public Health workers Community leaders	Specific information tailored to the group addressed; can be interactive.	Labor intensive; primarily information transfer only.
Workshops Drug treatment centers Safer sex workshops	Increased risk groups Health workers	Provides detailed information and emphasizes skill development.	Labor intensive.
Outreach activities Bars Baths Bookstores Streets	Persons at increased risk, e.g., gay and bisexual men, IV drug abusers, prostitutes	One-on-one/peer group counseling to individuals at increased risk who are most difficult to reach through other means.	Very labor intensive.
Counseling and testing	Persons at increased risk	One-on-one counseling to individuals attempting to adopt or sustain positive health behaviors.	Very labor intensive.
Referral of sex and needle-sharing partners	Partners of those at increased risk due to sexual activity or IV drug use	Can offer counseling and testing for very high-risk people who have shared needles and syringes or who have had unsafe sex with an infected person and may not otherwise become aware of their risk status.	Very labor intensive.

Source: Reprinted from *Guidelines for AIDS Prevention Program Operations*, p. 12, U.S. Department of Health and Human Services, Public Health Service, Centers for Disease Control, 1987.

There is a standard structure and a standard format for a news release (Exhibit 22-1). Content is usually organized around the five *W*s: Who, What, Where, When, and Why. The story normally develops along the lines of an inverted pyramid; that is, as much information as possible is summarized in the opening paragraph. Subsequent paragraphs elaborate on lines in the lead paragraph, in order of their importance. Ideally, the first sentence should include the who, what, where, when, and why, or as much as possible. The second sentence elaborates on the most important part of the first sentence. The third sentence elaborates on the second most important part of the first sentence, and so forth, with the least important material coming last. This format allows readers to scan a page, get essential information, and read further if interested. Notably, it also permits editors to cut the story at any point to fit available space, while maintaining the appearance of a complete story.

Exhibit 22-1 Sample Press Release

Mount Pleasant Hospice Task Force
Carol Suhrland
110 East Maple
Mount Pleasant, Michigan 48858
(517) 773-7237

TO: CM Life   FOR IMMEDIATE RELEASE
FROM: Carol Suhrland
TOPIC: Mount Pleasant Hospice Task Force Meeting
DATE: APRIL 29, 1994

The third meeting of the Mount Pleasant Hospice Task Force is scheduled for Tuesday, May 25 at 7:00 P.M., in the activity room of the medical care facility. Topics to be discussed at the meeting are a needs assessment of Isabella County, development of a constitution, and methods of educating the community about a hospice program.

The hospice program will provide medical services for the patient, as well as emotional support for both the patient and family. The services will be available from professionals and supervised volunteers on a 24-hour, on-call basis.

The meeting is open to anyone interested in the development of a hospice program for Isabella County. This offers an opportunity for C.M.U. students to become involved in a community concern.

For further information, contact task force chairpersons Lois Rank (772-2957), Susan Wainstock (773-2205), or Bob White (773-5649).

Source: Reprinted with permission from *Public Health Education Workbook*, Central Michigan University Press, Mount Pleasant, Michigan.

A press release should be typed double spaced on 8-1/2 x 11-inch paper, on one side of the paper only, with wide margins. It should normally begin about a third of the way down the first page to allow editors room for insertion of a heading. The pages are numbered consecutively, with *more* or *end* or other appropriate symbols at the bottom of each page. The writer's name, agency, and phone number ordinarily appear in the upper left-hand corner of the first page, with the date of release appearing in the upper right-hand corner.

A general press release can be sent to all media, including newspapers, radio, and television. Consideration should be given to deadlines of the various media. Morning papers, evening papers, and weeklies all have different deadlines, as do radio and television stations. It is recommended that a current list of newspapers and radio and television stations be maintained, noting their mailing addresses, contact people, telephone numbers, and deadlines.

Reporters or editors often rewrite a news release to fit available space, to give a particular emphasis, or to fit a particular format. The newspaper is a profit-making venture, with profits being based largely on the number of readers. Reporters and editors are charged with deciding what people want to read, as well as with discharging public responsibilities. They may decide that a weight loss clinic should be publicized in a regular column called "Health Happenings" and rewrite copy to fit that format. Similarly, the first week in January the same release may be rewritten into a feature article emphasizing New Year's resolutions. This is not to suggest that news releases are never used as submitted but rather that they may be changed significantly. Those submitting news releases should be satisfied with getting accurate coverage, rather than let pride of authorship result in a distressful reaction.

Some reporters prefer to receive fact sheets listing the who, what, where, when, and why. An experienced reporter can quickly convert this information into an article of desired size, emphasis, and format. Many health educators who use this approach hand deliver the fact sheets to the appropriate reporters and orally stress specific aspects of the events. With releases to a single newspaper this is feasible, whereas with multiple releases personal contact is impractical.

Health educators often are given press releases from state and federal agencies and are encouraged to submit them to the local press. As mentioned earlier, they should be localized so as to be newsworthy to local readers. A release accompanying a national immunization campaign on childhood disease causing disability and death can be localized with statistics, case studies, and local programs. The material in such a release can be readily incorporated into a story with the lead paragraph on a new immunization program. Many federal and national agencies prepare comprehensive press kits for local and state agencies prior to major campaigns, which can be used as are press releases.

Reporters may be interested in doing a feature story or a photo essay for a weekend issue. A good working relationship, submission of ideas, and an offer to help if the story is used may result in better-than-hoped-for publicity.

Similarly, editors, in their editorials, take public stands on matters involving public welfare. They are usually looking for appropriate issues. Health programs are often of interest. An editor may be willing to write an editorial on "The Needless Danger of Childhood Disease" or "The Economy of Prevention" if supplied with appropriate material.

Many newspapers carry a "Letters to the Editor" column, which is one of the most widely read parts of the paper. Health educators can write letters. Getting a key person to write a letter to the editor about cancer screening may be the most effective publicity available.

HOLDING A PRESS CONFERENCE

Occasionally, a health educator is called on to plan and conduct a press conference. This press conference may be focused on some other person in the organization such as the health director. The press conference should provide some new and dynamic information about an important health issue.

When a conference is needed, the health educator should have a week or more of advance notice. The press conference should be held at a convenient place for everyone and at a time that most everyone is available to minimize the effect of "scooping."

A letter from the department should state the reason for the press conference, and when and where it will be held, and should include an invitation to participate. The letter should describe the overall subject of the conference and mention that questions will be answered.

The health educator should then develop a one- or two-page fact sheet that gives accurate statistical and descriptive information in order for reporters to develop their own story. This fact sheet should be available only at the press conference, not before. A sample fact sheet is displayed in Exhibit 22-2.

Next, the health educator should plan for light refreshments, such as coffee, tea, soft drinks, and cookies to be available in the room for the press conference.

An agenda should be developed for the press conference and may be made available with the fact sheet.

A question-and-answer session should have a time limit (approximately 20 minutes). The length may vary depending on the complexity of the subject. The conference, however, should be concluded immediately following the question-and-answer session.

There is no doubt that press conferences, when properly conducted, can give the public more complete and accurate information about a health issue or problem than they would otherwise get. Hasty or extemporaneous press conferences called without proper planning often do just the opposite. Misinformation is disseminated, making the press, the agency, and the individual look bad.

Exhibit 22-2 Sample Fact Sheet

Fact Sheet on Crack

Contact: M. R. Hutsinger   "Crack Will Crack You" Campaign
833-3145   McDonough County Health Department
                                             Macomb, Illinois
                                             September 1994

1. Last year, in the United States there were over 9,000 cocaine-related deaths. In Illinois, over 300 of the drug deaths were due to "crack." In McDonough County there were at least 40 drug-related medical emergencies, with three deaths being due to crack.

2. The Macomb Police Chief has examined the crime records for last year and estimates that the 9 percent increase in robberies was due to drug users needing money to pay for drugs, especially crack. He noted that in the five large drug raids and many drug arrests, cocaine and crack were the major drugs involved.

3. Crack is made in crack houses, which are places where cocaine hydrochloride is converted to a base state in a process that uses baking soda and water, as opposed to the volatile chemicals in "freebasing."

4. The Health Department is initiating a "Crack Will Crack You" campaign over the next few months and asking local service clubs such as Kiwanis, Rotary, Lions, and the Jaycees to sponsor educational programs throughout the community and to help in a communitywide effort to save the community from this menace.

5. The Health Department is also asking the media and the schools to help with this program by presenting programs and information to the public.

RADIO AND TELEVISION CONTACTS

As noted earlier, press releases can and often should be sent to radio and television stations as well as to newspapers. Health topics and programs are usually of interest to listeners and viewers and may be included in newscasts or on community-calendar–type shows. Similarly, some radio and television personalities take public stands on local issues. As with newspaper editorials, submitting a suggestion with backup material may be an easy, yet effective, way to get exposure.

The most common format used by health educators when working with radio and television is the public service announcement (PSA). PSAs are part of the American way of life. "Next to the doctor or clinic where treatment is received, television PSAs are . . . the most important source of health information."[1] This is partly in response to their widespread usage and partly because they can combine sight, sound, motion, and color to maximize impact. PSAs are usually aired without charge because they are in the public interest and because the Federal Communications Commission considers a station's public service performance when deciding whether to renew its license. Equally as important, radio and television stations compete for listeners and viewers and endeavor to provide what people want. Many stations thrive on emphasizing local events and stories. These factors, combined with altruism, result in much free air time being available for PSAs.

Several options are available to health care professionals seeking air time. One is to submit a fact sheet suggesting or requesting preparation of a PSA. Another is to prepare and submit a series of spot announcements that are either original or localized versions of those distributed through a state or national campaign. In either instance a standard format is recommended, as are other guidelines to use in preparation.

PSAs generally rely on an emotional appeal for action. A dramatic opening is especially important in order to get the attention of listeners and viewers. Those preparing PSAs would be well advised to analyze the attention-getting techniques used in a dozen professionally prepared PSAs. Typically, there will be appeals to self-preservation, love of family, patriotism, and loyalty. Appropriate popular music may be used, as may easily recognized voices. A cliché may be turned around into a play on words, or impressive statistics can be used to get attention. Still others call for action, such as dialing a toll-free number for more information.

Regardless of the attention-getting device that is used, it must be successful if a PSA is to reach its audience. The spots between regular programming are times when many people do something else. A PSA must get their attention and hold it for the duration. Suggestions for developing messages for PSAs are presented in Exhibit 22-3.

Exhibit 22-3 Message Development Guidelines

Keep messages short and simple, just one or two key points.

Repeat the subject as many times as possible.

Superimpose your main point on the screen to reinforce the verbal message.

Recommend performing specific behaviors.

Demonstrate the health problem, behavior, or skills (if appropriate).

Provide new, accurate, and complete information.

Use a slogan or theme.

Be sure that the message presenter is seen as a credible source of information, whether authority figure, target audience member, or celebrity.

Use only a few characters.

Select a testimonial, demonstration, or slice-of-life format.

Present the facts in a straightforward manner.

Use positive rather than negative appeals.

Use humor, if appropriate, but pretest to be sure it does not offend the intended audience.

Be sure the message is relevant to the target audience.

Source: Reprinted from *Making PSA's Work: A Handbook for Health Communication Professionals*, p. 22, National Institutes of Health, 1983.

PSAs are usually 10, 15, 20, 30, 45, or 60 seconds long, with most lasting 30 seconds or less. This suggests that, for maximum effectiveness, the content must be group specific and must be prepared carefully so as to achieve a single behavioral objective. Precise timing is important in the broadcast industry, so music that fades in and out is commonly used to achieve the desired precision. Also, it is good practice to submit several PSAs of varying length, so that they can be selected to fit the time available.

PSAs are submitted in written form, unless recorded PSAs are available as part of a state or national campaign. In the latter situation, localizing a lead or a tail may be all the preparation that is necessary. Professionally prepared PSAs usually include an audience analysis, a behavioral objective, message testing, and an evaluation of the impact. Health educators must often, of necessity, settle for less. Usually an identification and description of intended target groups and developed behavioral objective is minimal. Knowing who is to be reached is critical to the selection of attention-getting content; knowing what behavior is desired is important in selecting content for the balance of the message.

PSAs are typed on 8-1/2 x 11-inch bond paper. Copy to be read is double spaced and typed in all capital letters. Descriptive or identifying materials are usually single spaced and are capitalized according to standard practice (Exhibit 22-4).

Exhibit 22-4 Sample Radio Spot

Northern Michigan Local Health Departments
Public Service Announcements
:30

WATCH YOUR CHILD AS HE READS. DOES HE SQUINT OR HOLD THE BOOK TOO CLOSE? PERHAPS HE NEEDS HIS VISION TESTED. BEFORE ENTERING SCHOOL, ALL PRESCHOOLERS ARE REQUIRED TO TAKE A VISION TEST. USING TRAINED VISION TECHNICIANS, YOUR HEALTH DEPARTMENT OFFERS A SCREENING PROGRAM FOR ALL AREA SCHOOLCHILDREN. FOR FURTHER INFORMATION, CALL YOUR LOCAL HEALTH DEPARTMENT.

:10

YOUR HEALTH DEPARTMENT OFFERS A VISION SCREENING PROGRAM FOR ALL AREA SCHOOLCHILDREN. FOR FURTHER INFORMATION ABOUT VISION PROBLEMS, CONTACT YOUR LOCAL HEALTH DEPARTMENT.

Source: Reprinted with permission from *Public Health Education Workbook,* Central Michigan University Press, Mount Pleasant, Michigan.

Scripts for television PSAs are usually done in two columns, with the graphics identified in the left column opposite the script to be read. The script is typed in capital letters. An X in parentheses is inserted to indicate when the graphic is to be changed. Illustrative material is most commonly in the form of slides, 16-mm film, or videotape. Slides are often preferred over videotapes because titles or printed captions can be readily used to reinforce oral messages and they can also be easily interchanged (Exhibit 22-5).

Exhibit 22-5 Sample Television Spot

Michigan Hospice Organization
205 West Saginaw St.
Lansing, Michigan 48933
(517) 485-4770
Public Service Announcement
:30

SLIDE 1: Person sitting alone in room with head in hands	ACCEPTING THE REALITY OF A TER-MINAL ILLNESS IS VERY PAINFUL, BUT THAT SITUATION NEED NOT BE FACED ALONE. (X)
SLIDE 2: Volunteer talking with patient	HOSPICE HAS THE ANSWER. THEIR PROGRAMS PROVIDE COMPREHEN-SIVE CARE THROUGH EMOTIONAL SUPPORT AS WELL AS MEDICAL SU-PERVISION. (X)
SLIDE 3: Patient and family talking with nurse	TO ALL CONCERNED, HOSPICE OF-FERS A LIFE-ORIENTED ALTERNA-TIVE. (X)
SLIDE 4: Address and phone number of Michigan Hospice Organization	FOR FURTHER INFORMATION, CON-TACT THE MICHIGAN HOSPICE ORGAN-IZATION, OR A HOSPICE PROGRAM IN YOUR AREA. (X)

Source: Reprinted with permission from *Public Health Education Workbook,* Central Michigan University Press, Mount Pleasant, Michigan.

A PSA may be useful in promoting an event in a given locality. It has the potential of raising the levels of awareness and interest in the event. If the PSA is played on a station that the members of the target group listen to or watch at a time when they tune in, and if the lead catches the attention of the intended audience, people may become interested enough in a screening event to participate, or to urge someone else to attend. There are enough variables in the preceding scenarios, however, to imply that too much relevance can be placed on this means of reaching the public. As indicated earlier, the media can be misused. This is done by applying undue relevance to poorly prepared material placed in media that the intended audience seldom uses. This syndrome can evolve into "blaming the victims" because they did not respond.

A more appropriate use of PSAs is to develop a campaign. Federal and state agencies have used several health promotion programs in which PSAs are an important, but not the sole, part of the health information campaign. Such a campaign involves identifying a target audience, establishing campaign objectives, selecting stations to be used, developing and testing messages, and assessing the effectiveness (Exhibit 22-6).

Exhibit 22-6 Outline of PSA Campaign Plan

PSA Campaign Plan Outline

I. The communication strategy statement
   A. Statement of the problem
   B. Statement of the information needs and perceptions of large audiences
   C. Campaign objectives
   D. Target audiences (primary and secondary)
   E. Communication strategies

II. Anticipated outcomes or effects of the campaign

III. Rationale and description of message and media selection decisions

IV. Plan for developing and pretesting campaign messages

V. Charts listing the media outlets to be sent campaign messages, the message formats and lengths to be delivered to each station, and the due dates for sending campaign messages

VI. Plan for coordinating the campaign with other agencies

VII. Plan for evaluating the campaign

VII. Budget and personnel requirements

IX. Monthly schedule of activities listed by task and personnel responsible for implementation

Source: Reprinted from *Making PSA's Work: A Handbook for Health Communication Professionals,* p. 16, National Institutes of Health, 1983.

TALK SHOWS

Radio and television have numerous talk shows during which hosts interview interesting guests. Health service professionals are usually interesting guests, with topics of current interest. Inquiries or suggestions often result in health educators or other staff members being invited to be guests on such shows.

Preparation is the key to a successful interview. The host and guest usually discuss content before the interview. A rough outline of the topic or a list of the key issues or main points can make the interview easy and enjoyable for participants and the audience. Particular attention should be paid to the final question. Backtiming is common in the broadcast industry and allows the discussion to progress to the point where there is just enough time remaining to answer the final question.

The host is responsible for an opening and closing statement and for asking leading questions in such a manner as to keep the discussion moving. Other participants should be prepared to present a point of view on the issues and respond to related questions. Material should be familiar enough so that notes are not necessary, except perhaps for statistics or quotations.

Guests should speak clearly and not too fast. Most people talk faster when they are nervous, so for the first several interviews it is wise to remember to slow down. Participants also commonly allow their voices to trail off at the ends of sentences rather than projecting them somewhat.

Generally, a talk show is most effective when the guest is relaxed and actually enjoying the experience. Memorizing responses is usually counterproductive because the guest usually forgets the response under duress. However, interviews can be rehearsed before going to the studio to the point where the interviewee is relaxed and can talk conversationally about the topic under consideration. If either party stumbles over a word or draws a blank during the interview, it is best to smile and go on as if off the air.

If the interview is being televised, it is also necessary for participants to appear relaxed. Arriving early so as to become familiar with the setting and the people is important. Last-minute arrivals are often disastrous. Smiling is the part of one's appearance that is noticed first. Good posture is especially critical, in that television tends to magnify poor posture.

Eye contact with other participants increases the effectiveness of a show and helps the participants to look natural. If a guest is making an extended statement, it is appropriate for him or her to look directly at the live camera, but usually this is not necessary. When in doubt, eye contact as used in normal conversation is the best alternative.

Another pitfall to avoid is looking down. If guests are seated, the camera is usually above them. This line of vision sometimes gives guests the appearance of having their eyes closed. This is another reason guests should not use notes, because they may appear to be asleep while on camera.

Guests may bring graphics with them to refer to as appropriate. Studio person- nel are accustomed to handling visuals and usually prefer it because television is, first and foremost, a visual medium. Slides are commonly used for this purpose. Lists of points to be made, graphs, addresses, telephone numbers, logos, and so on, can all be readily injected into an interview by advance preparation of appro- priate slides. Material pertaining to the topic can also be mounted on posterboard. Graphics should be the same size (9 x 14-inches is recommended) and should have a wide border and good color contrast.

A floor manager will give time signals to the host, so a guest should follow the host's lead and be prepared to condense or extend a comment to fit the time available.

Video News Releases and Sound Bites

Relatively new formats being used with media are video news releases and sound bites. Use of these formats can increase the frequency of radio and televi- sion coverage. Because they are so simple to use, and because they increase results, health educators should use them.

Both radio and television stations have limited news teams, and they frequently send teams only to cover the big news stories. However, astute agencies can send prepared videotaped or audiotaped messages along with a press release. If stations can easily "dub in" a 30-second, 60-second, or 90-second quote from a local expert on a topic that is currently newsworthy, they are more likely to provide air time than they are if they receive only a news release.

The sound bite format is easy to set up; a cassette tape recorder is all that is needed. The news release is written, and where quotes appear, a taped quote is submitted to supplement the written quote. This makes the news team appear to have been in the field gathering news, rather than simply using material brought to them by others.

The video news release uses essentially the same format, except a videotape camera (or camcorder) is used with a tripod, and the quotes are used on television. (They can be done in studios, of course, but can also be done effectively in the field.) Because it is a visual media, thought should be given to where the taping should occur. Beside a local landmark, near a hospital, in front of a display of cig- arettes, or next to a nurse immunizing a child are examples of backgrounds or set- tings that might be effective.

IN CONCLUSION

Using the media is a superb way to reach a large number of people with an economy of scale not attainable elsewhere. This communication method can be surprisingly effective when used properly or spectacularly ineffective when used improperly.

Media skills are assumed as a condition of employment. Although the basics have been presented in this chapter, readers should remember that real skill comes only through practice. Media skills are used in varying degrees of frequency, depending on the setting, but proficiency is assumed of all who bear the title of health educator.

***

Suggested Learning Activities

1. Visit a local newspaper or radio or television station.
2. Examine current health stories as to authorship, style, accuracy, impact, and so on.
3. Explore how a "satellite-produced" paper, such as *U.S.A. Today*, is produced and marketed.
4. Prepare 10-, 30-, and 60-second PSAs on a current community health program or problem.
5. Prepare and conduct a simulated TV interview using videotape equipment.

NOTE

1. *Making PSA's Work: A Handbook for Health Communication Professionals* (Bethesda, Md.: National Institutes of Health, 1983), 1.

SUGGESTED READING

Backer, T.E. 1992. *Mass media health campaigns: What works.* Newbury Park, Calif.: Sage Publications, Inc.

Wallack, L., et al. 1992. *Media advocacy and public health.* Newbury Park, Calif.: Sage Publications, Inc.

Ward, K. 1989. *Mass communication in the modern world.* Belmont, Calif.: Wadsworth Publishing Co.

Using Educational Media

Media used in educational settings is called by a variety of names, including educational media, instructional media, and audiovisual resources. The term *media* refers to both the equipment, or hardware, and the materials, or software, that are played in or on a piece of equipment.

Educational media has long been an important tool of educational specialists, as they have discovered, through experience, that learning is accomplished more effectively and efficiently through proper presentation of appropriate media.

A primary reason media is more effective is that it uses multisensory learning. When several senses are used concurrently, learning is usually enhanced. Thus, for example, a lecture that relies heavily on the sense of hearing may be effective but an illustrated lecture is more effective because learning can occur concurrently with what is heard and seen. In general the more senses that can be involved at once, the more effective and efficient the learning is going to be. Multimedia presentations are one way of using multisensory theory.

The other major reason media enhances learning is that it is capable of providing concrete examples of abstract concepts that are being presented verbally. Although demonstration and supervised personal experience are most effective, they cannot readily be provided for large numbers of people in different locations. These concrete examples can, however, be shown in a realistic setting while functioning, if appropriate. Functioning can be shown at actual speed, or it can be compressed or expanded, magnified or reduced, and so on.

Health educators should be able to use media effectively when appropriate. Competence comes through actual practice, but in this chapter, factors affecting successful usage are discussed.

WHEN IS USE OF MEDIA APPROPRIATE?

To state the obvious, media should be used to enhance learning. Media can be either the principal means of instruction or the integral part of instruction but should not be used as a substitute for teaching.

The use of media is appropriate when learners prefer it. Many people learn a great deal from viewing television for thousands of hours and prefer videotapes to printed material.

Media can also be used when the material being presented is complex or abstract and needs examples. A visual component will facilitate understanding, as, for example, when color or motion can illustrate the functioning of the pulmonary system.

Media can be helpful when self-paced learning is desirable. With the right equipment, information can be repeated as slowly or as often as necessary.

Sometimes people need to learn at different times and places. The logistics of many health care settings may make it impossible for all employees to hear a particular lecture at the time it is given, but they can view a videotape of the lecture.

The use of media is appropriate when standard content is needed. The essentials can be transmitted by videotape, with the assurance that all viewers were exposed to the same material. When people present information they often get sidetracked, and some material does not get covered.

Finally, media provides variety. Repetition is a basic law of learning. Using a media production can be an effective way to review material in a different format.

Effective media usage requires advance systematic planning. As suggested in the previous paragraphs, such usage should include an audience analysis and an analysis of the learning objective. It should include an analysis of both the material to be presented and the relevant media available. It should include an analysis of the logistics, such as room and audience size, seating arrangement, room-darkening capability, and electrical outlet availability.

It should include thorough previewing of material to determine its appropriateness. Appropriateness involves consideration of content level and general relevance of the material. Material might be appropriate in content and level but focus on urban rather than rural settings, or white populations rather than ethnic groups.

Additionally, effective media usage should include developing familiarity with the equipment so that minor repairs can be made if needed, with spare bulbs and extension cords readily available.

The material should be introduced adequately. Viewers need to be instructed on what to look for, what they will be seeing, and what is important. Planning needs to occur for some form of follow-up discussion. Clients should be encouraged to ask questions, which should be addressed as openly as possible. Key questions should be posed by the educator to ascertain if the viewers learned major concepts. Questions can be posed in a variety of ways to stimulate discussion or to see if clients can apply material to home-life settings.

VIDEOTAPES AND VIDEODISCS

When most people think of media they think of motion pictures or their subsequent formats, videotapes or videodiscs. Tapes and discs are especially appropriate for portraying real-life action. Because of this, they can be used to help change attitudes and to demonstrate desirable values. They are among the most effective ways of working with feelings, emotions, or other aspects of the affective domain.

The other special use of videotapes and discs is animation. Animation is the recording of a number of drawings that when projected are viewed as motion. Animation is useful for showing how equipment or organs work. As mentioned earlier, the material can be enlarged so that all in a large group can see it.

Tapes and discs are available in hundreds of titles and in high-quality sound and color. They can be purchased for multiple showings or rented for periodic use. Careful selection of all media is important. A form to assist in evaluating media is presented in Exhibit 23-1.

Exhibit 23-1 Worksheet Evaluating Audiovisual Aids

Title _____

Subject _____ Date _____

Publisher _____

Purchase Price _____ Rental _____

Type of Media

___ videodisc

___ 35mm slides

___ videotape

___ audiotape

___ slide tape program

___ transparencies

___ other

___ Color ___Sound ____Time

Purpose or theme_____

For what group is this material most appropriate? (Check all that apply.)

___ Men ___ Women ___ Pediatric ___Geriatric

Specific cultural groups_____

Specific occupational groups_____

A   B   C   D   Appeal: Does it get and hold attention?

A   B   C   D   Physical properties: Photography and sound?

A   B   C . D   Accuracy: Accurate, up-to-date?

A   B   C   D   Approach: Does it agree with approach used locally?

A   B   C   D   Organization: Logical, easy to follow?

A   B   C   D   Completeness: Sufficient detail; too much detail?

Strengths:

Weaknesses:

Recommendation:

Signed: _____

Date: _____

Source: Reprinted from *Hospital Health Education: A Guide to Program Development* by D.J. Breckon, p. 111, Aspen Publishers, Inc., © 1982.

With videotaping equipment becoming easier to use, health educators can realistically undertake a project to write a script and film it. Special lighting is not needed and sound can be included, with the final product being in color. This is especially appropriate for materials where local facilities or personnel are needed, such as a tour of the hospital for children.

Videocassette recorders make it feasible to tape and store for later use programs prepared for and shown on television. Although this is a common practice, the copyright laws governing such matters are an ongoing topic of discussion.

SLIDES AND TRANSPARENCIES

Slides are a commonly used "still projection" and are effective in a wide variety of situations. Health educators should be able to both produce and use slides and will usually encounter many opportunities to do so.

Slides are available commercially in 2 x 2-inch frames or can be readily produced with ordinary cameras and film. They are relatively inexpensive, especially when self-produced, and can be of locally used facilities, equipment, or personnel. Producing slides to go along with the presentation being prepared can be extremely satisfying and educationally sound.

Slides are easy to store and retrieve in trays. They can be selected for specific presentations in any sequence and can be changed or updated easily.

Slide presentations are equally appropriate for individuals, for small groups, or for large groups. Slide projectors are easy to operate and seldom need maintenance. They are portable and can be programmed with tapes into a slide-tape program.

Transparencies are commonly used with overhead projectors. The overhead projector is so named because it projects a picture over and above the head of the presenter, who faces the audience while the image is projected on the screen behind. It can be used to list major points so as to add structure, clarity, and interest to a lecture presentation.

The transparency is typically an 8 x 10-inch piece of acetate or similar material. The presenter can either write on it as if using a chalkboard or prepare it beforehand, using felt-tip pens or other special marking pens or pencils.

Transparencies are available commercially and accompany many educational programs. However, they are so easy to prepare that the majority of those used are prepared by presenters. Major points of a presentation can be typed on white paper with large primary type. They can then be converted into a transparency by simply running them through a copier. Charts, diagrams, graphs, and so on, can be photocopied from a book or journal or generated via desktop publishing and converted quickly and easily into a transparency. Many transparencies are also available commercially from health education materials companies.

Transparencies are inexpensive to prepare and enable the presenter to face the audience. They can be used in a normally lighted room. They are well suited for group presentations. They can be used as overlays, for example, with the first one showing the outline of the body, the second one showing the heart and lungs, a third showing arteries, and a fourth showing veins.

The "reveal technique" is often used with transparencies, so that material being presented can be progressively disclosed. This involves placing a piece of paper or cardboard over the material not to be shown, rather than presenting all the material at once and allowing audiences to race ahead. Also, the presenter can highlight whatever is being projected by turning the machine on and off when changing projectuals. The bright light suddenly on the screen is a good attention getter.

There are other methods in which still pictures can be used, including flip charts and posters. However, slides and transparencies are the most effective and easiest to use and are among the most common forms of educational media.

POSTERS, DISPLAYS, AND BULLETIN BOARDS

Posters, displays, and bulletin boards must be eye-catching to be effective. They are usually used in traffic flow areas and must get the attention of those passing by. This is the most important factor to consider in designing such items.

Planning begins with the target group, those passing by who need a health education message. An analysis of their needs and interests usually pays dividends in effectiveness. As with public service announcements, these materials can use eye-catching illustrations, color combination, clichés, a play on words, well-known personalities or cartoon characters, words to popular music, or other such techniques to cause those passing by to look for 10 or 15 seconds. The material should be personalized to the extent that it says, "This concerns you."

For a visual aid to be effective, it must have a single theme or topic. A specific behavioral objective should be prepared, delineating the desired behavior change. Planners must have clearly in mind what they want the viewer to know, feel, or do in order to get the desired response after only a 10- or 15-second exposure.

Posters, displays, and bulletin boards should have a center of interest that the eye is attracted toward. It may be the largest element, the most irregular, the most contrasting, or the nearest to the margin. This center of interest should be selected carefully.

There should be a normal flow of elements so that the viewer's eye follows from one element to another in proper sequence. This movement can be pre-planned so that arrangement of material contributes to effectiveness.

It is important to keep the visual simple and use only those elements that are necessary. Small items may be grouped so as to reduce their apparent numbers. Lettering and spacing should be used so as to promote clarity. The viewer should be able to comprehend the message at a glance.

Grouping of elements and other techniques should be used as necessary to provide a sense of unity. Elements can be tied together with lines or a superimposed design to minimize the impression of a group of disparate parts.

Similarly, a sense of balance is necessary. Items can be arranged so that they are compensated in size and color, from one side to the other and from top to bottom. This is not to be confused with symmetry. The center of interest is not usually dead center, so symmetry is not planned, but balance can and should be. For example, a group of small items on one side of a display might balance a large item on the other side.

Colors, backgrounds, and accessories that are seasonal or otherwise appropriate are effective in creating a pleasing and attractive appearance. Colors should have sufficient contrast and intensity to be readily visible. Color combinations most easily read at a distance are dark blue on white, black on yellow, white on red, green on white, and yellow on black. It is also useful to know that red, orange, and yellow attract, stimulate, and excite, whereas white, green, blue, and purple tend to be soothing, cool, and restful. Light colors appear to increase the size of objects; dark colors appear to decrease an object's size.

Although emphasis in this section has been on preparation of posters, displays, and bulletin boards, commercially prepared posters can be purchased or occasionally obtained free of charge. In such circumstances it is necessary to consider the appropriateness of the materials for the audience, using many of the same considerations as are used in construction. Checklists are presented in Exhibits 23-2 and 23-3 to assist in this analysis.

NEW FORMS OF EDUCATIONAL TECHNOLOGY

Educational technology changes from time to time, with many changes being improvements on old standbys. As in other arenas, microcomputer technology has been involved.

Software programs can quickly produce charts, graphs, and other training visuals. Copy machines have evolved into electronic imaging and allow all kinds of options of size, place, color, and dimension not previously possible.

The overhead projector is still basic, but custom-made transparency visuals are possible and often expected. Several companies make user-friendly products and equipment to make such visuals. Computers allow composition on a screen and then can have the graphic printed on a transparency for a group to view or on paper to be inserted into a report or as its cover. Improvements exist, however, when, instead of a transparency, pages are stored on computer disks. A portable unit can plug into any television, to display the charts stored on the disk at the presenter's cue, in full color. Of course, pointers have also improved. Most notably, hand-held laser pointers can project a colored arrow to help focus attention to items of concern.

Similarly, videotapes represent dramatic improvements over films, and new videorecorders make promotional videotapes feasible. A health educator can now

Exhibit 23-2 Worksheet Evaluating Posters and Charts

Title _____

Publisher _____

Cost_____ Approximate size_____ Language _____

Purpose or theme_____

For what group is this material most appropriate? (Check all that apply.)

   ___ Men ___ Women ___ Pediatric ___Geriatric

  Specific cultural groups_____

  Specific occupational groups_____

A   B   C   D   Appeal: Does it get attention quickly; hold attention?

A   B   C   D   Physical properties: Artwork, lettering, color, etc.

A   B   C   D   Accuracy: Accurate and contemporary?

A   B   C   D   Balance: Not symmetrical, but size and color is compensated for.

A   B   C   D   Movement: Center of interest not centered; flows in sequence.

A   B   C   D   Unity: Close together or tied together so as to appear a whole.

A   B   C   D   Simplicity: Only necessary elements; small elements grouped so as to reduce their apparent number.

A   B   C   D   Clarity: Good lettering, enough contrast; understood at a glance.

A   B   C   D   Color intensity: Attention-getting colors are yellow, orange, red, green, blue, indigo, violet. Colors read most easily at a distance are dark blue on white, black on yellow, white on red, green on white, blue on white.

A   B   C   D   Color appropriateness: Red, orange, and yellow attract and excite; green, blue, and purple are soothing, cool, and restful; light colors appear to increase the size of objects while dark colors appear to decrease size. Blue, green, and red are the most generally preferred colors.

Strengths:

Weaknesses:

Recommendation:

Signed: _____

Date: _____

Source: Reprinted from *Hospital Health Education: A Guide to Program Development* by D.J. Breckon, p. 110, Aspen Publishers, Inc., © 1982.

reasonably be expected to develop a script and do some of the camera work, although professional help in editing and captions will be required for the novice.

The cassette format of videotapes and the widespread ownership of videocassette recorders/players (VCRs) make possible in-home viewing by the client and family. (Portable VCRs can be loaned to people who do not own one.) The inexpensive nature of the tapes makes multiple copies feasible and minimizes the need to assemble people in larger groups to view the film. (Agency or community videotape libraries can handle the paperwork associated with a loan program.) Videotapes also can be sold to interested clients.

Equipment is available for in-office use that allows printing an image from a videotape or a computer. For example, a family planning client could view a

Exhibit 23-3 Evaluation of Exhibits

Conference_____
Sponsor _____
Address _____
_____
Contact Person_____
Phone No. (   )_____

A   B   C   D   Is it physically possible to read the exhibit from the point of observation?
A   B   C   D   Will all graphs, charts, and diagrams be understood by the intended audience?
                Has the use of statistical presentations been kept to a minimum?
A   B   C   D   Are the vocabulary and style of writing such that the intended audience can
                comfortably follow and understand the exhibit?
A   B   C   D   Does the exhibit sustain interest long enough to be read completely?
A   B   C   D   Does the exhibit employ supplementary items (qualified attendant present, visual
                aids used, visitor-operated devices used and contributing to exhibit,
                literature supporting the exhibit objectives)?
A   B   C   D   Does the exhibit impart the desired message?
A   B   C   D   Does the exhibit tie in with the visitors' interests?
A   B   C   D   Does the exhibit offer visitors a chance to participate in satisfying a personal
                purpose?

Strengths:_____
Weaknesses: _____
Recommendation: _____
                            Signed: _____
                            Date:_____

videotape that was stopped for discussion. A diagram on the screen could be printed and given to the client as a handout.

Similarly, items on a computer screen can be projected to a large screen for all of the audience in a large auditorium to see. Moreover, equipment exists that has capability for split-screen windows that permit side-by-side comparisons, as well as random access to the screens on file.

A major advance that is expected to dominate the market in future years is that of video laser discs, videodiscs and the closely related optical discs, that provide high-quality images, of real-life quality. They use hard rather than floppy disks and are recorded and read with low-power laser beams.

Videodiscs can use real-life photography, still photography or other print media in any combination. Animation and real-life photography can be blended. Illustrations can be live action, or clearer than live action. Graphics can be multicolored, multishaded, and multidimensional, in varying degrees of brightness, and can be slowed down, frozen, or repeated for critical analysis.[1]

Videodiscs use similar technology to that of microcomputers. When linked together, they are referred to as interactive videodiscs. Videodiscs have random-access features, which allow any frame to be displayed instantly. (Videotapes need to be reversed or fast forwarded to sequentially go through the frames until the right one is reached.) Microcomputers are interactive, too, meaning the learner interacts with the microcomputer and the software and the screen instantly displays whatever the learner requests.

> Imagine a program on alcohol with live subjects. Users can choose various levels of intoxication and see actual people in a variety of roles under these circumstances. Similarly, consider a family planning program in which the female reproductive system is diagrammed. Microphotography then could be used to show the ovulation process. Other segments could allow the user to choose between the forms of contraception. Assuming that the student selected abortion, the menu could be presented allowing a choice of a simple illustration with diagrams or actual procedures. Similarly, students could opt for discussion by clients who had abortions as to their feelings and experiences in the months following this procedure.[2]

Interactive videodiscs are still in their infancy, but their use seems to be increasing. They may, in fact, replace films and videotapes and become the new standard for educational technology. At this writing, costs are high and equipment is cumbersome. Videodiscs are being used in medical and nursing education. In the future they may be as commonplace as videotapes became in the 1980s.

Technology often develops so rapidly that users have difficulty understanding how to use it effectively. An old maxim seems to be worth remembering in this regard: "Be not the first by whom the new is tried, nor yet the last to lay the old aside."

IN CONCLUSION

Educational media can enrich and enhance almost any educational encounter. Health educators are expected to be media specialists, at least in using the common formats discussed in this chapter. Use of media can enhance instruction and increase the likelihood of reaching behavioral objectives.

A few simple rules can be followed to increase success rates during utilization. Whenever possible, translate information into pictorial form, such as graphs and symbols, and use this material as illustrations. Make the message interesting by using interesting examples. Keep the format simple, and repeat major points more than once in different formats. These techniques can be helpful in most situations that health educators encounter.

***

Suggested Learning Activities

1. Prepare an exhibit for a health fair.
2. Evaluate three health-related posters or exhibits using the forms in this chapter.
3. Prepare a slide-tape presentation on a specific health topic.
4. Contact the American Heart Association. Arrange for a class demonstration of their cardiopulmonary resuscitation interactive videodisc system.

NOTES

1. D.J. Breckon and R.M. Pennington, Interactive Videodisks: A New Generation of Computer-Assisted Instruction. *Health Values: Achieving High Level Wellness* 10, no. 6 (1986):53.
2. Ibid., p. 54.

SUGGESTED READING

Heinich, R., et al. 1993. *Instructional media and the new technologies of instruction.* New York: Macmillan Publishing Co.

Chapter 24

Developing and Using Printed Materials Effectively

Helping people to learn more about their own health and the health of others has been one of the key duties of health educators, whether employed by official, voluntary, or private organizations. Following the lead of the cooperative extension services from the land-grant colleges in the early 1900s, health educators have recognized the success of giving people short, concise, and accurate printed materials about subjects of interest. This practice was preceded by using libraries and newspapers as important disseminators of information.

The printed word, whether enhanced by graphics, pictures, or illustrations, is not only effective but also desired by those who want to learn. It is important, however, to communicate with the printed word in ways that people fully understand, using policies and guidelines in concert with agency policies that are ethically sound. If health educators have the primary responsibility for printed information about health matters, then it is their duty to become adept not only in selecting printed materials but also in creating them.

There is no doubt that the technology of information dissemination has evolved and will continue to do so. It is important, however, to stress that requirements and procedures for effective communication through the use of the written word will still be essential, regardless of the technology involved.

DETERMINING NEED

Turner and Wilbur advised health educators to make sure, in the early stages of planning, that the printed piece is in agreement with agency purposes and objectives.[1,2] Similarly, the item should be authorized by the administrative decision makers in the sponsoring agency.

Wants and needs are often expressed by individuals and groups requesting more and better information about an issue, problem, or situation.

Questions that are related to concerns about the proposed printed piece need to be answered. For example:

- What is the need for this information?
- What is the target population?
- Is the printed word the best way to disseminate this particular information?

If the answers to these questions call for the printed word, then preparation can proceed.

Other community problems may arise for which the health organization may want to provide specific information or instruction to the public. Also, the public's information needs should be reviewed by department representatives at regular administrative meetings. The health educator can then work with administrators to determine whether a publication will meet these needs and set priorities for its development.

STEPS IN DEVELOPMENT

Assuming that an analysis has shown that the printed word is desired, educators, using a combination of program development, priorities, completion date requirements, and cost estimates, can then proceed to produce the best possible product. The steps in the process, along with some direction to the activity, are provided in Figure 24-1.

CONCERNS

Almost everyone has observed people at meetings and programs picking up pamphlets and materials about a specific subject for later perusal. At first one is

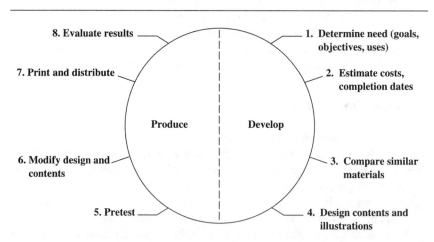

Figure 24–1 Steps for Printed Materials Development.

impressed with this active participation in self-directed learning. However, if the contents of a nearby waste receptacle were to be examined after the program activity, they would probably reveal a high percentage of the printed material picked up a few minutes earlier. This phenomenon should awaken health educators to the fact that if people are going to learn something from a written piece, the information must be truly useful to them.

Another concern related to the planning, design, and production of printed materials is the high cost of paper, inks, and printing processes. The expense involved forces one to examine carefully the purpose of the materials and its potential effectiveness before embarking on the venture.

TYPES OF PRINTED MATERIALS

Health educators are often involved in the planning, development, and distribution of a wide variety of materials, such as formal annual reports and planning documents for decision makers; informal annual reports and planning documents for consumers; and booklets, pamphlets, fliers, and stuffers.

Each example calls for a specialized design, content, and illustration method. There are, however, some similarities of the requirements for all of them.

Printed materials should meet certain criteria. They should be attractive, interesting, uncluttered, readable, concise, important, timely, clear, motivating, and accurate. They should express friendliness and be direct, sincere, and honest. In many cases they should suggest some action by the reader. These requirements may seem overwhelming at first, but with a little experience, a health educator can incorporate them into writing projects.

HUMAN WANTS

Before discussing specialized techniques for the written word, it is important to examine some things that people want. If educators write and design a piece using these "wants" to approach what is conceived to be the people's "needs," the probability of producing interesting and useful documents is increased.

Research indicates that people want to learn.[3] Among other things, they want to learn to improve their health, security, self-confidence, and use of leisure. People want to learn how to be good citizens and parents. They want to learn to express their personalities, resist domination, and improve themselves. They want to learn how to save time and money and how to avoid work, discomfort, worry, and risks. All these perceived learning needs relate to health educators. If a written piece appeals to some of these specific wants while providing useful information, it will be more successful.

READABILITY

Health educators hear many complaints about written materials. Some people say that they "can't understand it"; others say that "it's so simple it's boring." As a result, a question naturally arises: "How does one write for the best appeal and understanding of a target population?"

Those who would write for others are advised to conform their writing to meet the understanding or readability level of their audience. They should examine other writers' materials for acceptable readability before purchasing and using them.

Some unique approaches for measuring readability have been developed by several researchers. Regardless of their specific methods, they all use sentence length and word difficulty to estimate readability.

The Gunning Fog Index uses samples of approximately 100 words divided by the total number of sentences to give an average number of words per sentence. Then the number of words having three or more syllables is multiplied by 0.4 and an approximate grade level of readability is obtained. A worksheet for the Gunning Fog Index is present in Exhibit 24-1. This widely used method is often preferred because of its ease of use.

Exhibit 24-1 Assessing the Readability of Printed Materials: Gunning Fog Index—Worksheet

Title _____ Page No._____ Page No._____ Page No. _____
Author_____ From_____ From_____ From _____
Publisher _____ Date _____ To_____ To_____ To_____

1. No. of words in sample   _____   _____   _____
2. No. of sentences in sample   _____   _____   _____
3. Average no. of words per
   sentence (No. 1 ÷ No. 2)   _____   _____   _____
4. No. of words of 3 or
   more syllables in the
   sample   _____   _____   _____
5. Total (No. 3 + No. 4
   above)   _____   _____   _____
6. FOG Index (Total in No.
   5 x 0.4)   _____   _____   _____

Average FOG Index of _____samples _____
(This gives grade reading level directly)

Analyzed by _____ Date _____
Checked by _____ Date _____

Source: Reprinted with permission from the *Public Health Education Workbook,* Central Michigan University Press, Mount Pleasant, Michigan..

The most accurate and reliable test developed to date is credited to Professor Edgar Dale and a graduate student, Jeanne Chall, at the Ohio State University. Their formula for predicting readability interprets average sentence length and difficult words from words not on a familiar word list to produce raw scores, which can then be corrected to give results showing the grade levels of understandability from the 4th through 16th + grades. Because this process is rather lengthy and requires the use of word lists, no worksheet is presented.

A simpler way of determining readability, called the "Grasp Estimate," has been developed by John Harvey. Its findings estimate the reading difficulty of a piece in only three categories: easy, moderate, or difficult to understand. (With all these procedures, accuracy can be improved by taking more than one sample and averaging the results.) The procedure for conducting the Grasp Estimate is as follows:

1. Select a fairly large random paragraph.
2. Count the number of words in the first two sentences.
3. Count the number of words containing six or more letters.
4. Divide the number of words having six or more letters by the number of words in the two sentences.
5. Multiply this result times the sum of the words in the first two sentences plus the number of words having six or more letters.
6. A result near 8 or below indicates that the written piece is easy to understand. A score near 15 means that it is moderate. A score near 30 or above means that it is difficult to understand.

The following paragraph from Toffler's *The Third Wave* can be used to help clarify the Grasp Estimate procedure and compare its results with the other methods in use.

The computer will not only design the product the customer wants, Professor Hame explains, but select the manufacturing process to be used. It will assign the machines. It will sequence the necessary steps from, say milling or grinding, right down to printing. It will write the necessary programs for the subcomputers or numerical control devices that will run the machines. And it may even feed an "adaptive control" that will optimize these various processes for both economic and environmental purposes.[4]

The Gunning Fog Index indicates that this paragraph is written for grade 14, a college sophomore. The Dale-Chall readability procedure indicates that it is written for the 11–12 grade level.

The Grasp Estimate procedure and results, using only the first two sentences, follow:

1. 27 total words
2. 11 words with 6 or more letters
3. 11/27 = 0.41
4. 0.41 x 38 = 15.5
5. A "moderate" level of understandability

Microcomputer programs are now available to determine readability levels. Samples are typed into the machine, and, with an additional command, several readability scores are produced for comparison. Ease of use of this magnitude should preclude using inappropriate materials with target groups.

ANNUAL REPORTS

Annual reports, whether written for people serving in decision-making bodies or for public consumption, should follow a planned format. A typical format of an official annual report has the following components:

1. A cover with pictures or illustrations and the name and address of the organization
2. Introduction—a letter from the director describing some challenges, accomplishments, and problems of the previous year or a background statement of history and progress of the agency
3. Report of program activities and number of people served
4. A listing of the budget and how money was spent
5. An organizational table and listing of names and positions of boards and employees

Smaller, pamphlet-type annual reports for general public distribution may contain only some good pictures, statements of program activities and accomplishments, budgets, and a list of key people. Pie charts and bar graphs can save space and can show relationships of how the money was spent and the number and types of program activities.

Annual reports should meet all the requirements for readability, color, and type size/style that are necessary for other printed materials. It is a good idea to collect samples of annual reports from a wide variety of organizations and consider the use of the ideas and techniques of the better ones.

In larger organizations, department heads and others may submit their special section for inclusion in the report. These should be examined and edited to present a uniform writing style, readability, and verb tense. Another important consideration is having a general theme or slogan for everyone to use in writing their contribution to the report. This theme can then be stated on the front or back cover of the report, in the director's letter, and in different sections of the report to help weave threads of continuity throughout the document. This theme can be derived from considering situations, happenings, or program thrusts that occurred during the year and produced positive effects. Examples of such themes that have been used in the past include "people helping people," "progress," "good health for all," and "a year of progress." Sometimes a symbol can be developed that is unique to the program. This symbol can be combined with the slogan or theme and used on all publications of the agency, to give a readily identifiable image.

BOOKLETS, PAMPHLETS, FLIERS, AND STUFFERS

These materials are usually written in short sentences and easily understandable language. They need attractive illustrations and examples. Quality samples should be collected, categorized, and saved for ideas when developing new materials.

A flier is a single sheet, printed in a single color ink for use in attracting attention and making announcements. It usually gives the reader some directions to follow in order to solve a particular problem. Fliers are usually available at displays and counters for easy pickup and are promptly discarded after use.

A stuffer is an additional piece of printed material that is included in a mailed letter or statement. It is generally used to tell recipients about some additional program fact or service they might be interested in. Even though fliers and stuffers are usually inexpensive to produce and are thrown away after use, they should be designed and edited carefully so that they are useful to the reader and not just another nuisance.

PRODUCTION AND PRINTING

Much commercial printing is now done by the offset method. This method uses temporary photographic masters instead of lead slugs or lead plates. The offset process has eliminated the tedious, costly, time-consuming letterpress printing process of the past and moves instead to computer typing with automatic line adjustment and justification.

The developer of printed materials should visit the print shop in which the piece is to be printed and examine the options in type size, style, paper surface, paper colors, and inks as related to the cost and the developer's budget. Four color inks can reproduce from four different impressions a full-color picture, which, when combined with a heavy, slick paper, can be quite costly. Combinations of paper color with one or two colors of ink, however, can produce quite satisfactory materials if chosen carefully. Studies of colors for visibility and effect have disclosed that yellow and colors from yellow to red are the most visible. Green and blue are somewhat less visible. Black, blue, and red inks on white or yellow paper are highly visible. Red excites, whereas green and blue calm and sometimes depress. Experiments should be conducted for each printed piece to determine the most effective colors for the ink and paper combination.

Special effects can be produced for unique designs using combinations of either manual or machine cutting, folding, and assembly techniques. A triple fold of the traditional $8\frac{1}{2}$ x 11-inch paper, for example, produces a letter- or pocket-sized brochure or pamphlet. Triangular folds and staggered assembly can also give interesting results.

Bindings vary, depending on the thickness of the finished product. They range from a stapled cover sheet to one punched or drilled with plastic rings, to a glued binding such as those typically used in hard-covered documents.

DESKTOP PUBLISHING

For printing large numbers of brochures or newsletters, offset printing is still recommended. However, many items formerly done at a printing press can now be done at a health education agency, using desktop publishing. Desktop publishing is revolutionizing the preparation of printed materials and is another advantage of being computer literate.

Microcomputers now have large memories that can store a variety of fonts (print size and type), graphics (pictures and illustrations), borders, and formats. Software programs now are available to allow the user to prepare material on the screen, arranging type, headings, margins, and illustrations to look as desired. Copies can be printed in draft form, so that other staff can review and comment on the newsletter or brochure.

Some desktop publishing software programs are very sophisticated and require experience on the part of the user to produce finished work. Other programs, such as those to print newsletters, are easy to use and can be quickly used effectively by anyone with previous microcomputer experience. The more difficult-to-use programs also provide the most options, such as the ability to move illustrations around on the page and to make them larger or smaller as required in the final version. They also have a large inventory of illustrations and fonts from which to select.

The key to good quality desktop publishing is a good-quality printer, preferably a laser-jet printer. Laser printers provide sharp images for both type and graphics, producing print shop quality. If agencies do much printing, acquisition of this equipment can quickly pay for itself through reduced printing costs. Also, many commercial printers prefer to receive a computer disc of the job to be done, rather than the hard copy.

Desktop publishing will not eliminate the need to use offset printing presses, but it can reduce the frequency of use. Many smaller jobs can be done in-house.

Special-purpose newsletters, fliers, and brochures can be quickly generated. Either the needed number can be run by the printer or one "clean" copy can be taken to the copy center of the agency or community.

EVALUATION

If a reader is favorably impressed and is involved in the printed word, good things can happen. Various criteria and techniques of judging the quality and potential effectiveness of the printed word in its various forms have evolved over the years. These criteria are important to use in evaluating items that a health educator has produced as well as those available commercially. The worksheet shown in Exhibit 24-2 is a useful reminder of some of the basics of preparing and evaluating commercially prepared material.

Some general considerations for evaluating printed materials include the following:

Exhibit 24-2 Worksheet Evaluating Printed Materials

```
Title _____
Publisher _____
Cost_____ Date of Publication _____ Language Used_____
Purpose or Theme _____
For what groups is this material most appropriate? (Check all appropriate.)
    ___ Men ___ Women ___ Children ___Geriatric
    Cultural _____
    Occupational _____
A  B  C  D   Audience Appeal: Does it get attention, lead the reader on, keep attention?
A  B  C  D   Accuracy: Is it accurate and up-to-date?
A  B  C  D   Approach: Does it agree with the emphasis and approach used locally?
A  B  C  D   Organization: Is it logical, clearly developed, easy to follow, believable?
A  B  C  D   Completeness: Is there sufficient detail? Too much detail?
A  B  C  D   Tone: Is the message personal, supportive, positive, honest?
A  B  C  D   Physical Properties: Are the layout, print, illustrations, and color appropriate
             for the intended group? Is the piece attractive?
A  B  C  D   Graphics: Are the graphics simple and clear?
A  B  C  D   Vocabulary: Is the vocabulary familiar or explained for readers?
A  B  C  D   Readability: Are the sentences short? Has jargon been avoided?
Grade Level_____
Strengths:
Weaknesses:
Recommendation:
Signed: _____
Date: _____
```

• Is the purpose or theme expressible in one sentence?
• Is the writing consistently and effectively focused on the target group of people?
• Does the material quickly get and hold the reader's attention?
• Are the statements scientifically accurate?
• Are the sentences simple and nontechnical?
• Is the printing type easy to read?
• Is the layout attractive? Is there balance, unity, and movement and are facing pages in harmony?
• Are the illustrations scientifically accurate? Do they support the text? Are they printed sharply and cleanly?
• Is the paper durable and fairly inexpensive?
• Does the color of the inks and paper add to the appeal and effectiveness of the piece? Do they harmonize?

Dale and Hager have expressed their views and made suggestions for health educators developing printed materials.[5] They stated that authors need to

1. Be sure they get their main points across
2. Have the material well organized and in a logical order
3. Have subheadings short, clear, and supportive of the main body of text
4. Make sure that main points are briefly summarized in the right places and that important information is repeated in different ways
5. Be sure the writing has a warm, friendly, informal tone
6. Use concrete examples to explain difficult concepts
7. Use a specific to general application approach whenever possible (what it is and how it applies)
8. Be sure the reader knows why the subject is important
9. Tell the reader just how to do the things he or she should know

IN CONCLUSION

It is beyond the scope of this chapter to describe in detail all the considerations necessary for the health educator to become truly effective in the development and use of printed material. The health educator should consult the literature on particular interests and problems of the subjects involved, ask those who are knowledgeable for their advice, collect examples of good and bad documents, and experiment with various projects using the printed word. At minimum, health educators should develop a good working relationship with a local graphic arts and printing agency, much as they would with news media outlets.

***

Suggested Learning Activities

1. Determine the readability of three health-related pamphlets.
2. Prepare a health pamphlet suitable for printing.
3. Identify one or more local graphic arts and printing resources. Arrange either a visit or a class presentation.

NOTES

1. C.E. Turner, *CHECK . . . Community Health Educator's Compendium of Knowledge* (St. Louis: C.V.Mosby Co., 1951), 175–212.

2. M.B. Wilbur, *Educational Tools for Health Personnel* (New York: Macmillan Publishing Co., Inc., 1968), 177–178.

3. A. Tough, *The Adult's Learning Projects* (Toronto: Ontario Institute for Studies in Education, 1981), 17.

4. A. Toffler, *The Third Wave* (New York: William Morrow, 1980), 291.

5. E. Dale and H. Hager, *Some Suggestions for Writing Health Materials* (New York: National Tuberculosis Association, 1950), 25–26.

SUGGESTED READING

Blake, B. 1992. *Creating newsletters, brochures and pamphlets: A how to do it manual.* New York: Neal-Schuman Publishers.

Chapter 25

Evaluating Health Education Programs

Most administrators and educators in the health field no longer consider evaluation optional. They feel obligated to determine what has been accomplished as a result of their efforts. This feeling prevails partly because of the persistent writing and speaking of Suchman, Green, and others on this topic. Evaluation means different things to different people. For some, evaluation evokes images of statistics and computers; for others, it evokes images of simply reflecting on past practices. Both images may, in fact, be part of an evaluation process; yet neither extreme, in and of itself, is adequate. As the Healthy Communities 2000 project indicates, evaluation components are critical. As always, obtaining common understanding of what is expected is an important beginning place, as is an understanding of why it is expected and how it will be used.

THE POLITICS OF EVALUATION

Professionals constantly make judgments about programs, whether their own or those of others. Such judgments are subjective opinions that may reflect personal biases. Judgments are not usually quantified. The feelings or impressions may be vague and undefined or strong and focused. The judgments may prove to be useful in future program planning, or they may be so biased or vague as to be useless.

As quality assurance and accountability gained ascendancy in health planning, evaluation became imperative. It became necessary to move the judgments from the subjective realm to the objective realm and to become systematic in making such evaluations, so that the results would be more meaningful. Evaluation has always been an important management tool, but its value increases when it is used objectively.

Evaluation should be nonthreatening. Program planners should be creative, positive, and forward looking. Regardless of how well a program has been or is being done, it probably could have been more effective with different input during

253

the planning process and indeed can be done better the next time. Learning from experience and recognizing that hindsight is better than foresight are part of the philosophy of evaluation. Stated differently, evaluation implies a willingness to change, a desire to improve. When viewed in this context, it should not be threatening.

Evaluation studies can be done for other reasons. Funding agencies may want to know if funding should be continued. Administration may want to know if a different programmatic emphasis would be more effective. Even in such circumstances, evaluation should not be viewed as threatening or punitive. If used positively, it can be viewed as an opportunity to improve a program as it develops and as an opportunity to measure success, not failure.

Similarly, evaluation requires sound planning skills and a commitment not to manipulate the outcome. Although it is probably true that an evaluator can manipulate the outcome of a study to show a desirable outcome, it is obviously not ethical to do so. Evaluators need to use planning skills wisely, to avoid even the appearance of duplicity.

Program directors need to be careful to avoid covering failure by not doing an objective appraisal. They need to be careful to avoid the temptation to select for evaluation only those program elements that appear to be successful. It is important to be comprehensive, so as not to give the appearance of shifting attention from an essential part of the program that has failed to a minor program component.

Evaluation also has to be timely. It can be postponed or delayed to allow concerns to dissipate over time. Yet another political end can be served by attempting to make a program look effective because of internal conflict. Whether a program succeeds or fails, those who are involved are partisans. The evaluator and the evaluation design must show evidence of not being partisan if the results are to be credible.

Program evaluators, then, should ideally be devoid of political motives in planning and implementing an evaluation design. Additionally, some personal considerations sometimes emerge. Program directors may be afraid of looking ignorant about evaluation because of lack of experience. They may be concerned that the way things are done will be disrupted while evaluation is occurring, especially if the results are unfavorable. Others may fear that differing views of program objectives will be brought into the open.

A political climate that supports evaluation includes strong motivation to measure past success and reasons for that success. It includes organizational backing and adequate resources for evaluation. It includes some knowledge and skill in evaluation and realistic expectations.

EVALUATION FOR WHOM?

Another dimension of political consideration in evaluation centers on who will be reading the evaluation report. A variety of audiences exist, with some overlap, but expectations of primary audiences are a major determinant of evaluation strategies.

Frequently, some form of evaluation will be required by funding agencies. In grant applications the evaluation design usually has to be specified, at least in general terms. The adequacy of the evaluation design may well be a primary factor in the decision to fund a project. If money is being made available for a demonstration project, a determination needs to be made as to what was accomplished and on the possibility of widespread replication of that project. In such situations a strong evaluation component needs to be part of the grant and its terms must be adhered to completely on the time schedule specified.

Evaluation is also an important consideration for health educators in all situations in which others are making budgetary decisions on health education programs. In health departments, hospitals, and many other settings, health educators do not make the final decision on their budgets. Furthermore, health education budget requests usually compete for scarce resources with requests from other divisions. Administrators and budget committees respond more favorably to budget requests that are documented. Evaluation data indicating what was accomplished are impressive to such administrators and may be used to maintain a budget in an era of inadequate and shifting resources.

Even if funding is secure and evaluation data are not demanded, astute program directors should still be doing evaluation studies. The fiscal climate of any agency can change rapidly. A rapid change in the nation's inflation rates, a change in the fiscal health of an agency funding source, failure to obtain renewal of a major grant, and a change in the administrative superstructure of an agency can all result in the necessity to justify a program's existence, although it was not necessary previously. Unfortunately, in these cases, appropriate data cannot be gathered quickly, and health educators who cannot document the effect of their programs may find that there is simply not enough time to do the studies. Such a situation is especially tragic because more foresight in planning evaluation studies may have saved the program.

Health educators often are employed by agencies that are accountable to the public. Board members, trustees, or others representing political bodies or the public at large may demand evaluation data. It is good strategy to provide such data, whether demanded or not. Data are evidence that can be used to justify programmatic decisions by these bodies and may have publicity value.

Evaluation data may not be required by superiors but may be collected and made available to the media. Because people are interested in health education and in public accountability, the media is usually interested in related data. If a health educator can show a lowered readmission rate to area hospitals or a decrease in the incidence of problem pregnancy, for example, the media usually considers such data newsworthy.

Educators in agencies that need public support in the form of millage, capital fund drives, donations to annual operating budgets, or simply an ultimatum to continue health education services should be especially sensitive to the news value of evaluation data. Those working in voluntary agencies or hospitals that cultivate major donors need to be concerned about informing potential donors of the impact of health education programs. Similarly, many programs depend on public awareness to increase their number of clients. Evaluation data made available to the community through the media or other sources can increase the visibility of a program and generate new clients.

Ideally, in addition to some or all of the above reasons, health educators should know how they are doing and what they are accomplishing. One important element of professionalism is the desire to do the most possible and the best possible, even with limited resources. Collecting evaluation data is one way of determining what has been accomplished and suggesting strategies for improvement. This reasoning can be extended to indicate that health educators must evaluate their efforts professionally. Indeed, many consider it unethical to fail to do so.

At least one other audience exists for evaluation data, and that is professional colleagues. Health educators need to learn from one another if they are to maximize their impact. A major way of increasing the learning from other health educators is to publish evaluation studies.

Ideally, the needs of several groups can be incorporated in an evaluation design, especially if each group receives a separate report that is slanted to its particular needs. However, those planning the evaluation studies need to know who the studies are being done for, what the group or groups want to know, and what uses will be made of the data, so that these needs have a reasonable chance of being met. For example, program participants might want data on program effectiveness; governing boards might want data on average program costs; program directors may want to know how programs can be improved; and funding agencies may want all the above categories of information and more.

EVALUATION FOR WHAT?

Once it has been determined who wants the evaluation data and what they want to know, one of several common responses can be made. Such responses are best examined within the context of a discussion of types of evaluation studies.

Formative Evaluation

One of the main reasons for doing an evaluation study is either to help develop a new program or to improve an old one. Such an evaluation is usually built into the formative stages of a project. It is sometimes called a feedback loop because it provides more or less continuous feedback to program directors that enable them to make adjustments that will improve their programs. The evaluator may be the program developer or, if not, someone who must work collaboratively with program developers.

Formative evaluation focuses on monitoring programs in early stages. It may include needs assessment of the target group, development of goal consensus, or assessment of client reactions to the services that have been provided. Although formative evaluation often refers to studies that result in immediate program adjustments, this is not always the case. "Process evaluation" is also appropriate. This type of evaluation, besides including the above studies, may be a retrospective review of the processes used in planning and implementing a program. For example, staff members or others could review together whether enough people were involved in planning or whether the addition of key individuals would have improved the database and the planning process. Similarly, an assessment could be made of the adequacy of media coverage, the time schedule, or any problematic areas in program implementation. If problems are identified and analyzed from a perspective of what might have prevented them from occurring, useful information will be provided for subsequent attempts to develop similar programs. Because the emphasis is on data that are useful immediately, sophisticated research designs are not necessary for formative studies.

Summative Evaluation

Many individuals and groups are interested in knowing what was accomplished by a program, either at its end or at a specific interval, such as the end of the year. Such assessments are part of summative evaluation studies. Policy makers and funding agencies are especially interested in such data.

Summative evaluation usually focuses on whether goals and objectives have been accomplished. Often evaluators work independently of program developers to avoid research bias. It is not usually necessary to contract with outsiders to do the evaluation. Program developers can and often do conduct credible program evaluation by involving several persons in the process and by making a concerted effort to avoid bias in the evaluation design and report.

Summative evaluation studies require a more sophisticated research design than do formative evaluation studies. They also require more time, effort, and resources to implement.

EVALUATION QUESTIONS

An important early step in planning evaluation studies is to formulate evaluation questions. If desired, the questions may be stated as hypotheses. Hypothesis testing is an acceptable but not necessary part of program evaluation design. For beginners, it is easier and more effective to formulate questions that are to be answered. The questions should be specific, focused on the project to be evaluated. They should be written and rewritten until consensus is reached that indeed these are the questions that need to be answered. Preferably, an evaluation committee or those involved with program design and implementation should help formulate the questions. It is important to determine if the questions to be asked are appropriate, necessary, inclusive, objectively stated, and so on.

In formative evaluation, questions can focus on effort and efficiency. For example, evaluators might want to know the following: Was there enough input from the target group so that the program was implemented in such a way that prospective participants were able to attend? Was there enough support from influential people? Was the timetable appropriate? Was media coverage adequate? Were locations appropriate? Were there enough dollars spent? Were time, effort, and budget expended efficiently?

Once the questions have been agreed on, the evaluation design can be finalized. Methodologies should be selected that will provide the needed data most efficiently. A comparison of data collection methodology is presented in Table 25-1. Ease of use and cost are important variables in selecting evaluation strategies. Sometimes simple, inexpensive strategies are just as useful as those that are difficult and expensive.

The evaluation questions and possible methodologies for answering those questions should again be discussed by the planners to develop a useful design. For example, if only a few people are involved, an evaluation team may decide to interview them or send them an open-ended questionnaire. If a larger group is involved, a rating scale may be devised to quantify responses by phrasing questions as statements. Respondents would then check appropriate responses, such as agree or disagree or, more elaborately, strongly agree, agree, neutral, disagree, or strongly disagree. Other labels could be used on such a five-point scale, and frequencies, percentages, means, and ranges can all be used to summarize the data.

Formative studies are relatively easy to do and can yield useful information if done carefully. The results of such a study should be summarized in writing, with conclusions and recommendations; distributed to appropriate individuals or groups; and filed for future use. The results should be readily accessible to facilitate usage, which is the primary justification for doing process evaluation.

Questions focusing on outcome evaluation are also an important part of program evaluation. A significant amount of effort can be expended on a program—and quite efficiently—with little result.

Program objectives are essential to this phase of designing an evaluation and should be stated in measurable format. If objectives are not so stated, an important first step is to develop or rewrite them. The basic set of evaluation questions should determine whether the program objectives are being or have been accom-

Table 25-1 Comparison of Data Collection Methodologies

Method	Advantages	Disadvantages	Result Quality	State Requirements	Costs
Person-to-person interview	• High response rate • Highly flexible • Visual aid opportunity • Community input and morale builder	• High costs • Raises expectations • Travel expenses • Possible interviewer bias • Technical staff required • High agency effort • Possible computer needs • High call-back expenses	• Yields detailed and high-quality results • Most representative results • Quantifiable results	• Technical assistance for interview construction • Interviewer training • Technical assistance for data analyzation processing and interpretation	High
Telephone interview	• Easy to administer • Low call-back expense • Community input and morale builder • High response rate • Relatively low cost	• Possible interviewer bias • Possible computer needs • Raises expectations • Representativeness and sampling problems	• Quantifiable results • Relatively quality results • Unless corrected, some bias in results • Fairly detailed results	• Interviewer training • Several interviewers • Possible technical assistance for data analyzation • Technical assistance for interview construction	Medium
Mail-out questionnaire	• Low cost • Minimum staff time • Possible good response • Larger outreach	• Generally low return rate • Possible bias and unrepresentativeness	• Quantifiable results • Low to medium quality • Possible major bias	• Technical assistance for questionnaire construction • If hand-processed, one or two	Low

Source: Reprinted with permission from *Social Needs Assessment Handbook,* p. 115, League of California Cities, © 1976.

plished and, if so, by what percentage of the participants. Questions such as "How many clients are managing stress appropriately? have stopped smoking? are practicing breast self-examination?" should be asked. Specific criteria are necessary to evaluate an outcome. For example, how many people practice breast self-examination at least every other month or, by self-report, indicate that they follow a sodium-restricted diet at least 75 percent of the time?

Inasmuch as health educators are behavior change specialists, outcome evaluation should determine whether behaviors have indeed changed. Green stated that the majority of effort by practicing professionals should focus on this type of evaluation.[1]

Impact evaluation is a more difficult form of summative evaluation to use. Evaluation questions in this context should focus on, for example, whether the incidence of disease or disorder was affected, the hospitalization was prevented, the length of stay was shortened, the number of readmissions were decreased, and the health care costs were reduced. Cost-effectiveness studies and other impact evaluation studies are more sophisticated and expensive and generally more difficult to implement. They often are left to evaluation specialists, whether in agencies or universities. Frequently, graduate students undertake such studies for theses or dissertations and may be available to conduct such a study for practicing professionals.

QUALITATIVE ASSESSMENT

Not all evaluation has to be quantified. Indeed, subjective opinion has always been a part of evaluation. However, qualitative evaluation can be more meaningful if it, too, is quantified. For example, planners can feel that the planning process was very effective or ineffective. These choices or similar forced ones can be quantified on a numerical scale permitting computation of mean scores, ranges, etc., that are easily compared. Qualitative assessment also can involve open-ended questions. It is possible to read all responses, list all responses in logical sequence, and assign some point value to each response. Of course, qualitative evaluation does not need to be quantified to be useful, but it often helps.

IN CONCLUSION

Evaluation studies can be easy or difficult to do. Some people enjoy doing such studies, whereas others dread them. Some evaluation data are useful, whereas other data seldom, if ever, get used. More and more emphasis is being placed on evaluation. Health educators are expected to be able to do it. No evaluation design is universally acceptable. Yet the principles of program evaluation must be understood and used effectively. When the principles are used and the design is put in context of the program and the purpose of the evaluation, an evaluation committee can usually agree on an adequate plan. Entry-level health educators should be able to participate meaningfully in the process and should be able to implement the plans, once formulated.

***

Suggested Learning Activities

1. With a local health educator, discuss evaluation designs, forms, and so on, that he or she has used.
2. Identify popular evaluation techniques as determined by a recent literature review.

NOTE

1. L. Green, et al., *Health Education Planning: A Diagnostic Approach* (Mountain View, Calif.: Mayfield Publishing Co., 1980).

SUGGESTED READING

Green, L.W., and Lewis, F. 1986. *Measurement and evaluation and health promotion.* Mountain View, Calif: Mayfield Publishing Co.

McKenzie, J.S., and Jurs, J.L. 1993. *Planning, implementing and evaluating health promotion programs.* New York: Macmillan Publishing Co., Inc.

Sarvela, P., and McDermott, R. 1993. *Health education and measurement: A practitioner's perspectives.* Madison, Wis.: Brown & Benchmark.

Veney, J. 1991. *Evaluation and decision making for health services.* Ann Arbor, Mich.: Health Administration Press.

Chapter 26

Acquisition and
Management of Grants

Seldom are there enough dollars in an agency to support a health education or health promotion program adequately. Program managers usually are astute enough to see opportunities for improvement or expansion if additional money were available. In fact, if health educators are not actually planning for program expansion and seeking funds to implement such plans, they are not as effective as they could otherwise be.

Administrators often respond to requests for additional funding with the time-worn phrase, "I'd like to, but there isn't any money available." Perhaps there actually is no money available or maybe the priorities of the manager dictate that available dollars go elsewhere. Health educators often need to educate decision makers on the need for additional funding. It is typical to have to "fight for what you get."

Conversely, seldom does an administrator discourage a staff member from expanding program efforts through the acquisition of funds from external sources. Rather, such a staff member is encouraged, supported, and sometimes even promoted. Health educators who are successful in such pursuits usually develop larger and more effective programs, are valued highly by supervisors, and feel good about themselves and their efforts.

Clearly, skills in grant development and fund-raising are useful and should be developed. Like many other skills, they are best developed through practice. Although reading chapters like this one or taking courses or conferring with experienced grants personnel are all useful, there is no substitute for actually writing a small grant. Nonetheless, an introduction to and overview of the process is a useful place to begin.

FUND-RAISING AND RATIONAL PLANNING

Literally millions of dollars are available through grants and contracts from government agencies and private foundations. Additionally, individuals give billions of dollars in charitable donations each year. Although religious and related charities are the most popular recipients of such donations, health-related programs usually receive the second largest sum.

The dollar amounts fluctuate from year to year, but large sums of money are available each year and often go unclaimed. Grant writers must start with the assumption that the dollars are there and continue to be optimistic and enthusiastic.

Some grant writers chase grants and simply try to get a share of whatever grant money is available. This practice is not recommended, for various reasons. Most important, external funding dictates programming. It affects who the client group of an agency will be and what programs will be developed or emphasized. It affects what the existing staff will do with their time, as well as what kind of additional staff are to be acquired. Indeed, the overall image of an agency can shift perceptibly over time as a direct result of grant acquisition. Although the change may be desirable and needed, it ought to be chosen from alternatives as best for the agency and the community.

Agencies and institutions usually have mission statements, goals and objectives, and long-range plans to implement the goals and objectives and fulfill the mission statement. Possible grants should be reviewed and discussed in this context. Most important, grant applications should be prepared only for tasks that an agency would like to undertake, even if external money were not available.

Rational planning is also essential in development of the proposal. Grant reviewers look for a proposal that is stated clearly and convincingly. They look for documentation that a problem exists and for a plan that will help alleviate the problem. They look for measurable objectives that are feasible. They look at the credibility of the agency and the credentials of the staff. They look for the probability of success and how such a project will be evaluated.

Stated differently, agency personnel that review and act on grant applications are concerned that their money is spent wisely and that full value will be received. Rational planning and sound administrative practices are therefore essential parts of the grant preparation process and the program that is proposed.

The committee approach is recommended for grant development, although one person usually needs to do the actual writing for the proposal to be coherent. The value of having several people involved in generating ideas and in reviewing drafts cannot be overstated. If a proposal represents the best thinking of several people, it will be better than if it represents the good thinking of only one person.

The committee approach to grant development is, admittedly, time consuming. However, passage of time allows complex ideas to develop and form and usually results in a better proposal. Although a draft of a grant can be written over a weekend, a good proposal takes several months to develop fully and obtain administrative approval. A more rational plan usually results when there is adequate lead time for several people to discuss several drafts.

PROPOSAL DEVELOPMENT FOR STATE OR FEDERAL AGENCIES

A proposal is a positive statement that sets forth a program or a set of activities. It requires two parties. It is a statement of what an individual or agency intends to do. It is made to another agency or institution and should be uniquely suited to that agency. It is written for presentation to another party in order to gain its acceptance.

Several types of proposals can be developed, the most common of which is a program proposal that offers a specific set of services to individual families, groups, or communities. A program proposal may be to provide training and consultation to agency staff and members of the community, or it may be to provide a number of other direct services. Technical assistance is a feature of many grant applications. Some planning proposals detail a set of planning and coordinating activities, which usually result in a program proposal. Similarly, there are research proposals to study a specific problem, evaluate a service, and so on.

Proposals can be solicited or unsolicited. A solicited proposal is prepared in response to a formal, written request for proposal, called an RFP. RFPs are prepared and sent to prospective agencies and operations. Similarly, program announcements and guidelines are described in various publications. The *Catalog of Federal Domestic Assistance* and the *Federal Register* are helpful in locating grant money and are available in most libraries. There are also grant-oriented newsletters, some of which are free. Potential grant writers need only request that their names be placed on an agency mailing list. A number of commercial organizations also prepare and sell subscriptions that describe currently available grant money. Although such subscriptions are expensive, they can pay for themselves quickly in terms of time saved and dollars garnered.

Unsolicited proposals are also received and reviewed regularly. It is important in both cases to ascertain if a project is a priority in the agency that is being solicited. A telephone call to the agency will usually result in the needed information.

Once one or more potential sources of grant money have been developed, the agency (or agencies) should be contacted for available guidelines and application forms. Further, prospective grant writers should telephone or visit a contact person in the agency and describe the essence of what will be proposed. Such first-hand information and advice is readily available, and staff members prefer to provide it before the project is fully developed, rather than after. Seeking and using such advice can save a lot of time and energy, but more important, it can increase the probability of a project being funded.

Each funding agency has its own application forms and guidelines. It is imperative that the forms be filled out completely and accurately. Writing a grant is more complicated than filling in the blanks, but ability and willingness to follow directions completely is an important part of the process.

Despite the dissimilarities and their importance, grants have a great deal in common. There are common elements in the proposal. They may have different names, be grouped differently, or be in different sequence. These items should be included in a proposal in some fashion. In unsolicited proposals, in which no formal guidelines or application forms are available, these proposal elements can be used as guidelines.

The narrative need not be long. It is not uncommon for agency guidelines to set a page limitation on the narrative, typically 10 or 15 pages of double-spaced typing. Such restrictions cause grant writers to revise the narrative until it is clear and succinct, permitting reviewers to evaluate it in a shorter period of time.

Letter of Transmittal

The letter of transmittal, or cover sheet, is the first page of a grant but may, in fact, be the last part of the application to be prepared. It provides, at minimum, the name and address of the organization submitting the proposal, a concise summary of the problem, and the proposed program. In an initial attempt to establish credibility, it often includes a statement of the organization's interest, capability, and experience in the area. It must contain the contact person's name, address, and telephone number and an authorized signature from a chief administrative officer. The authorized signature is necessary because the proposal is offering to use agency space, equipment, and staff to do specific tasks. Grant reviewers want to know that the agency is committed to such tasks. When funded, such a project has the effect of a contract.

Table of Contents

If the application is large, a table of contents usually follows the letter of transmittal. Use of headings in the body of the proposal facilitates development of a table of contents. Headings also make it easier for reviewers to follow the organization of the project and should be used even if a table of contents is not needed.

Introduction

An introductory statement that puts the proposal in context is appropriate. The statement may or may not include a description of the problem; the description can be a separate section. In either case, it is important to establish that there is a problem and that is has serious consequences to the citizenry. Documentation is usually necessary at this point and, even if not necessary, is helpful.

Applicant Agency Description

Funding agencies need to know if the organization is able to carry out the proposed project. Items to describe include organizational structure, past experience, qualifications of the staff, and budget.

Target Group

The target group should be described in detail and put in the context of the geographical area in which the program will take place. The number and kind of clients is valuable information. A description of the client group's involvement in the project planning process is also important.

Objectives

The specific objectives should be included in measurable form. Although behavioral objectives are not necessarily required, they lend themselves well to grant application specifications. A timetable for accomplishing the objectives should also be included.

Procedures

The procedures that will be used should be detailed. A logical, sequential timetable for the work plan is helpful. Specific methods and materials should be identified, with emphasis given to the innovative features of the program.

Evaluation

A plan for evaluation should also be included and is often a key part of the proposal. The tools and methodology to be used should be described in enough detail to ensure funding agencies that the results of the program will be summarized accurately.

Budget

A budget sheet is usually included in the application form. Because this varies from agency to agency, the forms of the grant agency should be used when possible. However, grant budgets do have some commonality. Usually they list salaries, by position. Salary schedules of the applicant agency should be used in calculations. Fringe benefits are ordinarily figured on a percentage of salary. They include employer contributions to Social Security, health insurance, unemployment compensation, workers' compensation, and so on. The figures vary from agency to agency and from year to year but are usually about 25 percent of the total salary costs.

If consultants are needed on technical projects, a realistic per diem fee should be used in a separate section of the budget. Consultants are not entitled to fringe benefits.

Supplies and materials should also be described in a separate section. They should be itemized by major types, such as office supplies, mail, telephone, duplication costs, and printing.

Equipment is usually itemized in a separate category, giving such specifics as model number and vendor.

Travel should be categorized as in country/out of country, in state/out of state; it can be divided by personnel or by program function. Reviewers usually want to know how travel allowances are going to be used.

Indirect costs include such items as utilities, space, procurement, and accounting staffs. Governmental funding agencies usually have a maximum allowable indirect rate. The rate is often negotiated; it may approach 50 percent of salaries and wages for the project.

Matching Funds

If matching funds are being used, they should be described. They represent the portion of the project cost that the institution is providing. In some instances, in-kind contributions have been used for this purpose. Institutions may agree to provide space, office furniture, and so on, and place a monetary value on that. In other instances, matching funds are required. In any case the larger the amount of matching funds or in-kind contributions, the more attractive the application will be.

Assurances

When applying to government agencies it is also necessary to provide assurance compliances. There are a number of such assurances and they change from time to time. They might include such items as treatment of human subjects, following affirmative action procedures when hiring, handicapped accessibility, and accounting practices. Again, funding agencies can readily provide copies of such required assurances.

Appendices

As in other written documents, the appendices are used to include material that, if included in the body of the proposal, would interrupt the flow. Vitae of key personnel in the project and supporting letters of other agencies are usually appended. Brochures, flow charts, diagrams, and other supporting material may be included.

FOUNDATIONS

A foundation is a nongovernmental, nonprofit organization. It has funds and programs managed by its own board of directors. Foundations are usually established by wealthy individuals or corporations as an efficient way of dispersing grants to aid a variety of social causes. With few exceptions, they make grants only to other tax-exempt, nonprofit agencies.

A foundation may have either a narrow range or a wide range of problems it is interested in funding. Smaller foundations prefer to fund projects in their own geographical locale, whereas larger foundations may prefer projects that are state, regional, or national in scope. In either case it is important to locate one or two foundations whose interests somewhat match the interests addressed in the proposal.

The Foundation Directory is a good reference to use in identifying interested foundations. It describes the purpose and activities of specific foundations, the locale in which they make grants, and the general size of the grants they make.

An important follow-up step is to contact the foundation and ask for an annual report or material that describes the major thrust of the foundation. A careful review of such material usually reveals whether the foundation would be interested in funding the project. A program officer's first question usually is, "Is this the kind of activity that fits within our foundation's interests?" A second related question is, "Is the request for support the kind and amount that our foundation usually gives?" If proposal writers can anticipate these questions and submit to foundations that have a good "fit," the probability of funding increases.

Proposals for foundations are essentially the same as those for state and federal agencies, only smaller. Most foundations do not want a fully developed proposal as their first point of contact. Some small foundations prefer personal contact before any written proposal is submitted, and others prefer a letter and a summary. In some instances an expanded letter is preferred, whereas in the case of large foundations, application forms may be used.

In any case, grant developers need to state the problem clearly, describe the proposed program, articulate the expected accomplishments, and outline a budget. The general principles of proposal development as discussed in the earlier sections are applicable, but the final submission should be in condensed format. A five-page concept paper is somewhat typical for a first submission to a founda-

Exhibit 26–1 A Checklist for Grant Developers

- Have you written or telephoned the funding source to gather additional information?
- Have you used the team approach involving clients, other relevant agencies, and other members of your own agency?
- Has a demonstrable need been established?
- Have you demonstrated familiarity with the relevant literature, research, programs, etc.?
- Have you stressed innovative features?
- Does a cover page include the needed summary information, and is an authorized signature included?
- Has an individual outside your field read the proposal for clarity, organization, etc.?
- Have the computations been double-checked for accuracy, and is the budget realistic and explained adequately?
- Has agency credibility and competency of project staff been established?
- Does the proposal have an attractive format?
- Have agency requirements been met in terms of deadlines, number of copies, etc.?
- Are you prepared to negotiate the proposal or resubmit and/or implement the program as proposed if funding is denied?

tion; a more detailed submission will be required after the first screening. The first submission should be short, clear, and persuasive; it should state at the outset what is to be accomplished, who expects to accomplish it, how much it will cost, and how long it will take.

IN CONCLUSION

Grant development is an exciting task. It is not difficult, yet few are effective at it. Those who are effective have an awareness of "the big picture" and give attention to detail. It is an area of skill development that responds well to practice. The checklist in Exhibit 26-1 summarizes the major points used in the process.

***

Suggested Learning Activities

1. Locate a foundation directory in the library and list local, state, and national foundations that express interest in health education.
2. Use the *Catalog of Federal Domestic Assistance* and locate current sources of funding for health-related programs.

SUGGESTED READING

Frost, G.J. 1993. *Winning grant proposals.* Detroit, Mich.: The Taft Group.

Chapter 27

Community Fund-Raising

Health educators working in voluntary health agencies will have to spend a significant amount of time in fund-raising. The actual percentage varies from agency to agency but is in the vicinity of 30 to 40 percent of a work week. Individuals working in hospitals are similarly involved in periodic capital campaigns to finance an addition or purchase a major piece of equipment. Hospitals also often engage in annual fund-raising events, such as a "Hospital Ball," or a "Casino Night." Even health educators in tax-supported agencies occasionally may need to become involved in fund-raising. Matching funds for a grant application may need to be raised, or agency funds may not be available for a community project with sufficient appeal to attract community funding. In any case, health educators need to be familiar with the basics of community fund-raising.

A RATIONALE FOR COMMUNITY FUND-RAISING

An important place to begin a discussion of fund-raising principles is to address why agencies should engage in community fund-raising. On the surface of this issue, the answer is obvious: Agencies engage in fund-raising because the funds are needed for a worthwhile project that cannot be completed without additional resources. Such a reason is sufficient, but there are other good reasons for agencies to engage in this time- and energy-consuming process.

Fund-raising may be used as a means of organization building, as a means of deepening the commitment of board members, staff, and others in the community who will be involved in the activity. Soliciting funds for an agency requires more commitment than does serving it in other ways. A clear understanding of the agency's mission, clientele, problems, opportunities, and need for funds is necessary for effective solicitation. Preparation of such a case statement can clarify and enhance the need for personal and community support. As usual, learning enough about a campaign so that the volunteers can solicit funds results in the volunteers learning the most.

A well-organized fund-raising campaign also results in enhancement of pride of those associated with the organization. Pride evolves from a series of achievements, a sense of self-sufficiency, a sense of doing something worthwhile that would not otherwise be done, and a sense of doing it in the democratic way, of people helping people.

Organizations also benefit from the associated publicity necessary to conduct a successful campaign. Public awareness of an organization or agency is enhanced, as is the agency's image. This publicity may also facilitate recruitment of volunteers. For example, an interagency group may conduct a fund-raising campaign to establish a hospice. The fund-raising campaign will necessarily involve media coverage, which may in turn increase levels of awareness and interest among potential volunteers and clients.

Fund-raising campaigns in health agencies usually include health education materials. It is a teachable moment, in the sense that potential donors are thinking about a disease or disorder and may read or listen to health education messages at that time. Further, such messages can be delivered efficiently and inexpensively by using the same delivery system as for the fund-raising material.

GENERAL PRINCIPLES OF FUND-RAISING

A lot of do's and don'ts associated with fund-raising can be learned from the many books and manuals on the subject. This section combines and summarizes the most important concepts.

An overriding consideration in fund-raising is to be positive. It is necessary to think positively and to be positive in materials and media releases used in the appeal. Fund-raising is not a time to beg or to stress that survival is at stake. People generally like winners more than losers, so it is a recommended strategy to be positive in all contacts and appeals.

In this sense it is helpful to establish attainable goals so that success is feasible. A realistic budget is necessary, with realistic appraisal of revenue sources. However, it need not all come from individual donors. Corporations or foundations can be contacted for larger contributions. Such gifts are usually identified as advance gifts. Advance gifts should total at least half the required amount. If it is not possible to raise half the goal through advance large gifts, it may be appropriate to revise the goal accordingly. This strategy makes the advantage of an advance-gift campaign obvious. If half the required funds are successfully solicited before public announcement of the campaign, this breeds an aura of success and people are more likely to get on the "bandwagon" and become part of a successful campaign that the community is excited about. Conversely, the advance campaign allows adjustment of the goal downward if necessary, so that success will be inevitable and the goal will be met, regardless of the amount of dollars raised.

Advance campaigns are predicated on another fundamental concept of fundraising: Most of the dollars raised are usually from large donors. If this principle is accepted, it follows that most of the time and energy should be directed toward large donors.

The final outcome varies from campaign to campaign, but the overriding result is that most of the money comes from only a few of the people. This is sometimes stated as the 90 percent rule and postulates that 90 percent of the money will come from 10 percent of the prospects. In other instances, 80 percent of the money comes from 20 percent of the donors. In yet other campaigns, one-third of the money raised comes from the ten highest givers, one-third comes from the next 100 givers, and one-third comes from all others.

Development of a prospect list is important when preparing to solicit large donations. It is recommended that a specific amount be solicited. If solicitors make clear that $50,000 is needed and 50 people have been selected who will, it is hoped, contribute $1,000, success is more imminent than if the appeal is based on "give us whatever amount you can." Agency personnel should also think about why people give and prepare an appeal that capitalizes on these reasons.

One such reason is that "people give to people" and, more specifically, "people give to their peers." If, for example, someone from the neighborhood appears at the door and requests a contribution, the donation is more likely to be forthcoming than if a stranger appears. Similarly, if a businessman approaches another businessman that he knows, describes a program, and asks for a contribution, it is more likely to be forthcoming than if solicited by a stranger. Ideally, bankers should be solicited by bankers, attorneys by attorneys, physicians by physicians. This places heavy emphasis on recruitment and training of volunteers. Use of volunteers can help share the load at all levels of a campaign.

Part of the training of volunteer solicitors is to stress that they make their contributions before they solicit others. Such an act tends to increase the dedication of the volunteer. Additionally, it is common for peers to ask, "How much did you give," and solicitors should be ready to respond to such inquiries. Similarly, board members and staff members should contribute as part of the advance-gifts campaign. Potential donors sometimes ask how much the board or staff gave.

It is also important when training volunteers or preparing a case statement to emphasize what a contribution will buy. Soliciting is a form of selling. The agency soliciting funds must establish its legitimacy and credibility. People do not want to support an organization with questionable or unknown goals. Similarly, donors do not want to see money wasted or misused. The program or activity should be established as being needed and as likely to be successful. Donors should also be shown how the program can benefit them. It is nice to be altruistic, and most people are to some degree. Self-centered interests are usually stronger, however, and should be used when possible. An analysis of donor interests and an appeal of how a program might indirectly help a donor will have a higher probability of success.

Volunteers training for solicitation should also stress cultivation of donors. Experience shows that as many as two-thirds of prospects will not contribute the first time. It may not be a good time financially, it may not be the right person soliciting, or it may not be the right approach. However, education of the prospect can convert a contact from a failure to a success. If a presentation is made or material is left that describes the agency or the problem, awareness and interest can be enhanced so that a subsequent year's solicitor will be successful.

Another principle of fund-raising has to do with involvement of top-level management in soliciting. Many large donors want to speak with the executive officer. The personal involvement of members of the management team in media, large groups, and selected individual contacts can pay big dividends.

Fund-raising campaigns need to be well organized. Usually a pyramid form of organization is used as the basic unit of structure. It starts at the top with the selection of a campaign chairperson who is capable and influential. This person or the campaign committee selects people to chair key committees within the campaign. These people may be residential, business, or industry professionals or a host of others. After they have contributed or pledged, they each recruit five people to work in the campaign, who in turn each recruit five people. This process can accommodate large campaigns in urban areas by building in regions or zones. It also incorporates the principle of people giving to peers, since people are likely to recruit their peers.

Beyond the organization of volunteers, good administrative skills are necessary. It is important to plan with people, keep accurate records, maintain accurate files on donors, set realistic timetables, call for appointments, send prompt thank-yous and receipts, and follow through on all commitments. It is also important to respect the restraints that volunteers work under and to recognize adequately the effort of volunteers. Finally, donor recognition is important. Listing donors in annual reports, providing certificates for various levels of giving, or in other ways providing public recognition to donors will contribute to success in future campaigns. Although efforts should be concentrated on large donors, small donors should also feel big success. The principle of donor cultivation implies that small donors may become capable of making large donations some day and will do so only if predisposed to.

DOOR-TO-DOOR CANVASSING

Personal, face-to-face soliciting has been found to be most successful, so the preferable soliciting methodology is to prepare a prospective list of people who can give and might like to give for any of a variety of reasons and then contact them individually.

A similar technique is to go door-to-door soliciting funds. This emphasizes the face-to-face contact and is apt to result in many small donations.

Such a campaign relies heavily on organization and volunteers. A large number of people need to know exactly what to do, including where to solicit, how to solicit, how to respond to anticipated questions, and where to turn in the money. Usually a packet is prepared for each solicitor that includes the agency name and address, a contact person, a phone number for questions, a set of instructions, identification of the volunteer, contribution envelopes, receipts, and educational leaflets. The kit also usually contains some motivational material for the volunteer, such as a reminder of the number of preventable deaths caused by the problem, and a memento, such as a bookmark shaped like a key that says, "You are the key to fighting cancer. Thank you for calling on your neighbors to help us raise funds to save lives from this dreaded disease."

The door-to-door canvassing should be preceded by a media blitz, so that residents are expecting a caller. Volunteers should be reminded that they will be expected and welcomed, and that mealtime and bad weather are inconvenient times to solicit, but they are good times to find people at home. A standard opening greeting is often provided, such as a greeting with a smile, following by "May I come in and talk about . . . ?"

Instructions on what to do if no one is at home or if assigned to high-security condominiums or apartments are useful. Instructions on how to handle negative feedback are also appropriate.

A deadline by which collections are to be made is helpful to all concerned. A backup system is usually needed to cover areas not being solicited owing to the breakdowns in the system.

The campaign needs a public report to the media and some form of volunteer recognition to wrap it up. Such a campaign usually represents many hundreds of hours of volunteer work. Door-to-door canvassing gets easier and raises more funds when done annually, but it can be effective in a variety of circumstances.

DIRECT MAIL CAMPAIGNS

Another technique used as part of a fund-raising campaign is to write a letter. This method is not as effective as face-to-face solicitation, but it can be used, for example, when volunteer help is limited, when trying to reach the hard to reach, or when potential donors are spread around the state or nation.

Direct mail campaigns are expensive and may actually lose money the first time. Printing and mailing costs may be high, and a typical response is only 1 percent.

One of the keys to a successful campaign is to generate a good mailing list, as when generating a prospect list for personal solicitation for large gifts. Good donor records can be used to cut down the list to good prospects, so as to minimize the costs. This also allows for generation of several lists, so that specialized letters can be sent to various groups. These records may be computerized so that appropriate letters can be sent to large donors, to those who gave last year, to the families of people the agency has served, and to those on the registration list from previous community functions. This type of fund-raising is getting more sophisticated, primarily because computers can segment the various potential donor groups.

Another key ingredient in a direct mail campaign is the letter or other material that is mailed out. It should be prepared carefully and pilot tested. In general, a letterhead that is specially prepared for a fund-raising campaign is more effective. Including the names of the fund-raising committee at the bottom or side of the stationery is helpful and uses the principle of people giving to people.

The other difficult task is to get mailing lists correct. The agency should use preferred names, not address mail to deceased individuals, and be current on marriages and divorces as these are problems for those raising funds by this method.

Use of large, bright stamps, rather than a postage meter imprint, increases the chances of the letter being opened. The letter must avoid the appearance of junk mail. It has to get opened rather than thrown away.

Once the letter has been opened, it is usually just skimmed. It is therefore useful to highlight key ideas by using some device, such as capitalization or italics. Skimmers look to see who signed the letter, so selection of a person who will sign the letter is important. Similarly, when possible, it is preferable that the signature be in bright blue or black ink rather than photocopied.

The letter should generally command attention through getting in touch with the readership at once. The opening paragraph should not only get the reader's attention but should also promise some benefit. The big ideas should be covered first because skimmers do not necessarily read the entire letter. The letter should conclude with the action portion of the letter. The reader should know what action the writer is advocating, such as suggesting a reasonable gift in dollar amounts and an immediate return in the enclosed return envelope.

If the letter is not a formal letter from an executive to an executive, liberties can be taken with normal letter-writing style. Eye-catching techniques, such as capitalized words or material in boxes, are often appropriate. Such material is read by those who scan, as are postscripts. A postscript can get a final message to the reader and should be prepared carefully.

SPECIAL EVENTS

Yet another form of fund-raising activity is the special event. Literally hundreds of special events can be used successfully, such as golf outings, road races, and rock-a-thons.

Special events are social or recreational events used to raise money. These events can generate a lot of publicity for an organization, resulting in enlarging the base of support in the community.

Special events should be fun. They are usually seasonal and associated with existing activities in the community, such as golfing or skiing. If people like to do an activity, they will often pay more than usual to engage in that activity if the profit is going to a good cause. Accordingly, a bowling proprietor may donate a percentage of the revenue for alley fees. The entry fee will go to the cause, the proprietor will get good publicity, the participants will enjoy the evening, and the program or project will generate funds for programming.

In planning special events, it is wise to think about what special events are currently planned for the community and what additional special events would appeal to the community. Insofar as possible, it is also wise to get donations or consignments for necessary costs. An organization can lose money on special events if, for example, a large supply of tee shirts and trophies are purchased and the event has an unusually small turnout.

The easiest and most effective way to conduct a special event is to recruit a chairperson or an organization that will do most of the work and that knows the subtleties. If a golfer from a local country club can be recruited, the details will usually be familiar and the staff role will be one of supervision and assistance. A decision also needs to be made as to whether to do the event annually or only once. If the group decides to hold the event annually, it is helpful to have the chairperson for the event recruit a replacement for himself or herself.

An agency can raise a lot of money, generate a lot of favorable publicity, and have a lot of fun doing special events. It can also put in a lot of hours of work with little or no return. Advertising and publicity are factors that can make the difference between success and failure. Another such factor is inadequate supervision. If volunteers do not follow through on commitments, or if inadequate volunteers are recruited, a special event can be disastrous, not only losing money, but also creating negative publicity that will affect the image of the agency.

DEFERRED GIVING

The last method of fund-raising to be discussed in this chapter is deferred giving. It includes wills, estates, insurance policies, trust funds, and memorials.

Deferred giving allows a person to designate an agency, institution, or project as recipient of an amount, with that amount being paid after the person's death. This method of giving is growing rapidly as a source of revenue for social service agencies.

Programs of this nature are of necessity long range in scope because of the unpredictability of death. It may be a decade or more before such a program will generate actual revenue. Involvement in such a program may be as simple as running public service announcements reminding people that designation of an agency as the beneficiary of all or part of an estate can continue the "good will and good works" begun while alive. Large, deferred-giving programs, on the other hand, have estate planners, attorneys, and tax consultants available to assist prospective donors in planning and executing their estates.

In either case, deferred-giving programs usually involve working with the general public and with bankers, attorneys, and insurance company representatives. They often involve regular mailings describing agency services and urging professionals to encourage their clients to remember an agency or project in a will.

Memorials are often designated by survivors of the deceased "in lieu of flowers." They are sometimes referred to as living memorials and often include churches or research programs associated with the cause of death. Scholarship funds at colleges and universities are established in a similar manner.

Using memorials to generate revenue involves general media releases on a periodic basis to remind people of the opportunity and of the important programs of the agency that can be expanded. Additionally, such a program involves working with morticians to remind them of agency needs and providing them with memorial envelopes or other materials.

IN CONCLUSION

Fund-raising may be a distasteful thing to many who do not like to ask others for money. However, it can be an exciting and productive area in which to work. It can include a health education component or can finance such programs.

Anyone can raise funds through community projects like those described in this chapter. The skills of planning, implementing, and evaluating health education are easily transferrable to the task of fund-raising. Training and experience in fund-raising will help health educators be mobile, but equally as important, they will increase the effectiveness of health educators in educational programming.

***

Suggested Learning Activities

1. Discuss fund-raising costs with a voluntary agency fund-raiser. Identify the most difficult tasks of the job and strategies to ease them.
2. Volunteer to participate in some leadership role in one or more fund-raising drives.
3. Review the fund-raising databases described in Appendix E.

SUGGESTED READING

Lindahl, W. 1992. *Strategic planning for fund raising.* San Francisco, Calif.: Jossey-Bass.

Mengerink, W. 1992. *Hand in hand: Funding strategies for human service agencies.* Detroit, Mich.: The Taft Group.

Part IV

A Look Ahead

A glimpse of the past has been presented in this text, along with a detailed analysis of the present. From this perspective, a glimpse of the future can be seen, albeit "through a glass darkly." Yet it is fitting to project what lies ahead for the health education profession and its practitioners.

Chapter 28

Health Education
in the 21st Century

What is health education? What important historical foundations exist or are being built? Is it truly a profession, or merely an application of several disciplines to solving health problems? Where is health education now? Where is it going? When will it get there? These questions are an important part of a book such as this, which focuses on skills required of health educators in present practice, and are addressed in this concluding chapter.

THE PRESENT

Practitioners that have been in the field for a long time and future historians may call the last quarter of this century the golden age of health education. Many still in the field remember being asked, "What do you coach?" when indicating that they were a health educator. Others remember when health education referred to school health education, because community health education was seldom taught or thought about. Another large percentage of practitioners remember when health education was something that was done by people working in local health departments, because hospitals and other community agencies were too busy treating the acutely ill to see a role for themselves in prevention. Yet others remember when legislation mandating governmental leadership in planning, implementing, and evaluating health education was but a dream. Many others remember when funding programs for a reasonable opportunity of exerting an impact was a rare occurrence. Although not all this has changed in recent years, much of it has.

Many people are calling themselves health educators now who previously would not have heard or understood the term, or if they did, would have preferred being called something else. Some legislation exists at both the state and federal level mandating leadership in programming. Many large, innovative programs exist with large budgets and staffs. Health education is a mandated service that

Note: A major portion of this chapter is adapted from D.J. Breckon, "Reflections: Health Education in the Year 2000," *Health Values: Achieving High Level Wellness*, Vol. 12, No. 2, pp. 53–57, with permission of Charles B. Slack, Inc., © March/April 1988.

must be available in many agencies and institutions. Now, with national health objectives and widely disseminated strategies for implementing them, a healthy nation with healthy communities seems feasible at last.

How did this happen? When did it happen? Consensus does not exist on the answer to either question. Most would agree, however, that the appointment of the President's Committee on Health Education in 1973 marked one transitional point into the present era. The national exposure and credibility that grew out of this activity is impossible to measure, but it was of monumental significance. Those who conceived of such a task force and worked to implement it, combined with those who served on it and yet others who worked to implement its recommendations, are owed a debt of gratitude by today's health educators.

The research done by faculty, graduate students, and practicing professions has also resulted in more recognition and credibility for health education. Although a research base alone lends credibility, research on program effectiveness and cost effectiveness that showed that good health education not only works but also saves money for the health service delivery system has been of inestimable worth to the profession. Such data have served as ammunition in the battle to establish health education as a necessary program element. The researchers who accepted the challenge, discipline, and rigor to do high-quality studies similarly are owed a debt of gratitude by the profession. Although no single study changed the direction of the profession, the accumulation of a database had much to do with recent changes.

The efforts of those who played leadership roles in delineating and verifying the requisite skills of health educators will, with the passage of time, be seen as another event of epic proportions. The hundreds of meetings by hundreds of health educators that led to consensus on necessary skills, on curricula, on standards of practice, and on credentialing have been of immeasurable worth to the development of legitimacy of the profession. Health education has emerged into a profession as the body of knowledge needed for professional practice has become standardized, documented as to effectiveness, and required of practicing professionals and those institutions training them. Health education has matured far beyond what all but a few of its pioneers envisioned and has come of age. It has matured to the point where it can legitimately claim its rightful place in the health services delivery system of the nations of the world.

A common body of knowledge exists, undergraduate and graduate degree programs exist, jobs exist with salaries comparable to other professionals, policy statements exist, program funding exists, and the citizenry is demanding health education services. Indeed, at least when compared with years of the recent past, the golden age of health education has arrived. The culmination of these decades of work was the development of *Healthy People 2000: National Health Promotion and Disease Prevention Objectives.* These two documents are not only the culmination of work by several generations of health educators, but are a sound platform on which to build programs for the 21st century.

THE IMMEDIATE FUTURE

Examining the future requires emphasizing a new set of skills for most health educators, and it demands an optimistic viewpoint. As the fictional Don Quixote said, "It is madness to see life as it is, instead of how it can become." Much can be learned about the future from examining the present. As futurist Alvin Toffler suggested, "if we do not, we shall be compelled to relive it, and even worse, to endure the future we have created." The following scenario represents our views on what may occur in the next decade.

Programmatic emphasis in the rest of the 1990s will focus on the year 2000 objectives. Key issues facing health educators will include AIDS and the other leading causes of death and disability. In *Closing the Gap*, developed by the Carter Center of Emory University, the highest priority precursors for major national health problems were tobacco, alcohol, injury, unintended pregnancy, gaps in primary prevention, violence, depression, and substance abuse.[1] All of these have important implications for health education. Continued use of measurable objectives at all levels and in all settings will be the standard practice. "Objectives can be the building blocks for programs that work—programs that make a difference in public health."[2]

Despite a national trend in the 1990s toward better health, there continues to be a disparity in death, disability, and illness experienced by minority groups. An estimated 60,000 excess deaths occur among African Americans, Hispanics, Asian/Pacific Islanders, and Native Americans annually.[3] The Office of Minority Health has been established in the Department of Health and Human Services. Special emphasis on minority health has clear implications for health educators. Besides recruitment and training of health education professionals from disadvantaged and minority groups, several areas of emphasis will be continued regarding the planning and funding of health education programs:

1. Increasing the use of media serving special populations and other communications channels at the state and local level
2. Developing culturally sensitive educational materials and media messages
3. Aggressively disseminating the materials to special populations through community-based organizations[4]

When working with minority groups, health educators need to use all their skills in consultation and community organization. Of utmost importance is involving community citizens and existing resource persons in planning and program implementation. Involvement means a willingness on the health educator's part to work as a partner with the community, not to use it as a "ceremonial" advisor.[5]

Perhaps of most significance, health educators will have to begin thinking of minority group members as the emerging majority. Early in the 21st century,

Caucasians will cease being the majority in the United States. There will no longer be a majority unless non-Caucasian people are so grouped. The United States will truly become the "melting pot" it has been called.

Demographic studies have analyzed, described, and projected these changes. Yet it remains for health educators to analyze, describe, and project what the changes will mean for the profession. How will they affect natality, morbidity, and mortality rates and, therefore, programmatic emphasis? How will they affect funding and hiring, demographic characteristics of the profession, professional preparation in colleges and universities, and the next generation of textbooks? Assuredly, there will be an impact, and the issue demands the very best thinking of the profession.

Health educators in the year 2000 will include many of the current generation of educators and graduates of the next several classes. The class of 2000 will be the few selected from a large pool of applicants, much as occurs at medical schools today.

Health educators will be screened and trained so that they are all good role models. They will have successfully passed gene screening, so that only those most likely to remain good role models are admitted. Periodic testing for drugs, alcohol, and nicotine will occur. Psychological stress analysis that includes a computerized analysis for voice tremors will occur intermittently. Each health educator will carry a wallet card with the following inscription: "No written word or verbal plea can teach other hearts what they should be; not all the books on all the shelves, but what we as professionals are ourselves."

Health educators will have a solid background in both the natural sciences and the social sciences. They will have specialized training in two core disciplines: economics and politics. They will also be experts in resource acquisition and management and in the ability to recognize and use power.

Health educators in the class of 2000 will recognize the need to work with two rapidly increasing non–English-speaking populations that were formerly thought of as minorities. To work with the major population groups in the United States, new health educators will be fluent in at least two of the following three languages: English, Spanish, and Chinese.

In 2000, health educators will have new respect and prestige and will have graduated from approved or accredited university programs. The faculty in such programs will also be role models. Many will have joint appointments in a university and in a community-based program; those who do not will be required to have reality assignments for one semester of every eight, where they work in community-based programs. Health education faculty will do less "professing" and will be engaged with students in more community-based demonstration projects.

University classrooms will be adequately equipped with current technology, which will be used effectively in classes. Research will occur regularly on the appropriate mixture of technology and human interaction in the health education process.

Students who successfully complete the entry-level screening, periodic monitoring, and rigorous competency-based university training will then be required to take a certification or licensure examination. All who aspire to be a certified or licensed health educator must be graduates of an approved or accredited program with either a baccalaureate or master's degree. Individuals who successfully pass examination of their knowledge, attitudes, and skills will be so certified or licensed and will be required to maintain their certification through continuing education credits. All others who desire to be involved in the profession of health education will be titled as "health education aides."

Settings

More health educators in the year 2000 will be employed in medical care settings, in worksite programs, and in private practice. Educational specialists in medical care settings will focus on helping clients maintain and improve their wellness, rather than recover from their sickness. Such programs will be largely funded from some form of universal health care system, which will include cost-effective preventive services. Health educators in the worksite settings will increase and will be funded by the corporations, from dollars saved through prevention.

Health education in schools will continue to be advocated. Programs in the schools will be funded by national health insurance dollars and will be done in the name of primary prevention and medical care cost control.

Local health departments will continue to be the primary agencies responsible for carrying out public health functions. Health education in health departments will decrease in scope and prestige and will focus on the growing group of the poor and uneducated. (Robots will have replaced most of the unskilled workers because robots are more dependable, accurate, and cost effective. They also do not demand coffee breaks, sick leaves, or raises in pay.)

Foundations will continue to be important sources of funding demonstration projects because of continued high interest rates. Such innovative projects will be in remote colonies in space or under the ocean.

Much of health education will be done in the homes of clients, as an integral part of home health care. Homes will be the site for patient education, diagnosis, and treatment. Hospitals will provide tertiary care and will evolve into research centers. Outpatient clinics will proliferate and will substantially reduce inpatient care even further.

The medical establishment and the public health establishment will be increasingly irrelevant. Health promotion specialists know what must be done. Success will depend on teaching people where their daily decisions about environment and lifestyles are influenced and made. This means reaching them in schools, at work, and in other nonmedical settings in the community.

Use of Technology

When the issue of educational technology comes up, most people think first of microcomputers. Microcomputers have already had a "healthy" impact on people. At home, people use computers to design diets and analyze nutrients. Microcomputers are used to design exercise plans, records efforts, and analyze the effect of those efforts. Silicon chips similar to those in microcomputers are placed in running shoes, treadmills, rowing machines, and other exercise devices to record exercise automatically. Computer programs exist to assist people to design weight loss programs, measure stress, learn about drugs and alcohol, and so on. Immunization histories can be recorded and health risk appraisals can be done. Microcomputers can easily do readability tests, generate crossword puzzles or other learning aids, and generate personalized instruction sheets for in-home use. Of course, they can prepare charts, graphs, and diagrams to give to clients or to be converted to transparencies.

Computer-assisted instruction exists on most health topics. Computer-managed instruction exists on some topics, in which records of use and scores are kept. Some computer-managed instruction programs give diagnostic tests and generate individualized lists of reference materials, review tests, and records of mastery.

Some computer-assisted and computer-managed instruction is linked to interactive videodiscs, so that real-life photography can be used in the programs. Of course, the computer permits going to time lapse, slow motion, and freeze frame, making the result better than real-life photography. Health educators in the year 2000 will be adept in developing and using effective programs of this nature.

Microcomputers and the related microchips are affecting other aspects of health that have implications for educators. The blind can hear information that has been read and converted to sound. The deaf can read phone calls by use of devices that connect telephones to microcomputers. The deaf can read script in television programs that are closed captioned. The paralyzed can operate a variety of appliances by voice control because of microchips.

Picture phones are a reality, albeit an expensive one. They are now used in business and industry for conference calls and will be used for health care setting to home communication. Timed messages can be programmed to call a client at specific intervals, for example, to remind a patient to take medication. Facsimile machines will be used to transmit information almost instantly to homes as well as to places of employment. Interactive video conferences will also largely replace home visits.

Robots currently exist in industry and will be used to do repetitive, boring tasks for educators. Computer-assisted diagnosis that uses microchips on slides or in test tubes will permit physicians to do tests in the office. These "smart" test tubes and slides also will permit clients to do diagnostic tests in their homes. Clients will need additional education to know what to use and when.

Health Education Topics

The content of health education will also change significantly by the year 2000. Chronic diseases such as heart disease and cancer will have a gradually reduced incidence. The genetic marker for a common form of heart disease has already been found. By 2000, other genetic markers will be identified.

Gene therapy will be commonplace for major chronic diseases like heart disease and cancer. It will replace or alter deficient genes responsible for hereditary susceptibility to chronic disease. Gene therapy will also raise serious ethical questions that will need to be considered. Once scientists begin tinkering with human heredity, it may be difficult to know where to stop.

Morbidity rates for existing chronic diseases will be reduced as a result of the rapidly developing class of biodrugs that are being designed using information gained from genetic research. Scientific advances will generally make it easier to identify risk and exposure and will provide new opportunities for preventive measures and cure of diseases and conditions. However, new and different infections and chronic diseases will emerge.

Effective prevention and treatment regimens will exist for AIDS, and health educators will plan, implement, and evaluate health education to help people prevent AIDS and to participate in screening, and/or other diagnostic activities.

Of course, cigarette smoking will be largely nonexistent in 2000. It will be viewed as a socially undesirable, personal addiction. This major contributor to disease and death started in the 20th century and will end in the 20th century. The government will stop subsidizing the tobacco industry and stop letting the media advertise this major killer. Smoking will be prohibited in public places. The surgeon general's campaign to have a smoke-free generation will be successful, and this chief avoidable cause of death will be at last a thing of the past.

New problems and concerns will arise to replace those that are presently addressed by health educators. Of course, there will continue to be politically hot topics. Reuse of water and water rationing will be commonplace and will require continued education. The toxic chemical problem will continue to be significant as new classes of chemical compounds are found to be toxic. "Technostress" will increase, as will isolation and alienation. Computers will have reduced human contact or will have provided an excuse to avoid it. Health educators will give more and more emphasis to the mental, emotional, and social aspects of health. They will look for ways to implement John Naisbitt's concept of "high tech-high touch."[6]

There will be a high incidence of social and emotional disorders. People will be less tolerant of these conditions and other subclinical symptoms and will demand services. There will be more worksite programs to address these problems, as well as more fee-for-service programs for the growing "super class" of two-income families that can afford the best in health care. People of all classes will come to appreciate more fully that "the greatest medications are those that are swallowed by the mind."

Funding

Financing for health education will undergo dramatic shifts by the year 2000. Preventive health care will become a major component of some form of national health insurance. Business and industry will expend much more to promote high-level wellness. Corporate wellness programs will be necessary to recruit and retain employees. Corporations that have such programs will receive reduced rates for various forms of insurance.

The most rapidly increasing sector of health education will be commercial. Weight Watchers and health spas provide the prototypes of organizations that do health education well because people are able and willing to pay for it. Of course, the profit motive will speed research and improve effectiveness. For example, research on smoking clinics will result in diagnostic tests for smokers that will allow prescription of the one best method of stopping smoking for that individual. Much more emphasis will be on maintenance of health gains and on reinforcement of behavior change, so that weight loss and smokeless behavior remain permanent because of the profit motive. That which Toffler called the "prosumer ethic" will result in demanding such services, and the emerging super class will provide a profit motive that will ensure that it exists. Fee-for-service health education will be the most rapidly developing form of health education between now and the year 2000.

Lest We Forget

This book has examined community health education theory and practice, with special emphasis on settings, roles, and skills. It is an introduction to these topics, an overview for those preparing to enter the profession and for those preparing to take the Certified Health Education Specialist exam. However, readers must remember it is not the end of a course of study, but the beginning.

Although the book will have many uses, its primary audience is college students in baccalaureate degree programs. Obviously, master's and doctoral degree programs and professional reading will add depth of knowledge on each of the topics presented, especially theoretical considerations. From the group of experienced health educators with advanced degrees will emerge the leaders in the profession.

By interacting in conferences, professional journals, and computer networks, health education professionals will improve the theory and practice of health education. In so doing, they will collectively save millions of lives and millions of dollars.

Health educators are involved in matters of life and death. Therefore, there is a constant need for improved practice, for the best possible programs.

The Health Project is a public/private organization involving leading U.S. corporations, the labor movement, the academic community, public groups, and government agencies. In a 1993 press release, the project reminded the nation that prevention needs to be a greater part of health care. The following excerpts are appropriate for health educators to ponder.[7]

Preventable causes account for eight of the nine leading categories and for 980,000 deaths per year.

Americans are going to have to accept increasing responsibility for the state of their own health.

They can no longer afford to neglect much less abuse their bodies and expect their employers and the government to pay for extravagant use of the country's health care system.

Ideally, a society of people does not smoke, does not consume alcohol to excess, exercises regularly, eats wisely, uses seat belts, treats its hypertension, provides other preventive health services, and sees that care at the end of life is humane.

People assume more responsibility for their own health by requesting health services when such services can be of help, and avoiding them when they cannot. There is emphasis on both disease prevention and collective individual restraint.

Preventable illness makes up approximately 70% of the burden of illness and the associated costs.

A growing literature documents the potential of well formulated health promotion programs to decrease health care costs.

The costs should be borne by those who will ultimately have the savings—that is those now paying the costs. Insurers, industry and government can pay out of their potential savings.

There already are model programs that improve health and decrease costs. It is not knowledge that is lacking, but penetration of these programs into a greater number of settings.

IN CONCLUSION

There will always be a need for health educators. As the philosopher Mohan Singh admonished, we should "remember always to be grateful to the millions of people whose despicable habits make health education necessary."[8]

However, health education as it is known today will be as irrelevant in 2000 as the "blood and bones" health and hygiene of the early 1900s is today. Health education and health promotion will flourish with or without today's generation of health educators, or perhaps even in spite of them.

The society that now provides the very best care possible for those who are dying will change its priorities and will soon provide the very best health education for those who are living. The intermediate steps necessary to implement such a program are so large as to appear overwhelming, but the opportunity exists for today's health educators to make a difference. Some will choose to do so. The future described in this chapter for the year 2000 can be reality if today's generation of health educators commit themselves to making it happen.

***

Suggested Learning Activity

1. Read "The Top 10 Health Trends" (Suggested Reading) or any recent article on health trends. Identify health education needs and opportunities for each of the trends.

NOTES

1. R.W. Amler and H.B. Dull, eds. *Closing the Gap—The Burden of Unnecessary Illness* (New York: Oxford University Press, 1987).

2. J.M. McGinnis, *Using Health Objectives To Make a Difference, Management by Objectives in Public Health: A Slide Presentation* (Washington, D.C.: U.S. Department of Health and Human Services, Office of Disease Prevention and Health Promotion, January 1988), 1.

3. *Prevention Report* (Washington, D.C.: U.S. Department of Health and Human Services, Office of Disease Prevention and Health Promotion, August 1988), 1.

4. Strategies for Promoting Health for Specific Populations, *Journal of Public Health Policy* (1987): 375.

5. K. Evans, Disparity, *Ohio Health Promotion Network Newsletter* (Spring 1988): 1.

6. J. Naisbitt, *MegaTrends: Ten New Directions Transforming Our Lives* (New York: Warner Books, 1982), 35–36.

7. Press release, The Health Project, July 22, 1993.

8. M. Singh, *Cosmic Reflections of Health for All* (Ottawa, Ont.: Le Cercle des Amis de Mohan Singh, 1983), 3.

SUGGESTED READING

The Top 10 Health Trends. 1992. *US News & World Report*, 113, no. 16:67.

Bibliography

American Hospital Association. 1979. *Promoting health*. Chicago: American Hospital Association.

American Journal of Health Promotion. Birmingham, Mich.: American Journal of Health Promotion, Inc.

American Journal of Public Health. Washington, D.C.: American Public Health Association.

Ames, E.E. 1992. *Designing school health curricula*. Madison, Wisc.: Brown and Benchmark.

Backer, T.E. 1992. *Mass media health campaigns: What works?* Beverly Hills, Calif.: Sage Publications.

Bantuzo, R.M. 1988. *Health education: Index of modern information*. New York: ABBE Publishers Association.

Bates, I.J., and A.E. Winder. 1984. *Introduction to health education*. Palo Alto, Calif.: Mayfield Publishing Co.

Bedworth, A.E., and D.A. Bedworth. 1992. *The profession and practice of health education*. Dubuque, Iowa: Wm. C. Brown Publishing.

Behrens, R., and M. Longe. 1984. *Hospital-based health promotion programs for children and youth*. Chicago: American Hospital Association.

Bellingham, R., et al. 1993. *Designing effective health promotion programs*. Amherst, Mass.: Human Resources Development Press.

Bracht, N., ed. 1990. *Health promotion at the community level*. Newbury Park, Calif.: Sage Publications.

Breckon, D.J. 1987. *Ethical aspects of life and death*. Independence, Mo.: Herald House.

Breckon, D.J. 1982. *Hospital health education: A guide to program development*. Gaithersburg, Md.: Aspen Publishers, Inc.

Breckon, D.J. 1985. *Marketing yourself as a health educator*. Mt. Pleasant, Mich.: Central Michigan University, Center for Health Related Studies.

Breckon, D.J. 1987. *Microcomputer applications to health education and health promotion*. Muncie, Ind.: Eta Sigma Gamma.

Breckon, D.J., and R.M. Pennington. 1986. Interactive videodisks: A new generation of computer-assisted instruction. *Health Values: Achieving High Level Wellness* 10, no. 6:52–55.

Bunton, R., et al., eds. 1992. *Health promotion: Disciplines and diversity*. New York: Routledge Publications.

Deeds, S.G. 1992. *The health education specialist: Self-study for professional competence*. Los Alamitos, Calif.: Loose Canon Publications.

Derryberry, H., ed. 1987. *Educating for health: The selected papers of Mayhew Derryberry*. New York: National Center for Health Education.

293

Dignan, M.B. 1986. *Measurement and evaluation of health education.* Springfield, Ill.: Charles C. Thomas.

Foreman, S.G., ed. 1987. *School-based affective and social interventions.* New York: Haworth Press.

Glanz, K., et al., eds. 1990. *Health behavior and health education: Theory, research and practice.* San Francisco: Jossey-Bass Publishers.

Gottlieb, N.H., ed. 1987. *Ethical dilemmas in health promotion.* New York: John Wiley & Sons, Inc.

Green, L.W., and C.L. Anderson. 1982. *Community health.* St. Louis: C. V. Mosby Co.

Green, L.W., and M.W. Kreuter. 1991. *Health promotion planning: An educational and environmental approach.* Mountain View, Calif.: Mayfield Publishing Co.

Green, L.W., et al. 1980. *Health education planning: A diagnostic approach.* Palo Alto, Calif.: Mayfield Publishing Co.

Green, L., and F. Lewis. 1986. *Measurement and evaluation in health education and health promotion.* Palo Alto, Calif.: Mayfield Publishing Co.

Greenberg, J.S. 1987. *Health education: Learner centered instructional strategies.* Dubuque, Iowa: Wm. C. Brown & Co.

Greene, W.H., and B.G. Simons-Morton. 1990. *Introduction to health education.* Prospect Heights, Ala.: Waveland Press.

Health Education Quarterly. San Francisco: Society for Public Health Education.

Health Education Reports, 807 National Press Building, Washington, D.C. 20045.

Health Values: Achieving High Level Wellness. 1979. Thorofare, N.J.: Charles Slack, Inc.

Healthy Communities 2000: Model Standards. 1991. Washington, D.C.: U.S. Government Printing Office.

Healthy People 2000: National Health Promotion and Disease Prevention Objectives. 1991. Washington, D.C.: U.S. Government Printing Office.

Higgs, Z.R., and D.D. Gustafson. 1985. *Community as a client: Assessment and diagnosis.* Philadelphia: F.A. Davis Co.

Houle, C.O. 1980. *Continuing learning in the professions.* San Francisco: Jossey-Bass.

Katz, A. 1987. *Prevention and health: Directions for policy and practice.* New York: Haworth Press.

Kernaghan, S., and B.E. Giloth. 1988. *Tracking the impact of health promotion on organizations: A key to program survival.* Chicago: American Hospital Association.

Klarreich, S.H., ed. 1987. *Health and fitness in the workplace.* New York: Praeger Publishers.

Locating funds for health promotion projects. 1988. Washington, D.C.: Office of Disease Prevention and Health Promotion, Public Health Service.

Longe, M. 1985. *Innovative hospital-based health promotion.* Chicago: American Hospital Association.

Longe, M.E., and A. Wolf. 1984. *Promoting community health through innovative hospital-based programs.* Chicago: American Hospital Association.

Making PSAs work: A handbook for health communicator professionals. 1983. Bethesda, Md.: National Cancer Institute.

Manoff, R.K. 1985. *Social marketing: New imperatives for public health.* New York: Praeger Publishers.

Matthews, B.P., ed. 1982. *The practice of health education,* SOPHE Heritage Collection. Vol. 2. Oakland, Calif.: Third Party Publishing Co.

McKenzie, J.F., and J.L. Jurs. 1993. *Planning, implementing, and evaluating health promotion programs.* New York: Macmillan Publishing Co.

Meanes, R.K. 1988. *Resource handbook for health education.* New York: Benchmark Press.

Miller, D., and S. Telljohan. 1992. *Health education in the elementary school.* Madison, Wisc.: Brown and Benchmark.

National Center for Health Education. 1983. *Education for health: The selective guide.* New York.

O'Donnell, M., ed. 1993. *Health promotion in the workplace.* Albany, N.Y.: Delmar Publishers, Inc.

Opatz, J.P. 1993. *Economic impact of worksite health promotion.* Champaign, Ill.: Human Kinetics Publishers.

Parkinson, R.S., et. al. 1984. *Managing health promotion in the workplace.* Palo Alto, Calif.: Mayfield Publishing Co..

Patton, R., and W. Cissell. 1990. *Community organization: Traditional principles and modern applications.* Johnson City, Tenn.: Latchpins Press.

Planning hospital health promotion services for business and industry. 1982. Chicago: American Hospital Association.

Pollock, M. 1987. *Planning and implementing health education in schools.* Palo Alto, Calif.: Mayfield Publishing Co.

Programming ideas for target populations. 1984. Chicago: American Hospital Association.

Report of the 1990 Joint Committee on Health Education Terminology. 1991. *Journal of Health Education,* 22, no. 2

Rice, R., and W.J. Paisley. eds. 1982. *Public communication campaigns.* Beverly Hills, Calif.: Sage Publications.

Rorden, J.W. 1987. *Nurses as health teachers: A practical guide.* Philadelphia: W.B. Saunders Publishing Co.

Ross, H.S., and P.R. Mico. 1980. *Theory and practice in health education.* Palo Alto, Calif.: Mayfield Publishing Co.

Sarvela, P., et al. 1993. *Health education and measurement: A practitioner's perspectives.* Madison, Wisc.: Brown and Benchmark.

Shield, J., et al. 1992. *Developing health education materials for special audiences.* Chicago: American Dietetic Association.

Simonds, S.K., ed. 1982. *The philosophical, behavioral, and professional bases for health education,* SOPHE Heritage Collection. Vol. 1. Oakland, Calif.: Third Party Publishing Co.

Singh, M. 1983. *Cosmic reflections of health for all.* Ottawa: Le Cercle des Amis de Mohan Singh.

Teague, M.L. 1987. *Health promotion: Achieving high-level wellness in later years.* New York: Benchmark Press.

Wallack, L., et al. 1992. *Media advocacy and public health.* Newbury Park, Calif.: Sage Publications.

Ward, W.B., ed. 1988. *Advances in health education and promotion.* Greenwich, Conn.: JAI Press.

Wendel, S., ed. 1993. *Healthy, wealthy and wise.* Omaha: Wellness Council of America.

Windsor, R., et al. 1984. *Evaluation of health promotion programs.* Palo Alto, Calif.: Mayfield Publishing Co.

World Health Organization. 1992. *School health education to prevent AIDS and sexually transmitted diseases.* Albany, N.Y.

Zapka, J.G., ed. 1982. *Research and evaluation in health education,* SOPHE Heritage Collection. Vol. 3. Oakland, Calif.: Third Party Publishing Co.

Responsibilities and Competencies for Entry-Level Health Educators

RESPONSIBILITY I—ASSESSING INDIVIDUAL AND COMMUNITY NEEDS FOR HEALTH EDUCATION

Competency A: Obtain health-related data about social and cultural environments, growth and development factors, needs, and interests.

Sub-Competencies:
    1. Select valid sources of information about health needs and interests.
    2. Utilize computerized sources of health-related information.
    3. Employ or develop appropriate data-gathering instruments.
    4. Apply survey techniques to acquire health data.

Competency B: Distinguish between behaviors that foster, and those that hinder, well-being.

Sub-Competencies:
    1. Investigate physical, social, emotional, and intellectual factors influencing health behaviors.
    2. Identify behaviors that tend to promote or compromise health.
    3. Recognize the role of learning and affective experience in shaping patterns of health behavior.

Competency C: Infer needs for health education on the basis of obtained data.

Sub-Competencies:
    1. Analyze needs assessment data.
    2. Determine priority areas of need for health education.

Reprinted from *A Framework for the Development of Competency-Based Curricula for Entry Level Health Educators* by the National Task Force on the Preparation and Practice of Health Educators, Inc., with permission of the National Commission for Health Education Credentialing, Inc., © 1985.

RESPONSIBILITY II—PLANNING EFFECTIVE HEALTH EDUCATION PROGRAMS

Competency A: Recruit community organizations, resource people, and potential participants for support and assistance in program planning.

Sub-Competencies:
1. Communicate need for the program to those who will be involved.
2. Obtain commitments from personnel and decision makers who will be involved in the program.
3. Seek ideas and opinions of those who will affect, or be affected by, the program.
4. Incorporate feasible ideas and recommendations into the planning process.

Competency B: Develop a logical scope and sequence plan for a health education program.

Sub-Competencies:
1. Determine the range of health information requisite to a given program of instruction.
2. Organize the subject areas constituting the scope of a program in logical sequence.

Competency C: Formulate appropriate and measurable program objectives.

Sub-Competencies:
1. Infer educational objectives facilitative of achievement of specified competencies.
2. Develop a framework of broadly stated, operational objectives relevant to a proposed health education program.

Competency D: Design educational programs consistent with specified program objectives.

Sub-Competencies:
1. Match proposed learning activities with those implicit in the stated objectives.
2. Formulate a wide variety of alternative educational methods.

3. Select strategies best suited to implementation of educational objectives in a given setting.
4. Plan a sequence of learning opportunities building upon, and reinforcing mastery of, preceding objectives.

RESPONSIBILITY III—IMPLEMENTING HEALTH EDUCATION PROGRAMS

Competency A: Exhibit competence in carrying out planned educational programs.

Sub-Competencies:
1. Employ a wide range of educational methods and techniques.
2. Apply individual or group process methods as appropriate to given learning situations.
3. Utilize instructional equipment and other instructional media effectively.
4. Select methods that best facilitate practice of program objectives.

Competency B: Infer enabling objectives as needed to implement instructional programs in specified settings.

Sub-Competencies:
1. Pretest learners to ascertain present abilities and knowledge relative to proposed program objectives.
2. Develop subordinate measurable objectives as needed for instruction.

Competency C: Select methods and media best suited to implement program plans for specific learners.

Sub-Competencies:
1. Analyze learner characteristics, legal aspects, feasibility, and other considerations influencing choices among methods.
2. Evaluate the efficacy of alternative methods and techniques capable of facilitating program objectives.
3. Determine the availability of information, personnel, time, and equipment needed to implement the program for a given audience.

Competency D: Monitor educational programs, adjusting objectives and activities as necessary.

Sub-Competencies:
1. Compare actual program activities with the stated objectives.
2. Assess the relevance of existing program objectives to current needs.
3. Revise program activities and objectives as necessitated by changes in learner needs.
4. Appraise applicability of resources and materials relative to given educational objectives.

RESPONSIBILITY IV—EVALUATING EFFECTIVENESS OF HEALTH EDUCATION PROGRAMS

Competency A: Develop plans to assess achievement of program objectives.

Sub-Competencies:
1. Determine standards of performance to be applied as criteria of effectiveness.
2. Establish a realistic scope of evaluation efforts.
3. Develop an inventory of existing valid and reliable tests and survey instruments.
4. Select appropriate methods for evaluating program effectiveness.

Competency B: Carry out evaluation plans.

Sub-Competencies:
1. Facilitate administration of the tests and activities specified in the plan.
2. Utilize data-collecting methods appropriate to the objectives.
3. Analyze resulting evaluation data.

Competency C: Interpret results of program evaluation.

Sub-Competencies:
1. Apply criteria of effectiveness to obtained results of a program.
2. Translate evaluation results into terms easily understood by others.
3. Report effectiveness of educational programs in achieving proposed objectives.

Competency D: Infer implications from findings for future program planning.

Sub-Competencies:
1. Explore possible explanations for important evaluation findings.
2. Recommend strategies for implementing results of evaluation.

RESPONSIBILITY V—COORDINATING PROVISION OF HEALTH EDUCATION SERVICES

Competency A: Develop a plan for coordinating health education services.

Sub-Competencies:
1. Determine the extent of available health education services.
2. Match health education services to proposed program activities.
3. Identify gaps and overlaps in the provision of collaborative health services.

Competency B: Facilitate cooperation between and among levels of program personnel.

Sub-Competencies:
1. Promote cooperation and feedback among personnel related to the program.
2. Apply various methods of conflict reduction as needed.
3. Analyze the role of health educator as liaison between program staff and outside groups and organizations.

Competency C: Formulate practical modes of collaboration among health agencies and organizations.

Sub-Competencies:
1. Stimulate development of cooperation among personnel responsible for community health education program.
2. Suggest approaches for integrating health education within existing health programs.
3. Develop plans for promoting collaborative efforts among health agencies and organizations with mutual interests.

Competency D: Organize inservice training programs for teachers, volunteers, and other interested personnel.

Sub-Competencies:
1. Plan an operational, competency-oriented training program.
2. Utilize instructional resources that meet a variety of inservice training needs.
3. Demonstrate a wide range of strategies for conducting inservice training programs.

RESPONSIBILITY VI—ACTING AS A RESOURCE PERSON IN HEALTH EDUCATION

Competency A: Utilize computerized health information retrieval systems effectively.

Sub-Competencies:
1. Match an information need with the appropriate retrieval system.
2. Access principal on-line and other database health information resources.

Competency B: Establish effective consultative relationships with those requesting assistance in solving health-related problems.

Sub-Competencies:
1. Analyze parameters of effective consultative relationships.
2. Describe special skills and abilities needed by health educators for consultation activities.
3. Formulate a plan for providing consultation to other health professionals.
4. Explain the process of marketing health education consultative services.

Competency C: Interpret and respond to requests for health information.

Sub-Competencies:
1. Analyze general processes for identifying the information needed to satisfy a request.
2. Employ a wide range of approaches in referring requesters to valid sources of health information.

Competency D: Select effective educational resource materials for dissemination.

Sub-Competencies:
1. Assemble educational material of value to the health of individuals and community groups.
2. Evaluate the worth and applicability of resource materials for given audiences.
3. Apply various processes in the acquisition of resource materials.
4. Compare different methods for distributing educational materials.

RESPONSIBILITY VII—COMMUNICATING HEALTH AND HEALTH EDUCATION NEEDS, CONCERNS, AND RESOURCES

Competency A: Interpret concepts, purposes, and theories of health education.

Sub-Competencies:
1. Evaluate the state of the art of health education.
2. Analyze the foundations of the discipline of health education.
3. Describe major responsibilities of the health educator in the practice of health education.

Competency B: Predict the impact of societal value systems on health education programs.

Sub-Competencies:
1. Investigate social forces causing opposing viewpoints regarding health education needs and concerns.
2. Employ a wide range of strategies for dealing with controversial health issues.

Competency C: Select a variety of communication methods and techniques in providing health information.

Sub-Competencies:
1. Utilize a wide range of techniques for communicating health and health education information.
2. Demonstrate proficiency in communicating health information and health education needs.

Competency D: Foster communication between health care providers and consumers.

Sub-Competencies:
1. Interpret the significance and implications of health care providers' messages to consumers.
2. Act as liaison between consumer groups and individuals and health care provider organizations.

Summary List of Risk Reduction Objectives from *Healthy People 2000*

1. Physical Activity and Fitness Risk Reduction Objectives

A. Increase to at least 30 percent the proportion of people aged 6 and older who engage regularly, preferably daily, in light to moderate physical activity for at least 30 minutes per day.

B. Increase to at least 20 percent the proportion of people aged 18 and older, and to at least 75 percent the proportion of children and adolescents aged 6 through 17, who engage in vigorous physical activity that promotes the development and maintenance of cardiorespiratory fitness three or more days per week for 20 or more minutes per occasion.

C. Reduce to no more than 15 percent the proportion of people aged 6 and older who engage in no leisure-time physical activity.

D. Increase to at least 40 percent the proportion of people aged 6 and older who regularly perform physical activities that enhance and maintain muscular strength, muscular endurance, and flexibility.

E. Increase to at least 50 percent the proportion of overweight people aged 12 and older who have adopted sound dietary practices combined with regular physical activity to attain an appropriate body weight.

2. Nutrition Risk Reduction Objectives

A. Reduce dietary fat intake to an average of 30 percent of calories or less and average saturated fat intake to less than 10 percent of calories among people aged 2 and older.

B. Increase complex carbohydrate and fiber-containing foods in the diets of adults to five or more daily servings for vegetables (including legumes) and fruits, and to six or more daily servings for grain products.

C. Increase to at least 50 percent the proportion of overweight people aged 12 and older who have adopted sound dietary practices combined with regular physical activity to attain an appropriate body weight.

D. Increase calcium intake so at least 50 percent of youth aged 12 through 24 and 50 percent of pregnant and lactating women consume three or more servings daily of foods rich in calcium, and at least 50 percent of people aged 25 and older consume two or more servings daily.

E. Decrease salt and sodium intake so at least 65 percent of home meal preparers prepare foods without adding salt, at least 80 percent of people avoid using salt at the table, and at least 40 percent of adults regularly purchase foods modified or lower in sodium.

F. Reduce iron deficiency to less than 3 percent among children aged 1 through 4 and among women of childbearing age.

G. Increase to at least 75 percent the proportion of mothers who breastfeed their babies in the early postpartum period and to at least 50 percent the proportion who continue breastfeeding until their babies are 5 to 6 months old.

H. Increase to at least 75 percent the proportion of parents and caregivers who use feeding practices that prevent baby-bottle tooth decay.

I. Increase to at least 85 percent the proportion of people aged 18 and older who use food labels to make nutritious food selections.

3. Tobacco Risk Reduction Objectives

A. Reduce cigarette smoking to a prevalence of no more than 15 percent among people aged 20 and older.

B. Reduce the initiation of smoking by children and youth so that no more than 15 percent have become regular smokers by age 20.

C. Increase to at least 50 percent the proportion of cigarette smokers aged 18 and older who stopped smoking cigarettes for at least one day during the preceding year.

D. Increase smoking cessation during pregnancy so that at least 60 percent of women who are cigarette smokers at the time they become pregnant quit smoking early in pregnancy and maintain abstinence for the remainder of their pregnancy.

E. Reduce to no more than 20 percent the proportion of children aged 6 and younger who are regularly exposed to tobacco smoke at home.

F. Reduce smokeless tobacco use by males aged 12 through 24 to a prevalence of no more than 4 percent.

4. Alcohol and Other Drugs Risk Reduction Objectives

A. Increase by at least 1 year the average age of first use of cigarettes, alcohol, and marijuana by adolescents aged 7 through 17.

B. Reduce the proportion of young people who have used alcohol, marijuana, and cocaine in the past months.

C. Reduce the proportion of high school seniors and college students engaging in recent occasions of heavy drinking of alcoholic beverages to no more than 28 percent of high school seniors and 32 percent of college students.

D. Reduce alcohol consumption by people aged 14 and older to an annual average of no more than 2 gallons of ethanol per person.

E. Increase the proportion of high school seniors who perceive social disapproval associated with the heavy use of alcohol, occasional use of marijuana, and experimentation with cocaine.

F. Increase the proportion of high school seniors who associate risk of physical or psychological harm with the heavy use of alcohol, regular use of marijuana, and experimentation with cocaine.

G. Reduce to no more than 3 percent the proportion of male high school seniors who use anabolic steroids.

5. Family Planning Risk Reduction Objectives

A. Reduce the proportion of adolescents who have engaged in sexual intercourse to no more than 15 percent by age 15 and no more than 40 percent by age 17.

B. Increase to at least 40 percent the proportion of once sexually active adolescents aged 17 and younger who have abstained from sexual activity for the previous 3 months.

C. Increase to at least 90 percent the proportion of sexually active, unmarried people aged 19 and younger who use contraception, especially combined method contraception that both effectively prevents pregnancy and provides barrier protection against disease.

D. Increase the effectiveness with which family planning methods are used, as measured by a decrease to no more than 5 percent in the proportion of couples experiencing pregnancy despite use of a contraceptive method.

6. Mental Health and Mental Disorders Risk Reduction Objectives

A. Increase to at least 30 percent the proportion of people aged 18 and older with severe, persistent mental disorders who use community support programs.

B. Increase to at least 45 percent the proportion of people with major depressive disorders who obtain treatment.

C. Increase to at least 20 percent the proportion of people aged 18 and older who seek help in coping with personal and emotional problems.

D. Decrease to no more than 5 percent the proportion of people aged 18 and older who report experiencing significant levels of stress who do not take steps to reduce or control their stress.

7. Violent and Abusive Behavior Risk Reduction Objectives

A. Reduce by 20 percent the incidence of physical fighting among adolescents aged 14 through 17.
B. Reduce by 20 percent the incidence of weapon-carrying by adolescents aged 14 through 17.
C. Reduce by 20 percent the proportion of people who possess weapons that are inappropriately stored and therefore dangerously available.

8. Educational and Community-Based Programs Risk Reduction Objectives

A. Increase the high school graduation rate to at least 90 percent, thereby reducing risks for multiple problem behaviors and poor mental and physical health.

9. Unintentional Injuries Risk Reduction Objectives

A. Increase use of occupant protection systems, such as safety belts, inflatable safety restraints, and child safety seats, to at least 85 percent of motor vehicle occupants.
B. Increase use of helmets to at least 80 percent of motorcyclists and at least 50 percent of bicyclists.

10. Occupational Safety and Health Risk Reduction Objectives

A. Increase to at least 75 percent the proportion of worksites with 50 or more employees that mandate employee use of occupant protection systems, such as seatbelts, during all work-related motor vehicle travel.
B. Reduce to no more than 15 percent the proportion of workers exposed to average daily noise levels that exceed 85 dBA.
C. Eliminate exposures that result in workers having blood lead concentrations greater than 25 µg/dL of whole blood.
D. Increase hepatitis B immunization levels to 90 percent among occupationally exposed workers.

11. Environmental Health Risk Reduction Objectives

A. Reduce human exposure to criteria air pollutants, as measured by an increase to at least 85 percent in the proportion of people who live in counties that have not exceeded any Environmental Protection Agency standard for air quality in the previous 12 months.

B. Increase to at least 40 percent the proportion of homes in which homeowners/occupants have tested for radon concentrations and that have either been found to pose minimal risk or have been modified to reduce risk to health.

C. Reduce human exposure to toxic agents by confining total pounds of toxic agents released into the air, water, and soil each year.

D. Reduce human exposure to solid waste–related water, air, and soil contamination, as measured by a reduction in average pounds of municipal solid waste produced per person each day to no more than 3.6 pounds.

E. Increase to at least 85 percent the proportion of people who receive a supply of drinking water that meets the safe drinking water standards established by the Environmental Protection Agency.

F. Reduce potential risks to human health from surface water, as measured by a decrease to no more than 15 percent in the proportion of assessed rivers, lakes, and estuaries that do not support beneficial uses, such as fishing and swimming.

12. Food and Drug Safety Risk Reduction Objectives

A. Increase to at least 75 percent of households in which principal food preparers routinely refrain from leaving perishable food out of the refrigerator for over 2 hours and wash cutting boards and utensils with soap after contact with raw meat and poultry.

13. Oral Health Risk Reduction Objectives

A. Increase to at least 50 percent the proportion of children who have received protective sealants on the occlusal (chewing) surfaces of permanent molar teeth.

B. Increase to at least 75 percent the proportion of people served by community water systems providing optimal levels of fluoride.

C. Increase use of professionally or self-administered topical or systemic (dietary) fluorides to at least 85 percent of people not receiving optimally fluoridated public water.

D. Increase to at least 75 percent the proportion of parents and caregivers who use feeding practices that prevent baby-bottle tooth decay.

14. Maternal and Infant Health Risk Reduction Objectives

A. Reduce low birth weight to an incidence of no more than 5 percent of live births and very low birth weight to no more than 1 percent of live births.

B. Increase to at least 85 percent the proportion of mothers who achieve the minimum recommended weight gain during their pregnancies.

C. Reduce severe complications of pregnancy to no more than 15 per 100 deliveries.

D. Reduce the Cesarean delivery rate to no more than 15 per 100 deliveries.

E. Increase to at least 75 percent the proportion of mothers who breastfeed their babies in the early postpartum period and to at least 50 percent the proportion who continue breastfeeding until their babies are 5 to 6 months old.

F. Increase abstinence from tobacco use by pregnant women at least 90 percent and increase abstinence from alcohol, cocaine, and marijuana by pregnant women by at least 20 percent.

15. Heart Disease and Stroke Risk Reduction Objectives

A. Increase to at least 50 percent the proportion of people with high blood pressure whose blood pressure is under control.

B. Increase to at least 90 percent the proportion of people with high blood pressure who are taking action to help control their blood pressure.

C. Reduce the mean serum cholesterol level among adults to no more than 200 mg/dL.

D. Reduce the prevalence of blood cholesterol levels of 240 mg/dL or greater to no more than 20 percent among adults.

E. Increase to at least 60 percent the proportion of adults with high blood cholesterol who are aware of their condition and are taking action to reduce their blood cholesterol to recommended levels.

F. Reduce dietary fat intake to an average of 30 percent of calories or less and average saturated fat intake to less than 10 percent of calories among people aged 2 and older.

G. Reduce overweight to a prevalence of no more than 20 percent among people aged 20 and older and no more than 15 percent among adolescents aged 12 through 19.

H. Increase to at least 30 percent the proportion of people aged 6 and older who engage regularly, preferably daily, in light to moderate physical activity for at least 30 minutes per day.

I. Reduce cigarette smoking to a prevalence of no more than 15 percent among people aged 20 and older.

16. Cancer Risk Reduction Objectives

A. Reduce cigarette smoking to a prevalence of no more than 15 percent among people aged 20 and older.

B. Reduce dietary fat intake to an average of 30 percent of calories or less and average saturated fat intake to less than 10 percent of calories among people aged 2 and older.
C. Increase complex carbohydrate and fiber-containing foods in the diets of adults to five or more daily servings for vegetables (including legumes) and fruits and to six or more daily servings for grain products.
D. Increase to at least 60 percent the proportion of people of all ages who limit sun exposure, use sunscreens and protective clothing when exposed to sunlight, and avoid artificial sources of ultraviolet light (e.g., sun lamps, tanning booths).

17. Diabetes and Chronic Disabling Conditions Risk Reduction Objectives

A. Reduce overweight to a prevalence of no more than 20 percent among people aged 20 and older and no more than 15 percent among adolescents aged 12 through 19.
B. Increase to at least 30 percent the proportion of people aged 6 and older who engage regularly, preferably daily, in light to moderate physical activity for at least 30 minutes per day.

18. HIV Infection Risk Reduction Objectives

A. Reduce the proportion of adolescents who have engaged in sexual intercourse to no more than 15 percent by age 15 and no more than 40 percent by age 17.
B. Increase to at least 50 percent the proportion of sexually active, unmarried people who used a condom at last sexual intercourse.
C. Increase to at least 50 percent the estimated proportion of all intravenous drug abusers who are in drug abuse treatment programs.
D. Increase to at least 50 percent the estimated proportion of intravenous drug abusers not in treatment who use only uncontaminated drug paraphernalia ("works").
E. Reduce to no more than 1 per 250,000 units of blood and blood components the risk of transfusion-transmitted HIV infection.

19. Sexually Transmitted Diseases Risk Reduction Objectives

A. Reduce the proportion of adolescents who have engaged in sexual intercourse to no more than 15 percent by age 15 and no more than 40 percent by age 17.
B. Increase to at least 50 percent the proportion of sexually active, unmarried people who used a condom at last sexual intercourse.

20. Immunization and Infectious Diseases Risk Reduction Objectives

A. Increase immunization levels as follows:
  • Basic immunization series among children under age 2: at least 90 percent
  • Basic immunization series among children in licensed child-care facilities and kindergarten through postsecondary education institutions: at least 95 percent
  • Pneumococcal pneumonia and influenza immunization among institutionalized chronically ill or older people: at least 80 percent
  • Pneumococcal pneumonia and influenza immunization among noninstitutionalized, high-risk populations, as defined by the Immunization Practices Advisory Committee: at least 60 percent
  • Hepatitis B immunization among high-risk populations, including infants of surface antigen-positive mothers, to at least 90 percent; occupationally exposed workers to at least 90 percent; IV-drug users in drug treatment programs to at least 50 percent; and homosexual men to at least 50 percent
B. Reduce postexposure rabies treatments to no more than 9,000 per year.

21. Clinical Preventive Services Risk Reduction Objective

A. Increase to at least 50 percent the proportion of people who have received, as a minimum within the appropriate interval, all of the screening and immunization services and at least one of the counseling services appropriate for their age and gender as recommended by the U.S. Preventive Services Task Force.

SOPHE Code of Ethics
for Health Education

Health educators take on profound responsibility in using educational processes to promote health and influence human well being. Ethical precepts that guide these processes must reflect the right of individuals and communities to make the decisions affecting their lives.

RESPONSIBILITIES TO SOCIETY

Health educators must do the following:

- Affirm an egalitarian ethic, believing that health is a basic human right for all.
- Provide people with all relevant and accurate information and resources to make their choices freely and intelligently.
- Support change by freedom of choice and self-determination, as long as these decisions pose no threat to the health of others.
- Advocate for healthful change and legislation, and speak out on issues deleterious to the public health.
- Be candid and truthful in dealings with the public, never misrepresenting or exaggerating the potential benefits of services or programs.
- Avoid and take appropriate action against unethical practices and conflict-of-interest situations.
- Respect the privacy, dignity, and culture of the individual and the community, and use skills consistent with these values.

RESPONSIBILITIES TO THE PROFESSION

Health educators must do the following:

- Share their skills, experience, and visions with their students and colleagues.
- Observe principles of informed consent and confidentiality of individuals.
- Maintain their highest levels of competence through continued study, training, and research.
- Further the art and science of health education through applied research and report findings honestly and without distortion.
- Accurately represent their capabilities, education, training, and experience, and act within the boundaries of their professional competence.
- Ensure that no exclusionary practices are enacted against individuals on the basis of gender, marital status, age, social class, religion, sexual preference, or ethnic or cultural background.

Report of the 1990 Joint Committee on Health Education Terminology

One of the essential underpinnings of any profession is a body of well-defined terms used to enable members to communicate easily and with the clarity necessary for understanding among themselves and with others. The field of health education has changed dramatically in the past two decades. The definitions in this report provide a common interpretation of terms frequently used by health educators in a variety of settings. Therefore, the terms presented here are defined for use by the professional health educator as well as by other individuals and groups.

The committee recognized that other health professionals (e.g., physicians, nurses, etc.) are concerned with and involved in health education as a part of their professional role and that they may have a different orientation. Consequently, they may use different terminology from that contained in this report. It is hoped, however, that the terms defined will be of help to these groups to clarify terminology used by health education professionals.

Words referring to health service and related personnel (e.g., *patient educator, health counselor*) or words which are in general use and understood by a variety of professionals (e.g., *mass communication, objectives, self-help, self-care, evaluation*) are not included. The committee chose to define community and school health education and associated terminology, because degrees are offered in these areas. Other areas (e.g., patient and worksite health education) were omitted because they tend to be areas of emphasis rather than degrees.

There may be other interpretations of the words defined; however, those presented in this report are as many health educators view them today. The terms included reflect trends, concepts, and practices. They help to explain what the profession is, who its practitioners are, and how they function.

CONTEXTUAL DEFINITIONS

Health education takes place within the broad context of health. Certain health terms are defined to clarify how health education functions.

Health   There are many definitions written for the word *health*. Three examples are provided:

A state of complete physical, mental, and social well-being, and not merely the absence of disease and infirmity.

A quality of life involving dynamic interaction and independence among the individual's physical well-being, his mental and emotional reactions, and the social complex in which he exists.

An integrated method of functioning which is oriented toward maximizing the potential of which the individual is capable. It requires that the individual maintain a continuum of balance and purposeful direction with the environment where he is functioning.

Health promotion and disease prevention   Health promotion and disease prevention is the aggregate of all purposeful activities designed to improve personal and public health through a combination of strategies, including the competent implementation of behavioral change strategies, health education, health protection measures, risk factor detection, health enhancement, and health maintenance.

Healthy lifestyle   A healthy lifestyle is a set of health-enhancing behaviors, shaped by internally consistent values, attitudes, beliefs, and external social and cultural forces.

Official health agency   An official health agency is a publicly supported governmental organization mandated by law and/or regulation for the protection and improvement of the health of the public.

Voluntary health organization   A voluntary health organization is a nonprofit association supported by contributions dedicated to conducting research and providing education and/or services related to particular health problems or concerns. (Note: Private voluntary organization [PVO] is the term used outside the United States to denote a voluntary health organization; in some countries and in connection with the United Nations, the term nongovernmental organization [NGO] is used.)

Private health agency   A private health agency is a profit or nonprofit organization devoted to providing primary, secondary, and/or tertiary health services, which may include health education.

PRIMARY HEALTH EDUCATION DEFINITIONS

Certain health education terms are generic and are defined here, as follows:

Health education field The health education field is a multidisciplinary practice, that is concerned with designing, implementing, and evaluating educational programs that enable individuals, families, groups, organizations, and communities to play active roles in achieving, protecting, and sustaining health.

Health education process The health education process is the continuum of learning that enables people, as individuals and as members of social structures, voluntarily to make decisions, modify behaviors, and change social conditions in ways that are health enhancing.

Health education program A health education program is a planned combination of activities developed with the involvement of specific populations and based on a needs assessment, sound principles of education, and periodic evaluation using a clear set of goals and objectives.

Health educator A health educator is a practitioner who is professionally prepared in the field of health education, who demonstrates competence in both theory and practice, and who accepts responsibility to advance the aims of the health education profession.

Examples of settings for health educators and the application of health education include, but are not limited to, the following:

- Schools
- Communities
- Postsecondary educational institutions
- Medical care institutions
- Voluntary health organizations
- Worksites (business and industry)
- Rehabilitation centers
- Professional associations
- Governmental agencies
- Public health agencies
- Environmental agencies
- Mental health agencies

Certified health education specialist A Certified Health Education Specialist (CHES) is an individual who is credentialed as a result of demonstrating competency based on criteria established by the National Commission for Health Education Credentialing, Inc. (NCHEC).

Health education coordinator A health education coordinator is a professional health educator who is responsible for the management and coordination of all health education policies, activities, and resources within a particular setting or circumstance.

Health education administrator A health education administrator is a professional health educator who has the authority and responsibility for the management and coordination of all health education policies, activities, and resources within a particular setting or circumstance.

Health information Health information is the content of communications based on data derived from systematic and scientific methods as they relate to health issues, policies, programs, services, and other aspects of individual and public health, which can be used for informing various populations and in planning health education activities.

Health literacy Health literacy is the capacity of an individual to obtain, interpret, and understand basic health information and services and the competence to use such information and services in ways that are health enhancing.

Health advising* Health advising is a process of informing and assisting individuals or groups in making decisions and solving problems related to health.

DEFINITIONS RELATED TO COMMUNITY SETTINGS

The terms that relate more specifically to community or public health education are defined here.

Community health education Community health education is the application of a variety of methods that result in the education and mobilization of community members in actions for resolving health issues and problems that affect the community. These methods include, but are not limited to, group process, mass media, communication, community organization, organization development, strategic planning, skills training, legislation, policy making, and advocacy.

---

* The committee believes that *health counseling* is a term that should be defined by the health counseling profession.

Community health educator A community health educator is a practitioner who is professionally prepared in the field of community/public health education, who demonstrates competence in the planning, implementation, and evaluation of a broad range of health promoting or health enhancing programs for community groups.

DEFINITIONS RELATED TO EDUCATIONAL SETTINGS

The terms that relate more specifically to school health education are defined here.

Comprehensive school health program A comprehensive school health program is an organized set of policies, procedures, and activities designed to protect and promote the health and well-being of students and staff, which has traditionally included health services, healthful school environment, and health education. It should also include, but not be limited to, guidance and counseling, physical education, food service, social work, psychological services, and employee health promotion.

School health education School health education is one component of the comprehensive school health program that includes the development, delivery, and evaluation of a planned instructional program and other activities for students pre-school through grade 12, for parents, and for school staff, and is designed to positively influence the health knowledge, attitudes, and skills of individuals.

School health services School health services are that part of the school health program provided by physicians, nurses, dentists, health educators, other allied health personnel, social workers, teachers, and others to appraise, protect, and promote the health of students and school personnel. These services are designed to ensure access to and the appropriate use of primary health care services, prevent and control communicable disease, provide emergency care for injury or sudden illness, promote and provide optimum sanitary conditions in a safe school facility and environment, and provide concurrent learning opportunities that are conducive to the maintenance and promotion of individual and community health.

School health educator A school health educator is a practitioner who is professionally prepared in the field of school health education, meets state teaching requirements, and demonstrates competence in the development, delivery, and evaluation of curricula for students and adults in the school setting that enhance health knowledge, attitudes, and problem-solving skills.

Comprehensive school health instruction Comprehensive school health instruction refers to the development, delivery, and evaluation of a planned curriculum, pre-school through 12, with goals, objectives, content sequence, and specific classroom lessons that include, but are not limited to, the following major content areas:

- Community health
- Consumer health
- Environmental health
- Family life
- Mental and emotional health
- Injury prevention and safety
- Nutrition
- Personal health
- Prevention and control of disease
- Substance use and abuse

Postsecondary health education program A postsecondary health education program is a planned set of health education policies, procedures, activities, and services that are directed to students, faculty, and/or staff of colleges, universities, and other higher education institutions. This includes, but is not limited to, the following:

- General health courses for students
- Employee and student health promotion activities
- Health services
- Professional preparation of health educators and other professionals
- Self-help groups
- Student life

Databases

Online databases can usually be accessed through terminals at large libraries for a fee.

Commerce Business Daily. Includes the complete text equivalent of the printed publication *Commerce Business Daily*, which is issued every weekday to announce products and services wanted or offered by the U.S. government.
Producer: U.S. Department of Commerce, Room 1304, 433 West Van Buren Street, Chicago, IL 60607; 312-353-2950. **Vendor:** DIALOG Information Services, 3460 Hillview Avenue, Palo Alto, CA 94304; 800-334-2564.

FAPRS (Federal Assistance Programs Retrieval System). Contains summaries of over 1,050 federal assistance, loan, and grant programs. The user specifies eligibility characteristics and subjects of interest, and the system responds with programs that meet these criteria. Updated monthly. Contains information from the *Catalog of Federal Domestic Assistance.* **Producer and Vendor:** General Services Administration, Ground Floor, Reporters Building, 300 Seventh Street, S.W., Washington, DC 20407; 202-453-4126.

Federal Register Abstracts. Provides comprehensive indexing of the *Federal Register*, the daily official government publication for agency pronouncements, including announcements of RFPs and RFAs. **Producer:** National Standards Association, 5161 River Road, Bethesda, MD 20816; 301-951-1313. **Vendor:** DIALOG Information Services, 3460 Hillview Avenue, Palo Alto, CA 94304; 800-334-2564.

Federal Research Reports. Contains full text of the *Federal Research Report,* a newsletter covering U.S. federal research, development funding, grants, and contracts. **Producer:** Business Publishers, Inc., 951 Pershing Drive, Silver Spring, MD 20910; 301-587-6300. **Vendor:** NewsNet, Inc., 945 Haverford Road, Bryn Mawr, PA 19010; 800-345-1301.

Foundation Directory. Provides descriptions of more than 3,500 foundations with assets of $1 million or more that makes grants of $100,000 or more annually.

Corresponds to the printed publication of the same name. **Producer:** The Foundation Center, 79 Fifth Avenue, New York, NY 10003; 212-620-4230. **Vendor:** DIALOG Information Services, 3460 Hillview Avenue, Palo Alto, CA 94304; 800-334-2564.

Foundation Grants Index. Contains information on grants awarded by more than 400 major American philanthropic foundations, representing all records from the *Foundation Grants Index* section of the bimonthly *Foundation News*. **Producer:** The Foundation Center, 79 Fifth Avenue, New York, NY 10003; 212-620-4230. **Vendor:** DIALOG Information Services, 3460 Hillview Avenue, Palo Alto, CA 94304; 800-334-2564.

Grants. Contains grants offered by federal, state, and local governments; commercial organizations; associations; and foundations. Does not include contracts. **Producer:** Oryx Press, 2214 North Central at Encanto, Phoenix, AZ 85004; 602-254-6156. **Vendor:** DIALOG Information Services, 3460 Hillview Avenue, Palo Alto, CA 94304; 800-334-2564.

Health Planning and Administration. Contains citations to the literature of health and health-related topics, including health promotion. **Producer and Vendor:** National Library of Medicine, MEDLARS Management Section, 8600 Rockville Pike, Bethesda, MD 20894; 800-638-8480, 301-496-6193. **Other Vendors:** DIALOG Information Services, 3460 Hillview Avenue, Palo Alto, CA 94304; 800-334-2564. BRS Information Technologies, 1200 Route 7, Latham, NY 12110; 800-345-4BRS.

MEDLINE. Provides citations to biomedical journal articles from both U.S. and foreign journals. **Producer and Vendor:** National Library of Medicine, MEDLARS Management Section, 8600 Rockville Pike, Bethesda, MD 20894; 800-638-8480, 301-496-6193. **Other Vendors:** DIALOG Information Services, 3460 Hillview Avenue, Palo Alto, CA 94304; 800-334-2564. BRS Information Technologies, 1200 Route 7, Latham, NY 12110; 800-345-4BRS.

National Foundations. Offers recent data on U.S. private foundations; overlaps and supplements the *Foundation Directory*. This file is especially useful in obtaining comprehensive listings of foundations by geographical designation. **Producer:** The Foundation Center, 79 Fifth Avenue, New York, NY 10003; 212-620-4230. **Vendor:** DIALOG Information Services, 3460 Hillview Avenue, Palo Alto, CA 94304; 800-334-2564.

For more information about available online databases, consult the following directories:

Database Director Service, Knowledge Industry Publications, 701 Westchester Avenue, White Plains, NY 10604; 800-248-5474.

Directory of Online Databases, Cuadra Associates, 11835 West Olympic Boulevard, Los Angeles, CA 90064; 213-478-0066.

NATIONAL CENTER FOR CHRONIC DISEASE PREVENTION AND HEALTH PROMOTION

Health professionals working to promote health awareness or prevent disease will find the Chronic Disease Prevention (CDP) File can be a powerful tool to assist them. CDP File is a CD-ROM produced by the Technical Information Services Branch, National Center for Chronic Disease Prevention and Health Promotion, Centers for Disease Control and Prevention. CDP File is a collection of six databases of information about health promotion and disease prevention. The CD-ROM includes these databases:

- The Health Promotion and Education Database (HE) contains abstracts of journal articles, monographs, proceedings, reports, curricular materials, and unpublished documents and descriptions of health programs. The materials cover such topics as community health education, worksite health promotion, self-care, maternal and infant health care, professional training and education, and research and evaluation.
- The AIDS School Health Education Database (SA) is a resource for AIDS education providers. It contains abstracts of teaching guides, curricula, reports, books, journal articles, government policies, papers, statements, and speeches.
- The Cancer Prevention and Control Database (CP) contains entries emphasizing the application of effective breast and cervical cancer early detection and control program activities and risk reduction efforts.
- The HE/SA/CP combination database allows health educators to search the HE, SA, and CP databases simultaneously.
- The Chronic Disease Prevention Directory includes the names and addresses of people and organizations who are key contacts in health promotion and disease prevention.
- The State Profile is useful to scan for information on programs or key contacts by state.

If you have a DOS-based microcomputer with a CD-ROM drive, you can have this vast compilation of valuable health information at your fingertips. CDP File is available from the Superintendent of Documents, Government Printing Office, Washington, DC 20402, 202-783-3238; order #017-022-01165-4. For more information, contact Technical Information Services Branch, National Center for Chronic Disease Prevention and Health Promotion, Centers for Disease Control and Prevention (CDC), 4770 Buford Highway N.E., Mailstop K13, Atlanta, GA 30341-3724; 404-488-5080.

Subfiles on the Combined Health Information Database

Health Promotion and Education Database

The Health Promotion and Education Database (HPED) is produced by the Center for Chronic Disease Prevention and Health Promotion. The database contains more than 19,000 entries describing health promotion/health education information emphasizing methodology and the application of effective health promotion/health education programs and risk-reduction interventions.

The HPED provides bibliographic citations and abstracts for journal articles, books/book chapters, reports, conference proceedings, curricular materials, and program descriptions on a variety of topics including the following:

• Chronic disease prevention and education
• Community health education
• Family life and sex education
• Health education methodology
• Patient health education
• Risk reduction interventions
• School health education
• Self care
• Worksite health promotion and education

In addition, the database provides source and availability information for these materials so that users may obtain the items directly.

The Combined Health Information Database (CHID) and subfiles are available for online searching through BRS Online, a division of InfoPro Technologies, 8000 Westpark Drive, McLean, VA 22102 (800-289-4277) and may be accessed using a telecommunicating computer terminal or through libraries and information centers that subscribe to BRS. The subfiles are also available through CDP-File, a CD-ROM produced by CDC's National Center for Chronic Disease Prevention and Health Promotion.

Comprehensive School Health Database

The Comprehensive School Health Database (CSHD) is also produced by the National Center for Chronic Disease Prevention and Health Promotion. An expansion of the AIDS School Health Education Database, CSHD contains information on various components of comprehensive school health programs, including school health education, school-linked or school-based health services, healthy school environment, physical education, school food service, and integrated school and community health promotion efforts. A core component of the CSHD includes information on resources to help educate children and youth about HIV and AIDS.

The CSHD provides bibliographic citations and abstracts for journal articles, books/book chapters, reports, conference proceedings, curricular materials, and program descriptions.

The primary focus of the CSHD will be on comprehensive school health education related to the following topics:

• Nutrition
• Physical activity
• Injury control
• Use of tobacco, alcohol, and other drugs
• Sexual behaviors that result in HIV infection, other sexually transmitted diseases, and unintended pregnancies

In addition, the database provides source and availability information for these materials so that users may obtain the items directly.

Cancer Prevention and Control Database

The Cancer Prevention and Control Database (CPCD), produced by the National Center for Chronic Disease Prevention and Health Promotion, contains entries emphasizing the application of effective breast and cervical cancer early detection and control program activities and risk reduction efforts.

The CPCD provides bibliographic citations and abstracts for journal articles, book chapters, technical reports, proceedings, papers, policy documents, legislation, monographs, unpublished documents, educational materials, curricula, and descriptions of cancer prevention programs and risk reduction activities at the national, state, and local levels. Topics covered by the database include the following:

• Quality assurance
• Public education
• Public information
• Professional education and training
• Regulation, legislation, and administration
• Research and evaluation
• Special populations
• Surveillance
• Worksite interventions

In addition, the database provides source and availability information for these materials so that users may obtain the items directly.

Chronic Disease Prevention File

The Chronic Disease Prevention File (CDP File) on CD-ROM is a collection of six databases of information about health promotion and disease prevention. In addition to bibliographic databases, CDP File includes the *Chronic Disease Prevention Directory* (CDPD). The CDPD database includes the names and addresses of people and organizations that are key contacts in health promotion and disease prevention.

The user may search for information by specifying a variety of elements, such as state name, name of contact, name of affiliation, and so forth, or by specifying output of the entire record or of applicable data in mailing label format.

Available Health Risk Appraisals

Name of Health Risk Appraisal:	**AVIVA**
Available from:	Cleveland State University 2121 Euclid, UC532 Cleveland, OH 44115
Contact:	Farrokh Alemi
Telephone Number: *Fax Number:*	216-687-5243 216-687-9317
General Description:	AVIVA (patent pending) is a computerized risk appraisal that anyone can access by calling 216-687-9217 and entering an access code. A "talking" computer will answer the call. It will ask a number of questions about the caller's lifestyle. Based on the caller's answers, the computer will provide an immediate evaluation of the individual's hospitalization health risks. The computer will help the caller gain access to additional resources (usually videotapes). Finally, the computer allows the caller to register for existing or future risk modification programs. AVIVA produces reports on requests for risk modification programs. As such, it can be used in planning prevention activities.
Overall Use:	Participants use a telephone to enter data on a computer, which then advises them of their major modifiable health risks.
Age Appropriate:	Adult (19–64)
Specifically Targeted Populations:	General audience; African-American; male; female

Name of Health Risk Appraisal:	**Wellness Inventory**
Available from:	Wellness Associates 12347 Dupont Road Sebastopol, CA 95472
Contact:	John W. Travis, M.D., President
Telephone Number:	707-874-1466
General Description:	The Wellness Inventory is designed to complement health risk assessments (HRAs) that look only at high-risk behaviors without exploring the test-taker's underlying beliefs and attitudes. A quick introduction to wellness, it provides a graphic scoring wheel that the test-taker fills in once scores are obtained in 12 areas of wellness: self-responsibility, breathing, sensing, eating, moving, feeling, thinking, community, playing/working, sex, finding meaning, and transcending. Similar to Wellness Inventory, the interactive software presents the 10 questions in a section and, after they are answered, updates the scoring chart on-screen. It then continues with the next section in a similar manner, giving encouraging comments along the way. On completion, a listing of test-taker's areas of concern are displayed on screen (as well as a printed listing). Data are saved on disc for optional statistical use later.
Overall Use:	Self-administered, self-scored health education tool; computerized interactive—participant answers questions directly into computer
Target Audience:	For "healthy" individuals; for those with chronic illness
Specifically Targeted Populations:	General audience

Name of Health Risk Appraisal:	**Healthstyle**
Available from:	National Health Information Clearinghouse (Office of Disease Prevention and Health Promotion) P.O. Box 1133 Washington, DC 20013
Contact:	Any Information Specialist
Telephone Number:	202-245-7611 or 800-336-4797
General Description:	A basic, self-scored HRA, giving participants a quick and easy way to find out about their health in six areas
Overall Use:	Self-administered, self-scored health education tool
Age Appropriate:	College-aged (18–22); adult (19–64)
Specifically Targeted Populations:	General audience

Name of Health Risk Appraisal:	**Hope Health Appraisal**
Available from:	Hope Publications—Exclusive Distributors International Health Awareness Center 350 E. Michigan Avenue, Suite 301 Kalamazoo, MI 49007
Contact:	Debra E. Seeley, Operations Coordinator
Telephone Number: *Fax Number:*	616-343-0770 616-342-6260
General Description:	The package consists of the following pieces: • The "Say Ahh" booklet, which contains 12 sections you can score yourself • The "Ahh" booklet, with tips that can help you make simple changes in your lifestyle to look better, feel better, and possibly live longer • The "HOPE Health Appraisal Wallet Card," designed to give a person the courage to be an assertive, questioning patient • The "HOPE Health Appraisal Poster," which is a two-in-one poster with an eating guide on one side and 50 proven stress reducers on the other
Overall Use:	Self-administered, self-scored health education tool
Age Appropriate:	Adult (19–64)
Specifically Targeted Populations:	General audience

Name of Health Risk Appraisal:	**School-Aged Health Inventories**
Available from:	Response Technologies, Inc. 3399 South County Trail East Greenwich, RI 02818
Contact:	James E. Dewey, Ph.D., President
Telephone Number:	401-885-6900
Fax Number:	401-885-6905
General Description:	Four health risk inventories make up this series: elementary (grades 4–6), junior high school (grades 7–8), senior high school (grades 9–12), and college. Each HRA is a stand-alone package, designed for immediate response health messages and aggregate reports.
Overall Use:	Stand alone with immediate response
Age Appropriate:	Fourth through sixth grade; young adult (middle and high school); college-aged (18–22)

Name of Health Risk Appraisal:	**The Healthier People Network Health Risk Appraisal**
Available from:	The Healthier People Network, Inc. 1549 N. Clairmont Road, Suite 205 Decatur, GA 30033
Contact:	Edwin B. Hutchins, Ph.D., President
Telephone Number:	404-636-3127
General Description:	The Healthier People Network, Inc. (HPN) health risk appraisal for mid-life adults, ages 19–65, is a mortality-based instrument. It covers 42 causes of death and yields 10-year estimates of risk of dying based on 23 risk factors. Four components define the HRA: (1) An epidemiologic and clinical database, (2) a self-reporting questionnaire, comprising 43 core questions, (3) a series of algorithms that relate the individual's database to the epidemiologic database to produce, (4) a set of probabilities related to the 42 causes of death that form the basis of a computer-generated report.
Overall Use:	Stand alone HRA suitable for mailing to participant; counseling tool for individual or group interpretation; HPN primary goal to foster the scientific development of health risk appraisal and to make this available to other HRA developers and health care providers
Target Audience:	For "healthy" individuals; those with chronic illness; elderly population; persons with disabilities
Age Appropriate:	Adult (19–64); senior (65+)
Specifically Targeted Populations:	General audience; African-American; American Indian

Name of Health Risk Appraisal:	**HealthMax**
Available from:	Health Examinetics, Inc. 15330 Avenue of Science San Diego, CA 92128
Contact:	Bruce H. Meyer, Vice-President
Telephone Number: *Fax Number:*	800-232-2332 619-485-8133
General Description:	HealthMax is the first health risk appraisal based on the actual dollar cost of individual behaviors. HealthMax rates a person's potential health costs based on clinically validated lifestyle-related data. A 1–100 point risk index is awarded to each participant. When teamed with health plan cost shifting and incentives, HealthMax is an extremely effective short-term cost containment and long-term behavior modification/ risk reduction tool for an employer. The HealthMax individual report provides year-to-year tracking of an individual's lifestyle and suggestions on positive behavior changes. The group reports show potential group health plan costs and will cost justify the program yearly.
Overall Use:	HealthMax clinically assesses an individual and provides a risk index score (1–100 points) based on the potential health plan costs their lifestyle represents.
Age Appropriate:	College-aged (18–22); Adult (19–64); senior (65+)
Specifically Targeted Populations:	General audience

Name of Health Risk Appraisal:	**Health Potential Assessment Program**
Available from:	Health Examinetics, Inc. 15330 Avenue of Science San Diego, CA 92128
Contact:	Bruce H. Meyer, Vice-President
Telephone Number: *Fax Number:*	619-485-0933 619-485-8133
General Description:	The Health Potential Assessment Program combines a self-administered lifestyle questionnaire with physiological data to provide a positive and motivational lifestyle evaluation. Tests include blood pressure, lipid screening, liver function, blood sugar, far visual acuity, tonometry, stool for occult blood, frame size, and body fat percentage. Testing is performed on-site at the client's location by Health Examinetics' staff of licensed medical professionals. Results are mailed directly to the participant, ensuring complete confidentiality. Group summaries are sent to the client.
Overall Use:	Questionnaire is self-administered; physiological data are collected by Health Examinetics' staff.
Target Audience:	For "healthy" individuals; those with chronic illness; those with disabilities
Age Appropriate:	Young adult (middle and high school); college-aged (18–22); adult (19–64); senior (65+)
Specifically Targeted Populations:	General audience

Name of Health Risk Appraisal:	**Personal Wellness Profile**
Available from:	Wellsource, Inc. P.O. Box 569 Clackamas, OR 97015
Contact:	Regional Sales Manager
Telephone Number:	503-656-7446 or 800-533-9355
Fax Number:	503-650-0880
General Description:	Personal Wellness Profile (PWP) provides a comprehensive employee health risk assessment and information management system. PWP gives worksite wellness coordinators a tool for raising employee health awareness, motivating lifestyle improvement, identifying employees at risk, and monitoring wellness program effectiveness. Participating employees fill out a questionnaire. Basic health and fitness tests can be added. The data are then computer analyzed, and participants receive a personal report, which compares their health status with established norms and guidelines from leading national health organizations. Four levels of PWP provide the flexibility to conduct both a relatively simple, nonclinical appraisal or a comprehensive health and fitness assessment.
Overall Use:	Stand alone HRA suitable for mailing to participant; counseling tool for individual or group interpretation
Age Appropriate:	Young adult (middle and high school); college-aged (18–22); adult (19–64); senior (65+)
Specifically Targeted Populations:	General audience

Name of Health Risk Appraisal:	**Personal Risk Analysis**
Available from:	Eris 4548 Scotts Valley Drive Scotts Valley, CA 95066
Contact:	Lou Kern, Director of Marketing
Telephone Number: *Fax Number:*	408-438-6601 408-438-6603
General Description:	Eris's Personal Risk Analysis modular software system offers basic HRA, interactive HRA, nutrition profile, cardiac risk analysis, and clinical systems review. Alternate report formats are available, and Spanish, Portuguese, and UK English are available for most modules. Eris software can process questionnaires immediately and return personalized reports with text and graphics to respondents on the spot. The system relies on very portable and opscan data entry systems for immediate turnaround. Questionr.aires for opscan or keyboard data entry are available. The system can be customized with your own questions and reports.
Overall Use:	Stand alone HRA suitable for mailing to participant; counseling tool for individual or group interpretation; computerized interactive—participant answers questions directly into computer
Age Appropriate:	Adult (19–64)
Specifically Targeted Populations:	General audience; American Indian; Latin/Hispanic
Languages Available	Spanish, Portuguese, UK English

Name of Health Risk Appraisal:	**Personal Health Evaluation**™
Available from:	Occupational Health Strategies, Inc. Charlottesville, VA 22903
Contact:	Barry A. Cooper, Vice-President, Marketing and Sales
Telephone Number: *Fax Number:*	804-977-3784 804-977-8570
General Description:	The Personal Health Evaluation™ System emphasizes a positive health focus and encourages individuals to build on current strengths as they improve their lifestyles. The PHE report is highly personalized to each individual and allows incorporation of client organization name, logo, and specialized messages, referring high-risk participants to company programs. Available with the PHE is immediate, confidential feedback and referral with the organization's toll-free health information hotline (staffed by health educators). The Corporate Health Evaluation™ group reports help target programs where they are most needed and feature customized graphics to help build top-management support, by allowing for effective, visual presentations.
Overall Use:	Stand alone HRA suitable for mailing to participant; counseling tool for individual or group interpretation; computerized interactive—participant answers questions directly into computer
Target Audience:	"Healthy" individuals and those with chronic illness; includes special paragraphs for individuals with history of various illnesses
Age Appropriate:	College-aged (18–22); adult (19–64); senior (65+)
Specifically Targeted Populations:	General audience

Name of Health Risk Appraisal:	**LifeView™ and HealthView™**
Available from:	Windom Health Enterprises 2600 Tenth Street Berkeley, CA 94710
Contact:	Michael D. McDonald, M.P.H., President
Telephone Number: *Fax Number:*	510-848-6980 510-848-6982
General Description:	LifeView™ and HealthView™ together represent a family of health risk assessments. LifeView™ is an introductory health risk assessment based on the Carter Center "Healthier People" 4.0. HealthView™ draws on the same vital statistics and same epidemiology for its calculation of life risk but also adds a wellness report covering quality of life, morbidity, and functional life capacity. More specific follow-up assessments on back care and video display terminal–related problems are also available. Interactive versions are available on the Macintosh.
Overall Use:	Stand alone HRA suitable for mailing to participant; counseling tool for individual or group interpretation; computerized interactive—participant answers questions directly into computer
Age Appropriate:	College-aged (18–22); adult (19–64); senior (65+)
Specifically Targeted Populations:	General audience; Latin/Hispanic
Languages Available:	English, Spanish, French

Name of Health Risk Appraisal:	**Lifestyle Assessment Questionnaire**
Available from:	National Wellness Institute 1319 Fremont St. Stevens Point, WI 54481
Contact:	Linda R. Chapin, D.D.S., M.S., Director of Operations and Special Projects
Telephone Number: *Fax Number:*	715-346-2172 715-346-3733
General Description:	The Lifestyle Assessment Questionnaire (LAQ) is a comprehensive assessment tool that promotes awareness and provides education. The LAQ is used by companies interested in containing cost, reducing absenteeism, and increasing productivity. The LAQ program: • Examines an individual's lifestyle behaviors • Provides a health risk appraisal • Identifies positive lifestyle behaviors and suggests ways to improve others • Provides a bibliography for selected topics of personal growth • Includes strategies for behavioral change planning and implementation
Overall Use:	Stand alone HRA suitable for mailing to participant; counseling tool for individual or group interpretation; computerized interactive—participant answers questions directly into computer; batch processed by key input or scanned using optical mark reader
Age Appropriate:	College-aged (18–22); adult (19–64); senior (65+)
Specifically Targeted Populations:	General audience

Name of Health Risk Appraisal:	**Health Risk Appraisal**
Available from:	University of Michigan Fitness Research Center 401 Washtenaw Avenue, 103 CCRB Ann Arbor, MI 48109-2214
Contact:	Elaine Schnueringer, Manager, Corporate Operations
Telephone Number: *Fax Number:*	313-763-2462 313-763-2206
General Description:	This health risk appraisal identifies major health risks, provides personalized evaluation (including a 20-year risk projection), recommends lifestyle behavior changes, highlights negative and positive lifestyle behaviors, and provides target goals and information to help the participant to set realistic goals for lifestyle changes. Health risk estimation is calculated from the National Center for Health Statistics and is recently updated to include the 1986–1987 mortality tables. Comparison and group summaries are developed from an in-house database collected over the last 12 years from over 600,000 individuals nationwide with diverse demographics. Questionnaires may be key punched, optiscanned, and customized. Individual and organizational reports may also be designed upon specification.
Overall Use:	Stand alone HRA suitable for mailing to participant; counseling tool for individual or group interpretation; computerized interactive—participant answers questions directly into computer; used for tracking lifestyle behaviors; used for evaluation of health promotion program
Age Appropriate:	Adult (19–64)
Specifically Targeted Populations:	General audience

Name of Health Risk Appraisal:	**Health Profile 500/900**
Available from:	Johnson & Johnson Health Management, Inc. 410 George Street New Brunswick, NJ 08901
Contact:	John Sherman, Product Director
Telephone Number:	908-524-2144
Fax Number:	908-524-2519
General Description:	The Health Profile (HP) 500/900 includes 22 questions on lifestyle practices that have the highest impact on health risk, as well as five key biometric measurements to determine health status: height, weight, blood pressure, cholesterol (total and HDL), and percent body fat. Biometric measures are self-reported by the participant. Lifestyle questions focus on exercise, nutrition, driving, smoking, alcohol, stress, and personal and family medical history. In the HP 500, the clinical data are self-reported; in the HP 900, the data are reported by a health professional.
Overall Use:	Self-administered, self-scored health education tool; stand alone HRA suitable for mailing to participant; counseling tool for individual or group interpretation; computerized interactive—participant answers questions directly into computer
Age Appropriate:	College-aged (18–22); adult (19–64); senior (65+)
Specifically Targeted Populations:	General audience

*Name of Health Risk
   Appraisal:*   **HealthPath®**

Available from: StayWell Health Management System
                      1285 Corporate Center Drive, Suite 100
                      Eagan, MN 55121

Contact: John Tarbuck, Vice-President, Marketing

Telephone Number: 612-454-3577
Fax Number: 612-454-4062

General Description: HealthPath focuses on health habits. Using this habit-based approach, while maintaining the science of actuarial-based mortality, makes HealthPath suitable for participants of various ages and ethnic backgrounds in different settings. HealthPath features habit-based feedback, year-to-year comparisons, personalized messages, priority-ranked health risks; motivational education, and special screening options. The Management Summary, Focused Intervention Program, and Management Information System are added features that help management reduce costs.

Overall Use: Stand alone HRA suitable for mailing to participant; counseling tool for individual or group interpretation

Age Appropriate: Young adult (middle and high school); college-aged (18–22); adult (19–64)

*Specifically Targeted
   Populations:*   General audience

Languages Available   English, Spanish

Name of Health Risk Appraisal:	**HealthLogic**™
Available from:	HMC Software 3001 LBJ Freeway, Suite 224 Dallas, TX 75234
Contact:	Michael Dehn, President
Telephone Number: *Fax Number:*	214-247-4080; 800-255-6809 214-247-6259
General Description:	HealthLogic covers medical history, preventive exams, CDC-based risk appraisal with risk age, Framingham heart disease risk, smoking, blood pressure, cholesterol, exercise and fitness, stress profile, osteoporosis, nutrition, cancer, motor vehicle accidents, and back and home safety. HealthLogic also collects optional human resource data on claims/leave usage, job satisfaction, and productivity. Group reports cover aggregate data for the entire database or subgroups. Custom queries can be performed and used to generate data listings, form letters, and mailing labels. Over 100 user-definable questions and measurements can be added to the database.
Overall Use:	Stand alone HRA suitable for mailing to participant; counseling tool for individual or group interpretation; computerized interactive—participant answers questions directly into computer
Age Appropriate:	Adult (19–64)
Specifically Targeted Populations:	General audience

Name of Health Risk Appraisal:	**Health Hazard Appraisal**
Available from:	Prospective Medicine Center 6220 Lawrence Drive Indianapolis, IN 46226
Contact:	Pamela Hall, Executive Program Director
Telephone Number: *Fax Number:*	317-549-3600 317-549-3100
General Description:	The Health Hazard Appraisal (HHA) form is backed by an up-to-date data and statistical support system to measure health risk. It can specify courses of action to reduce risk. 　　The system is the culmination of more than 25 years of research, study, and scientific validation. Using data from a vast variety of sources, the HHA is used to compute a person's life expectancy based not just on his or her age, but also on the health risks present in his or her lifestyle. These risks include such factors as family health history, weight, blood pressure, cholesterol, smoking habits, driving habits, and other factors known to increase the risk of dying.
Overall Use:	Self-administered questionnaire entered at office (data entry person); stand alone HRA suitable for mailing to participant; can be used via group or individual for counseling interpretation; computer analyzed.
Target Audience	For "healthy" individuals; those with chronic illness (alcoholism, C.A.H.D.)
Age Appropriate:	For any age
Specifically Targeted Populations:	General audience; Latin/Hispanic

Name of Health Risk Appraisal:	**Adolescent Wellness Appraisal**
Available from:	University of Michigan Fitness Research Center 401 Washtenaw Avenue Ann Arbor, MI 48109-2214
Contact:	Marilyn Edington, Manager, Health Communications
Telephone Number: *Fax Number:*	313-763-2462 313-763-2206
General Description:	The Adolescent Wellness Appraisal (AWA), developed by the University of Michigan Fitness Research Center and used in the Michigan Model for Comprehensive School Health Curriculum, provides a 55-question assessment aimed at promoting awareness of basic health knowledge and behaviors that most influence the health of adolescent participants. The AWA is different from the adult HRA since no mortality calculations are used. The report includes an overall wellness scale followed by supportive comments on each positive health behavior. Recommendations are given for the reported negative health behaviors. Standard height/weight tables are included with the manual for distribution and discussion with participants. The program also generates a group summary. A unique aspect of the program allows the generation of a separate interactive disc called "What If." No printed report is generated with this section, but it allows the student to see the impact of various answers on-screen.
Overall Use:	Self-administered, self-scored health eduction tool; stand alone HRA suitable for mailing to participant; counseling tool for individual or group interpretation; computerized interactive—participant answers questions directly into computer.
Age Appropriate:	Young adult (middle and high school)
Specifically Targeted Populations:	General audience

Name of Health Risk Appraisal:	**LifeStyle Directions Report**
Available from:	LifeStyle Directions, Inc. 300 Ninth Street Monaca, PA 15061
Contact:	Alane M. Conte, R.D., Health Enhancement Director
Telephone Number: *Fax Number:*	412-775-4660 412-775-0341
General Description:	LifeStyle Directions, Inc., is morbidity based and considers the most common causes of a disease, not the most probable causes of death. The LifeStyle Directions Report shows risk scores for preventing diseases and not for preventing death. It has the following functions: • Gives a continuing, long-term program for reducing risks for major illnesses and diseases • Directs participants to the choices that will help them move from higher to lower risks over a period of time • Redirects lifestyle habits—both physically and emotionally—to help participants make positive choices about their health and vitality • Charts improvements over time and monitors health on a long-range basis to give participants a continuing program for preventive health care.
Overall Use:	Stand alone HRA suitable for mailing to participant; counseling tool for individual or group interpretation; interacts with existing programs to give a company second- and third-generation disease prevention/health enhancement programs
Taregt Audience	For "healthy" individuals; those with chronic illness; those with disabilities
Age Appropriate:	Adult (19–64); senior (65+)
Specifically Targeted Populations:	General audience

Name of Health Risk Appraisal:	**LifeScore Plus HRA**
Available from:	The Center for Corporate Health, Inc. 10467 White Granite Dr., Suite 300 Oakton, VA 22124
Contact:	Terry Goplerud, General Manager—Communications
Telephone Number: *Fax Number:*	703-218-8411 703-218-8467
General Description:	LifeScore Plus combines a health risk appraisal with a comprehensive management report. LifeScore Plus helps individuals gauge their personal health status, risk of death over the next ten years, and probable longevity. The numerous graphs present data in a four-color personal report. Employees are provided with confidential data on projected and achievable lifespans and comparisons of actual with risk-related age.

The management report compares company results with national norms, gives ten-year company death projections for heart disease, data on absenteeism, employee health interest, and figures on the costs of smoking and other specific habits of employees. The system can compare year-to-year results, both to the individual and company. |
Overall Use:	Stand alone HRA suitable for mailing to participant; counseling tool for individual or group interpretation
Age Appropriate:	College-aged (18–22); adult (19–64); senior (65+)
Specifically Targeted Populations:	General audience

Name of Health Risk Appraisal:	**Health Profile 1000, 3000, 4000***
Available from:	Johnson & Johnson Health Management, Inc. (JJHMI) 2500 Broadway, Suite 100 Santa Monica, CA 90404
Contact:	Phillip Crib, Product Director
Telephone Number: *Fax Number:*	310-315-8128 310-453-6250
General Description:	The Health Profile assesses an individual's lifestyle and health status using a set of 189 questions. Biometric data can be either self-reported (HP 1000) or professionally collected (HP 3000 or 4000). The data collected are used to generate a complete picture of each individual's health. The 19-page questionnaire is designed to facilitate completion as well as to provide educational information in terms of the impact of lifestyle on health. Completed questionnaires are processed either on-site or at JJHMI Central Profile Processing. Turnaround time for centrally processed profiles is 5-10 working days. Each participant receives a nine-page, highly personalized report that includes a picture of current health risk status, positive reinforcement of currently healthful lifestyle practices, and detailed action steps that will help the individual improve his or her health.
Overall Use:	Stand alone HRA suitable for mailing to participant; counseling tool for individual or group interpretation
Age Appropriate:	College-aged (18–22); adult (19–64)
Specifically Targeted Populations:	General audience

*Series number related to level of service included.

Name of Health Risk Appraisal:	**HealthPlan Plus**™
Available from:	General Health, Inc. 3299 K Street, NW, Suite 310 Washington, DC 20007
Contact:	Julie L. Buren, Account Manager/Marketing Representative
Telephone Number: *Fax Number:*	202-965-4881 202-337-3726
General Description:	HealthPlan provides risk estimation data that benefit both employers and employees. HealthPlan enables employers to reduce the risk of preventable illnesses and associated costs, improve employee productivity, and demonstrate management commitment to the health and well-being of their employee group. Employees, likewise, are empowered with personalized wellness information that enables them to take control of their health. How lifestyle choices affect wellness and necessary steps to prevent serious health problems before they occur are also detailed. HealthPlan can be offered as a stand-alone program, as it links employees to both community-based providers and to General Health, Inc., health professionals for further advice.
Overall Use:	Stand alone HRA suitable for mailing to participant; counseling tool for individual or group interpretation
Age Appropriate:	College-aged (18–22); adult (19–64)
Specifically Targeted Populations:	General audience, Latin/Hispanic
Languages Available:	English, French, Spanish

Name of Health Risk Appraisal:

Health and Lifestyle Questionnaire

Available from:

Health Enhancement Systems, Inc.
9 Mercer Street
Princeton, NJ 08540

Contact:

John H. Rassweiler, Ph.D., President

Telephone Number:
Fax Number:

609-924-7799; or 800-437-6668
609-497-0739

General Description:

This HRA is an epidemiological quality health and lifestyle questionnaire that emphasizes current quality of life over medical risks. The 54-question, 150-data point questionnaire collects and analyzes data on health habits, psychological and job attitudes, stress (especially workplace related), and social relationships. The two-page profile report assigns scores ranging from "excellent" to "immediate attention."

Overall Use:

Stand alone HRA suitable for mailing to participant; counseling tool for individual or group interpretation

Target Audience:

For "healthy" individuals

Age Appropriate:

College-aged (18–22); adult (19–64)

Name of Health Risk Appraisal:	**HealthCheck**
Available from:	Life Plans, Inc. d/b/a Network Health Systems, Inc. 89 Centennial Trail, Bozeman, MT 59715 or P.O. Box 30514, Columbia, MO 65205
Contact:	James P. Bangs, President
Telephone Number: Fax Number:	406-587-5624 also 406-587-7740; or 314-446-6100 314-446-8036
General Description:	This health risk appraisal uses mortality and morbidity (hospital-episode days) data for 51 diseases and conditions affected by 44 risk indicators. Individual reports and group reports are furnished. Group reports give cost estimates and potential savings on replacement costs, sick leave, and hospitalization using unit costs furnished by client. Risk (stressor) factors use published data, federal government data, and clinical judgment of a health professionals panel. Calculations use risk factor and non-reversible risk factor databases.
Overall Use:	Stand alone HRA suitable for mailing to participant; counseling tool for individual or group interpretation; computerized interactive—participant answers questions directly into computer
Age Appropriate:	College-aged (18–22); adult (19–64); senior (65+)*
Specifically Targeted Populations:	General audience

---

*Age 15 data being compiled; over 65 data aggregate.

Name of Health Risk Appraisal:	**Health Appraisal Projections**
Available from:	Computerized Health Systems, Inc. 4775 Tait Road Dayton, OH 45429
Contact:	Richard L. Miller, M.D., President
Telephone Number: *Fax Number:*	513-298-0082 513-435-2175
General Description:	A concise (3 page), computerized statistical analysis of an individual's risks of morbidity and mortality including the following: • Longevity projections: at present age and compared with all like individuals • Factors improving longevity: listed in order of importance with computer number of added years projected longevity per factor • Projected mortality risks: computed statistically significant risks of death over succeeding ten years; in order of importance with contributing factors listed • Morbidity probability: of ensuing 12 months • Also available—female breast cancer risk: one-page statistical analysis at present age compared to all like females with contributing factors listed (used to outline and stimulate examination regimen)
Overall Use:	Stand alone HRA suitable for mailing to participant; counseling tool for individual or group interpretation; on-line computer operator use by modem interconnect
Age Appropriate:	Kindergarten through third grade (via parent); fourth through sixth grade; young adult (middle and high school); college-aged (18–22); adult (19–64); senior (65+)
Specifically Targeted Populations:	General audience

Name of Health Risk Appraisal:	**CompuHealth**
Available from:	CompuRisk, Inc. 325 Plant Avenue St. Louis, MO 63119
Contact:	Robert J. Wheeler, Ph.D., President
Telephone Number:	314-961-8679
General Description:	Using morbidity and mortality data, this system predicts the likelihood of an individual becoming hospitalized or dying prematurely because of 47 diseases or health conditions increased by 44 risk indicators. A personal report gives overall current and achievable health scores and ages, major risks and probability of having major health problems, and personalized comments about each of the assessed risks. An organizational report predicts health care costs and potential savings broken down by impact for hospitalization, job absence, and replacement and by the associated risk indicators. A composite report gives the incidence of risks for the group broken down by sex and job level.
Overall Use:	Stand alone HRA suitable for mailing to participant; counseling tool for individual or group interpretation; predicted costs and potential savings for groups and organizations to assist in planning cost-effective allocation of resources for particular health promotion and disease prevention activities
Age Appropriate:	College-aged (18–22); adult (19–64); senior (65+)
Specifically Targeted Populations:	General audience

Name of Health Risk Appraisal:	**Building a Healthier You**
Available from:	Health Management Resources 59 Temple Place, Suite 704 Boston, MA 02111-1345
Contact:	Dr. Gordon Kaplan, Director of Research
Telephone Number:	617-357-9876
Fax Number:	617-357-9690
General Description:	The Health Management Resources (HMR) system includes the HMR Risk Factor Questionnaire, Profile, and Individual Report. Also available are an optional 50-page booklet and a two-hour seminar. As questionnaires are scanned by HMR's computer in Boston, responses are translated into scaled scores and graphed onto profiles. A follow-up score can be graphed on the same profile as an initial score. This HRA is a tool for participants to learn simple changes that may substantially improve their health. The HRA and seminar have been used for 8 years with high-risk patients and are now available for use in corporate, clinical, and community settings.
Overall Use:	Stand alone HRA suitable for mailing to participant; counseling tool for individual or group interpretation
Target Audience:	For "healthy" individuals; those with chronic illness (cardiovascular disease, high blood pressure, diabetes, obesity)
Age Appropriate:	College-aged (18–22); adult (19–64); senior (65+)
Specifically Targeted Populations:	General audience

Index

Fund-raising, 263, 271, 272
See also Grant writing
Future of health education, 283

G

Grant writing, 263, 264
See also Fund-raising
Graphics, 177, 228, 241
Grasp estimate, 245
Group skills, 199, 200–203
Gunning Fog Index, 244
See also Readability tests

H

Health, 316
administrator, 318
advising, 318
behavior and education, 138, 141
departments, 53, 54, 287
educators, 3, 4, 319
information, 318
literacy, 318
promotion, 5, 6, 54, 80, 89, 316
See also Wellness Council of
America
risk appraisal, 177–178, 327–354
status objectives, 119
Health care reform, 76
Health communication theory, 167
Health communication wheel, 168
Health education, 3, 4, 121, 315
administrator, 318
coordinator, 318
databases, 178
definitions, 3, 4, 315, 317
specialists, 5, 54, 75
Health Education Quarterly, 23, 111
*Health Education Research: Theory and
Practice*, 32
Health Project, The, 29
Healthy Communities 2000, 48, 49, 53,
60, 64, 253
Healthy lifestyles, 316

Healthy People 2000, 29, 49, 53, 119,
120, 132, 133, 284, 305
HIV
See AIDS
HMOs 71, 73
Hygie, 23

I

Immunization, 31, 56, 312
Impact evaluation, 260
Institute, 188
Interactive videodiscs, 239, 288
International Union for Health
Promotion and Education, 23, 27
Intervention, 146
Interviews, 104–109, 227, 259

J

Job bank, 101, 110
Job descriptions, 7, 56, 96, 99
*Journal of American College Health
Association, 23*
Journal of Health Care Education, 23
Journal of School Health, 23

L

Laser printers, 248
Learning environment, 131
Learning theory, 129, 137, 138
Lecture, 143, 162, 185
Legalistic approach, 142
Letters, 102–104, 156, 266
Liability, 37, 38
Listening, 160, 188

M

Marketing, 209–211, 213
Mass media, 216
Maternal and infant health, 309
Media, 57, 215
Meetings, 183–185, 193

Videotape, 232, 236
Violence, 56, 308
Voluntary health agency characteristics
  and staff functions, 63, 65, 316
Volunteers, 64, 66–68, 101, 273, 274

W

Washington Business Group on Health,
  28
Wellness Council of America, 29
Word processing, 173

Workshop, 187, 218
Worksite health promotion, 54, 79
World Health Organization, 27, 33
Written communication, 163

Y

YMCAs, 83

Z

Zero population growth, 31

About the Authors

DONALD J. BRECKON, M.A., M.P.H., Ph.D., is president of Park College in Parkville, Missouri, a suburb of Kansas City. He was born, raised, and educated in Michigan, with his degrees being from Central Michigan University, the University of Michigan, and Michigan State University. He also spent a year studying as a postdoctoral fellow with the American Council on Education.

Dr. Breckon served in a variety of faculty and administrative roles at Central Michigan University, working there for twenty-four years. He served as Professor of Health Education and Health Science, while concurrently serving in consecutive appointments as Assistant Dean of Health, Physical Education, Recreation, and Athletics; Associate Dean of Education, Health, and Human Services; and Acting Dean of Graduate Studies/Associate Vice Provost for Research.

While at Central Michigan University, Dr. Breckon developed the undergraduate and graduate degree programs in Public Health Education and Health Promotion, Hospital Health Education and Health Promotion, and Allied Health Education. He has published approximately one hundred articles in more than thirty professional journals, along with 12 chapters in various books of readings, 12 monographs, and two nationally used college and university textbooks. He prepared the first edition of this book while at Central Michigan University.

Dr. Breckon has been active in state and national professional health education organizations, serving in both elected and appointed leadership roles. He has also been active in local and state government, serving as mayor of Mt. Pleasant, Michigan, on Governor's taskforces, and in various appointed roles in Missouri. He has received more than two dozen awards, commendations, and recognition, including being listed in *Who's Who in America.* Dr. Breckon is married and has four daughters. He views his position as college president and his political involvement as evidence that health education skills are applicable to a wide range of positions and settings.

JOHN R. HARVEY, M.P.H., Ph.D., received his bachelor's degree from Purdue University, majoring in food science and minoring in chemistry and bacteriology. He did graduate work at Massachusetts State University in Bridgewater. He received his Master of Public Health degree at the University of Michigan in 1968. He served as Director of Health Education for the City-County Health Department in Ann Arbor and then served as the health commissioner of the Butler County Health Department in Ohio. He received his doctorate from Ohio State University. He has taught at Eastern Michigan University, the University of Kansas, and East Tennessee State University and is presently Associate Professor of Health Sciences at Western Illinois University.

Dr. Harvey's teaching interests are in health administration, aging, and research and computer applications. He has served as a consultant in management and as director of continuing education for the health professions. He is active in professional organizations and community service. Dr. Harvey is married and has four children.

R. BRICK LANCASTER, M.A., C.H.E.S., was born, raised, and educated in Michigan. He has a bachelor's degree in biology and health education and a master of arts degree in health education from Central Michigan University. He has also had postgraduate continuing education from the University of Michigan School of Public Health, Johns Hopkins University School of Public Health, Rutgers University School of Alcohol Studies, and the Arizona State University School of Business.

Mr. Lancaster has more than twenty years of experience in local and state public health departments. He has held leadership positions in state and national health education professional organizations and was vice-president of the Society for Public Health Education in 1982, as well as President of the Association of State and Territorial Directors of Public Health Education in 1991 and 1992.

He has served as a local health educator in a six-county rural health department and as a statewide public health education consultant and is a former chief of the Community Health Education Section of the Michigan Department of Public Health. He also served as a local health department administrator in Grand Rapids, Michigan. He served as Chief of the Office of Health Promotion and Education for the Arizona Department of Health Services and currently serves as Associate Director for Health Education Practice and Policy, Division of Chronic Disease Control and Community Intervention, National Center for Chronic Disease Prevention and Health Promotion for the Centers for Disease Control and Prevention. Mr. Lancaster is married to a health educator and has two children.